"This is the book I would recommend to family, friends and business associates who are interested in learning about the contributions Hispanics have made to the growth and development of our nation. *The ABCs and Ñ* packages facts, history and future trends in an informative and entertaining journalistic style."

— Linda G. Alvarado
Co-owner, Colorado Rockies Baseball Team
President & CEO, Alvarado Construction Company, Inc.
Denver, CO

"A most concise and comprehensive look at the influence and positive impact the Hispanic community has had on our country. Jim provides wonderful details and a positive outlook for the direction our community is going and an invaluable guide for the future."

— Clara R. Apodaca
Former First Lady, State of New Mexico
Executive Director, NHCC Foundation
Albuquerque, NM

"The book provides an insiders perspective to how Latinos and Corporate America can become effective partners in the 21st century. Definitely a 'must read' for corporate executives trying to enter Latino markets and for Latinos trying to venture forth as economic partners with Corporate America."

— Jaime Chahín, Ph.D.
Dean, College of Applied Arts
Texas State University, San Marcos
San Marcos, TX

"A 'must understand' description of U.S. Latinos. In ten years there will be two kinds of executives in our country; those who read and understood *The ABCs and Ñ* and those who will wish they had. It should be a textbook in our schools and a college class for all executives whose companies and organizations interact with Latinos."

— Jorge Haynes
Senior Director, External Relations, Office of the Chancellor
California State University System
Long Beach, CA

"This book brings all of the essential facts, figures and historical evolution of this complex community together into one easy-to-read and comprehensive book about U.S. Latinos. It provides a road map on how to navigate the cultural and ethnic byways and highways of what our nation has been — but more importantly, of what it will become."

— John C. Lopez
Founder/Chairman Emeritus, Lopez Foods, Inc.
Co-Founder/Managing Partner, Sueños, LLC
Oklahoma City, OK

"An incredible read! The blend of the historic, contemporary and future views of what the book means to the Hispanic Consumer Market, and the U.S. population in general, is very revealing. A 'must read' for corporate and community leaders wanting to better understand, strategize and connect with Latino consumers and communities."

— Louis Olivas, Ed.D.
President, American Association of Hispanics in Higher Education
W.P. Carey School of Business, Arizona State University
Tempe, AZ

"If you want to understand why Latinos are not all the same, you should read this book. *The ABCs and Ñ* is the cliff notes of Latino political and socio-economic history in the United States. It provides a great deal of information and explains how different geographic backgrounds have created a segmented Latino population in the U.S. with one common goal: the American dream."

— Veronica Villafañe
Editor and Publisher, Media Moves
Ex-officio President, National Association of Hispanic Journalists
Los Angeles, CA

The ABCs and Ñ of America's Cultural Evolution

The ABCs and Ñ of America's Cultural Evolution

A Primer on the Growing Influence of Hispanics, Latinos, and mestizos in the USA

JIM ESTRADA

TATE PUBLISHING
AND ENTERPRISES, LLC

Published by Tate Publishing & Enterprises, LLC
127 E. Trade Center Terrace | Mustang, Oklahoma 73064 USA
1.888.361.9473 | www.tatepublishing.com

Tate Publishing is committed to excellence in the publishing industry. The company reflects the philosophy established by the founders, based on Psalm 68:11,
"The Lord gave the word and great was the company of those who published it."

Book design copyright © 2013 by Tate Publishing, LLC. All rights reserved.
Cover design by Joel Uber
Interior design by Joana Quilantang

Published in the United States of America

ISBN: 978-1-62510-424-3
1. History / Latin America / General
2. Social Science / Ethnic Studies / Hispanic American Studies
13.04.19

Dedication

I dedicate this book to the giants on whose shoulders I have stood.

Acknowledgments

I would like to acknowledge my parents *Ramón* and *Julia* for instilling in me a healthy pride in my culture, an appreciation for learning, the ability to celebrate life, and for teaching me basic life skills that have allowed me to stand confidently and proudly on my own two feet; my siblings *Manuel*, Angie, Eugene, *Martín*, Victor, and Ernie, who shared with me the love, respect and nurturing environment that allowed me to express my creativity, differences of opinion, and pursuit of my life's goals; my sons Raymond and Ron (and their wives Teresa and Roxana), who inspire me to continue growing, intellectually and emotionally; my grandsons Nicolas and Daniel, who are already continuing the family's commitment to make our world a better place for all; and the members of my extended family (*abuelos, tías y tíos, primos, padrinos, compadres, familia política y mis queridos amigos*) who helped me to learn and grow as a person, father, friend, and author.

I would be remiss not to thank those in my life who helped me to conceptualize, research, draft, and revise, revise, and revise the many drafts for this book. And especially to Carol, whose love, faith and support enabled me to focus on bringing this project to fruition.

Mil gracias y abrazos a todos.

Table of Contents

Foreword

JOHN C. LOPEZ

It is common knowledge in most Latino communities and schools across the nation that the positive aspects of our community have gone missing from most US History, news media, and entertainment accounts. Even today, individuals and the organizations that were great influences on my peers and me remain some of the best-kept secrets in our nation; people like César E. Chavéz of the United Farm Workers, Bert Corona of the Mexican American Political Association, Dr. Hector P. García of the American G.I. Forum, Mario G. Obledo of the Mexican American Legal Defense & Educational Fund, William "Willie" C. Velasquez of the Southwest Voter Registration & Education Project, Raúl Yzaguirre of the National Council of La Raza, and many others who changed the economic, educational, and political environments for Hispanics in the United States.

Like many of my ethnic brethren, I am the son of a first generation US citizen and a native of the US Southwest. My parents were entrepreneurs and operated a small neighborhood meat market in Glendale (just outside of Phoenix, AZ) where they instilled in my brothers and me a strong commitment to family and community. Monies earned from hard work provided all the needs of our family, with enough left over to give back to our extended families and community. Upon graduating from high school I attended Northern Arizona University, where I played football and majored in Economics.

I pursued a career in banking and in the early 1970s became a staff member of the Southwest Council of La Raza (SWCLR), a fledgling, grass roots, civil rights organization that years later was to become the National Council of La Raza (NCLR), one the most renowned advocacy groups in the country. Among its many services was the advancement of Latino entrepreneurs. It was during this phase of my career that I had the opportunity to meet a number of like-minded Latinos. Among them was Jim Estrada, who was one of the first Mexican American television news reporters in San Diego. He was involved in the development of the Chicano Federation of San Diego County—a SWCLR affiliate.

In 1978, my wife Pat and I benefitted from my work at SWCLR with our acquisition of the first of four McDonald's restaurants in Los Angeles, CA. Shortly thereafter we again crossed paths with Jim, who happened to be a McDonald's Corporation marketing executive for the San Diego, Arizona, and Nevada markets. He worked closely with many of my fellow Hispanic McDonald's Owner/Operator Association (HMOA) colleagues across the nation. He had already developed a reputation for his culturally relevant marketing and community relation initiatives.

In 1992 Pat and I embarked on a journey that was to become another major benchmark in our business lives. We left the world of franchisees to enter a new one as meat suppliers to the McDonald's national system in Oklahoma City, OK. It was during the start-up phase of our newest business endeavor that we learned from mutual friends that Jim had established his own Marketing and Public Relations agency in the neighboring state of Texas. He was the logical choice to help us introduce Lopez Foods, Inc. to key audiences. That was some twenty years ago.

Our business and personal relationships continue to this day. With the counsel of Estrada Communications Group, Inc., Pat and I launched our latest business endeavor—*Sueños* LLC, a hospitality industry company through which we own and operate hotels. The glue that bonds our business and personal relationships is based on common business, community, and cultural backgrounds, along with family values that are reflected in our respective families and companies. I believe many Hispanics, Latinos, and *mestizos* share many of the same experiences (and emotions) that he so clearly describes in this book. I know I do.

Over the years I have read many articles and books that have attempted to explain the diverse characteristics of our community. *The ABCs and Ñ of America's Cultural Evolution* not only explains—in an easy-to-read and informational collection of essays—the many common and distinctive characteristics of this segment of society, but it also provides essential facts, figures, and historical benchmarks not readily available in traditional textbooks or educational curricula. This book provides the insights to help readers navigate the cultural byways and highways of our nation's fastest-growing and largest ethnic population. More importantly it provides clues on how it will continue to influence the future of our society.

In order to gain an advantage in their efforts to interact with an increasingly diverse population, businesses, public agencies, and nonprofit organizations must actively explore ways to attract and increase participation by Hispanics, Latinos, and *mestizos* in their overall operations: employment, philanthropy, governance, and economic development. Unlike marketing and community relation efforts of the past, today one must be fully aware of the needs and preferences of the evolving marketplace and fast growing nonwhite population.

Regardless of what labels are used to describe them, they are expected to reach the 100 million population mark by the year 2050. The size and diversity of our nation's Hispanic population will continue to challenge those of us in business, education, public, and nonprofit organizations wishing to address the implications of that growth. What resources can leaders from these various sectors look to for help in understanding and resolving future social, economic, and political issues? I suggest they start with *The ABCs and Ñ of America's Cultural Evolution.*

— John C. Lopez
Founder/Chairman Emeritus, Lopez Foods, Inc.
Co-Founder/Managing Partner, Sueños, LLC
Oklahoma City, OK

Introduction
to the ABC's and Ñ

Olvidado y nunca sabido vienen a ser lo mismo.
Translation: Forgotten and never known come to be the same.
Transcreation: The palest ink is better than the best memory.

United States President Harry S. Truman once said, "The only thing new in this world is the history that you don't know," (Miller, *Plain Speaking*). This quote seems to fit the situation in which we find ourselves relative to the US Hispanic, Latino, and *mestizo* population. The phenomenal rate of growth by this US ethnic group is arguably the most significant demographic event in the history of our young nation; yet, a review of historical records, educational textbooks, and media exposure finds most non-Hispanic whites—as well as a substantial number of the fifty million US-born, naturalized and undocumented immigrant Latinos—are unaware of the contributions this segment of the population has made to the growth and advancement of the Americas.

In what seems like a blink of the eye, retailers, marketers, and organizations from the private and public sectors have taken notice of Latinos and their incredible growth rate, as well as their potential consumer, social, and political power. They are an imposing consumer force with an annual purchasing power of approximately $1 trillion—and projected to grow to $1.5 trillion by 2015—an amount greater than the economies of all but eight countries in the entire world.

INCONVENIENT TRUTHS

This consumer power has captured the attention of many US corporations, nonprofit organizations, and public sector staffs wishing to establish, or improve, relationships with the various sub-groups that constitute the US Hispanic population. A proliferation of products, services, and initiatives aimed at Latinos is a direct result of the aforementioned interests attempting to shift their respective branding, image building, and outreach efforts toward a changing marketplace and increasingly diverse population.

Trends identified in earlier US Census counts hinted of such a population explosion, but it wasn't until the 2000 Census trumpeted the arrival of this relatively unknown ethnic group that the nation's non-Hispanics actually began to take notice. Latinos had become a blip on the nation's radar screen and our nation was reaching a "tipping point" in matters regarding ethnicity and "majority-minority" race relations. By 2011 the Hispanic population had grown to over fifty million, approximately 17 percent of the nation's total of 308.7 million. This number did not include the 3.9 million US citizens who reside in the Commonwealth of Puerto Rico, nor a complete count of the traditionally under-counted ten to twelve million undocumented immigrants estimated to be living, working, and paying taxes in the USA.

According to a 2008 report by the Pew Hispanic Center the number of unauthorized immigrants entering the USA was declining; but it is unclear if the decrease was a result of a sagging US economy or stepped-up anti-immigration enforcement efforts. Still, some estimated the number of Hispanics in the US in 2011 to be over fifty million, or closer to 18 percent of our nation's total population. The USA is already home to the world's second largest population of Latinos, trailing Mexico's 115 million. With a growth rate five times greater than that of non-Hispanic whites (NHWs), Latinos are expected to continue their explosive population growth well into the 21st century.

The top twenty US Hispanic media markets during the past decade reflect that growth:

Rank:	Market:	2008 Population:	% of Total:
1	Los Angeles, CA	8,507,000	48.1
2	New York, NY	4,434,700	21.1
3	Miami-Fort Lauderdale, FL	2,152,300	9.2
4	Houston, TX	2,064,300	34.5
5	Chicago, IL	1,942,700	20.3
6	Dallas-Fort Worth, TX	1,757,500	25.9
7	San Francisco/San Jose Bay Area, CA	1,712,300	23.7
8	Phoenix-Prescott, AZ	1,378,200	27.4
9	San Antonio, TX	1,259,400	54.6
10	Brownsville/Harlingen /McAllen, TX	1,153,20	96.5
11	San Diego, CA	998,200	3.1
12	Fresno-Visalia, CA	982,300	51.3
13	Sacramento/Stockton /Modesto, CA	886,100	23.4
14	El Paso, TX/Las Cruces, NM	817,200	85.9
15	Denver, CO	791,000	20.8

Rank:	Market:	2008 Population:	% of Total:
16	Albuquerque/ Santa Fe, NM	767,600	45.0
17	Washington, DC/ Hagerstown, MD	688,600	11.1
18	Philadelphia, PA	626,500	7.9
19	Atlanta, GA	623,500	10.1
20	Las Vegas, NV	532,500	28.5

Despite the economic slowdown during the millennium's first decade, the Selig Center for Economic Growth at the University of Georgia predicted Hispanic consumer spending would reach $1 trillion per year by 2010 and rise to $1.5 trillion in 2015, accounting for nearly 11 percent of the nation's total buying power (Fahmy, *Despite Recession*). These consumer levels show no signs of ebbing as Latinos continue to attract attention from Corporate America, private nonprofit institutions, public agencies, and even major political parties and their candidates.

Yet, the consumer potential of Latinos—given its size, young median age, and spending potential—remains underdeveloped. This is due mainly to a general lack of knowledge about the history, culture and ties to the various motherlands that influence their attitudes, behaviors and levels of assimilation into our nation's mainstream society.

The ABCs and Ñ is a "primer" for people whose careers—or curiosity—require them to understand the Who? What? Where? When? and Why? of the largest ethnic segment of the US population. This collection of essays is intended to provide readers with the knowledge of forgotten and omitted facts that may help readers become better equipped in their efforts to reach out to, and effectively interact with, the fastest-growing consumer, employee, student, taxpayer and voter groups in the USA. *The ABCs and Ñ of America's Cultural Evolution* reminds readers of our lack of appreciation for the past, present (and future) influence of our country's fastest growing segment of its population.

Language is the Archive of History

El idioma es el mejor reflejo de una etnia, pueblo o comunidad.
Translation: Language is the best reflection of ethnicity, a town or a community.
Transcreation: One does not inhabit a country; one inhabits a language.

Poet, statesman, and writer Victor Hugo wrote: "Human society, the world, and the whole of mankind is to be found in the alphabet" (Ouaknin, *Mysteries of the Alphabet*). That may explain why the "ABCs" of the English alphabet are emblematic of the basics for most things in our society; but the Hispanic demographic explosion occurring in our country may require the addition of a Spanish alphabet letter to the three letters we routinely equate with the fundamentals of things.

The modern Spanish language alphabet contains the same twenty-six letters in the English alphabet, plus the *ñ*, which is pronounced **en**-yeh. It came into existence in the twelfth century when Spanish scribes made copies of documents by hand and placed diacritical accent marks—*tildes*—over letters to indicate they were doubled; "aa" became *ã* and "nn" became *ñ*. Over time its application to other letters fell out of use, and by the fourteenth century, the *ñ* was the only letter written with the tilde, or diacritical mark.

Use of the *ñ* can be seen in the word *año* (year), which was derived from the Latin word *anno.* As the phonetic nature of the Spanish language solidified, the *ñ* came to be used for its own individual sound, not just for words that included the double n.

Other Spanish words that use the *ñ* include: *baño* (bath), *cañon* (canyon), *campaña* (campaign), *mañana* (tomorrow), *señal* (sign) and *piñata* (not yet translated into English).

The evolution of the *ñ*, in the Spanish alphabet is similar to the evolutionary path of *mestizos* and their hybrid culture in the Americas, in that Spain and its language contributed to the existence of both.

Recently, the *ñ* has come to be closely associated with the increasing number of Latinos in the US who trace their ancestry to Spanish *conquistadores* and pre-Colombian indigenous people—both of whom inhabited the Western Hemisphere long before the arrival of the first Anglo-Saxon Protestant émigrés to the continent. Several organizations—*Instituto Cervantes*, a worldwide non-profit organization created by the Spanish government in 1991 to promote the study and teaching of Spanish language and culture and the National Association of Hispanic Journalists, a nonprofit US organization dedicated to the recognition and professional advancement of Latinos in the news industry—have adopted the *ñ* as their organization's logo and as a symbol of their Spanish language and heritage.

Both the *ñ* and *mestizos* have withstood the tests of time and continue to contribute to their own cultural and social transformation, as well as their geographic surroundings throughout the Americas; the evolution of both continues to connect the past, present, and future of the Americas..

The ABCs and Ñ of America's Cultural Evolution is intended to provide readers with the basics about our nation's fastest growing ethnic consumers, students, taxpayers, voters, and workers. The pages of this book contain insights into the historical and social identities, attitudes, and contributions of an ethnic population with a rich and diverse past that is still evolving and is projected to leave an indelible mark on America and mainstream society.

Culture Clash

No hay mal que por bien no venga.
Translation: There is no bad from which some good doesn't result.
Transcreation: The bitterest trials are often blessings in disguise.

The serendipitous landing by the Spanish on the shores of the "New World" is one of the most significant and important events in the history of the Western Hemisphere, and perhaps the world. The use of the word "discovery" is purposely avoided due to the fact the millions of indigenous people living in the Western Hemisphere were not "lost."

Like most colonization efforts related to the New World, exploration and conquest by European powers of their time were driven by the acquisition of material wealth, power, and religious conversion. A major distinction between the English and Spanish colonial conquests was the levels of interaction between the invaders and the indigenous people. Unlike the English, who enacted anti-miscegenation laws in the Maryland colony as early as 1661, the Spanish appeared to be more concerned with survival and sustainability of their expeditionary forces than they were about their European racial purity. In their efforts to facilitate control of the natives the Spaniards not only procreated with, but also converted, their conquered subjects to Christianity in efforts to attain their economic, political, and ecclesiastical objectives.

Following the Spanish defeat of the Aztec Empire (c.1520), governance of the Spanish colonies was placed exclusively in the hands of Spanish-born colonists, or *peninsulares* (natives of the Iberian Peninsula) in order to ensure the complete conquest of

New Spain. *Peninsulares* governed an area that included much of today's North America: including Canada, present-day Mexico and Central and South America. Spain's influence can still be seen many areas of the USA west of the Mississippi River and in the states bordering along the coast of the Gulf of Mexico.

Inheritance rights of heirs born in New Spain soon became an issue, prompting the establishment of a caste system to protect the wealth and influence of the *peninsulares*. Inasmuch as Spaniards sired *mestizo* children, the rights of potential heirs had to be defined and prioritized in accordance with the degree of Spanish purity. The system for determining lineage used convoluted formulae for defining offspring from Spanish and indigenous parents, listed in declining rank and social status.

Whenever an infant was baptized in the church it was assigned to a caste by a baptismal priest. This made the priest very influential since he decided to which caste the baby would be assigned. This practice led to corruption in the priesthood, since a well-placed bribe could improve one's standing for the rest of their lives. If the priest were angered or upset, he could assign one's child to a lower caste.

The social stratification created by the caste system was rigidly enforced and since it was based on race, it was impossible to move from ones birth caste into a higher category. It also led to many problems and hatreds between the castes, which resulted in discrimination, violence, subjugation, and exploitation among the members of the different castes in their efforts to move up in status and be allotted the benefits associated with being more "Spanish" than their cohorts.

The farther away from "pure" Spanish bloodlines the farther away from being granted inheritance claims. This extensive caste system began with the *criollo*—the New Spain offspring of parents born in Spain—that by royal edict could never hold official titles; down to the very bottom of the caste was often referred to metaphorically as *"allí te estás"* (and there you shall remain).

Ironically, Spaniards and *criollos* referred to themselves as "pure-blooded" Europeans. However history reminds us the Iberian Peninsula (Spain, Portugal, Andorra, Gibraltar, and a small area of France) and the bloodlines of its inhabitants were intermingled as a result of nearly eight hundred years of Moorish rule. The Moors (African Muslims), a mixture of Berbers and Arabs, infused Spain with their genes, culture and social practices over several centuries. Moorish influence resulted in tolerance (and partial acceptance) of mixed bloodlines and cultures that resulted in Spain's diverse ethnic, racial and religious population.

Yet, white European ancestry did carry certain social and financial "advantages" in the New World.

SURVIVAL OF THE FITTEST

Among the first natives of the Western Hemisphere the Spaniards encountered were the *Azteca*—derived from the *Náhuatl* language word *Aztecatl* meaning "people from *Aztlán*" or "people from the North." According to some historians, the *Azteca* are also referred to as the *Mechica* people of *Tenochtitlán* (modern day Mexico City)—considered the elite of the indigenous militaristic empire at the beginning of the sixteenth century—who with the allied city-states of *Texcoco* and *Tlacopán* formed an alliance known as the "Aztec Empire."

The Spanish conquest of the Aztecs is attributable to several factors, one of them being revenge for the practice of human sacrifice. Many of the *Mechica's* sacrificial victims were from neighboring and subjugated tribes, which resulted in motivated allies ready to help the Spanish invaders defeat the mighty *Azteca*.

Another common premise maintains that the *Azteca* believed their god *Quetzalcoatl* would return to destroy their empire. This god was expected to appear as a man with light-colored hair and skin; to the indigenous people, the Spaniard *Hernán Cortés* was the reincarnation of that god. To this day, modern scholars question this reference to the resurrection of *Quetzalcoatl* and consider it historical revisionism.

A third factor, which from a strategic point of view may have been the most important, was the use by *Cortés* of *Malinche*—also referred to in historical accounts as *Malintzín, Malinalli* or *Doña Marina* (Cypess, *La Malinche*).

Malintzín's mother (who remarried a ruling tribal official with whom she had a male heir) gave her daughter away to another tribe and into a life of servitude. *Malinche* became one of many slaves given to *Cortés* by the natives of *Tabasco*. She became his mistress and gave birth to his first son, *Martín*, thought to be one of the first *mestizos* in the Americas.

The Mexican Gulf coast native acted as interpreter, advisor, lover, and intermediary for *Cortés* in his dealings with the various tribes the Spaniards encountered during their forays into Central Mexico—the latter is a great example of the effective ethnic marketing principle: "Knowledge of your target audience's language and culture provides a tremendous advantage." With all due respect to *Pocahontas* and *Sacagawea* this had to be the first historical instance of the use of "cultural relevance" in cross-cultural communications in the Americas.

"*La Malinche*" is still referred to in a variety of disparaging to venerating remarks throughout Mexico and the Southwestern US. Among indigenous sympathizers, she is either the embodiment of treachery or the quintessential victim; for others she is considered the symbolic mother of the *mestizo* people. Yet, to this day the term *malinchista* is used by many Mexicans and Latinos of Mexican heritage to describe disloyalty.

The most credible factor leading to the conquest of the Aztec Empire was the importation of communicable diseases; the modern day equivalent of "weapons of mass destruction" that we now know as smallpox, measles, scarlet fever, typhoid, typhus, influenza, whooping cough, tuberculosis, cholera, diphtheria, chicken pox and venereal diseases. Collectively, the diseases eradicated a substantial number of the indigenous population, which was estimated at thirty million strong in 1518. Some fifty years later those numbers had been reduced to three million, and by 1620 the number had dwindled to approximately 1.6 million. No one knows for sure how many members of the Aztec Empire died from Spanish-borne European diseases, but historians referred to this epidemic devastation as the "Great Dying" (Wolf, *Europe*).

By virtue of these aforementioned factors, *Cortés* succeeded in overpowering the once great *Azteca* civilization. Efforts by indigenous tribes to defend their ways of life and customs against Spanish diseases, armies, and miscegenation proved to be futile. Of the many *dichos* (sayings) used among Spanish-speakers perhaps the most literal way to describe this cultural, physical and psychological confrontation remains: *"Lo que no te mata, te fortalece."* (What doesn't kill you makes you stronger.)

DIFFERENTIAL PERSPECTIVE

Náhuatl was the language spoken by the *Mechica* and remains to this day a legally sanctioned language in Mexico. It is spoken by more than a million people in the central regions of Mexico and has a legal status equal to Spanish. Popular Spanish and English words rooted in this pre-Colombian language remain in use today in both Spanish and English languages: *"aguacatl"* (*aguacate*/avocado), *"chilli"* (*chile*/chili pepper), *"chilpoctli"* (*chipotle*/chipotle*), '*coyotl*' (*coyote*/coyote), *"tomatl"* (*tomate*/tomato) and '*xocoatl*' (*chocolate*/chocolate) are a few of these words.

Other languages spoken in the Mesoamerican western hemisphere have given many words to the Spanish language. *Choclo*, the word used to describe both corn, and its kernels, is from the *Quechua* language of the *Inca*, which is also still spoken today. Another word for corn, *"maíz,"* was first discovered in the diary of *Cristobál Colón* (aka: Christopher Columbus in English and *Cristoforo Colombo* in Italian). Its roots are from the indigenous *Taino* language once spoken in the Caribbean islands: the *Bahamas, Cuba, Jamaica, Puerto Rico,* and others.

Other Uto-Aztecan language-speaking tribes flourished throughout pre-Colombian Mexico and the western US and have left traces of their existence; among them are: the *Tarahumara* (from the Mexican state of *Chihuahua*), the *Yaquí* (in the Mexican state of *Sonora*), *Tohono O'odham* (in the Mexican state of *Sonora* and Arizona in the US), and the *Huichol* (in the Mexican mountain states of *Nayarit, Jalisco, Zacatecas* and *Durango*).

US indigenous tribes that could be considered distant cousins of the Uto-Aztecans—are the *Gabrielino* (Los Angeles), *Hopi* (Northern Arizona), *Paiute* (Southwest), *Shoshone* (Idaho), and the *Ute* (Utah) (Schmal, *Are You Related?*).

Many of the natives adopted some form of the Spanish language, political system and religious practices. Vestiges of their religious conversion are evident in many of today's *mestizo* social and cultural practices. Perhaps the most obvious signs of cross-cultural influence were the birth names given indigenous and *mestizo* children. For generations, newborns were given *nombres de pila* (*pila* is the church font in which babies are baptized) in honor of the Roman Catholic Church's Holy Family or the Saints' day on which they were born.

Girls were often named *María* in honor of the Holy Mother. Names like *Dolores* (Sorrows) and *Mercedes* (Mercy) were also taken from titles associated with the Virgin Mary, while others such as *Anunciación, Concepción,* and *Guadalupe* refer to religious events related to the Mother of Christ. Common among boys' names were *Jesús* (Jesus), *Manuel* (Emmanuel), *Adán* (Adam), *Géronimo* (Jerome), *José* (Joseph), *Juán* (John) and *Pedro* (Peter).

Christianity may have prevailed in the New World, but it was indelibly marked with a facade created by its indigenous people. The natives imbued Catholicism with some of their own practices and perspectives; among them the adaptation of religious icons similar to the Catholic Church's Virgin Mary.

- The dark-skinned, indigenous-looking *Virgen de Guadalupe* is Mexico's patron saint and a revered religious and cultural icon. She was reported to have appeared in *Tepeyac* near Mexico City to *Juan Diego Cuauhtlatoatzín* (canonized as the first Mexican saint in 2002). *La Virgen de San Juan de Los Lagos* (Our Lady of St. John of the Lakes), who is claimed to have appeared to residents in *San Juan de Los Lagos*, in the state of *Jalisco*.

- *Nuestra Señora de la Caridad del Cobre* (The Virgin of Charity in El Cobre) is Cuba's Madonna.

- *La Virgen de Copacabana* (or Blessed Virgin of the *Candelaria*) is the patron saint of Bolivia.

- *Nossa Senhora Aparecida* (Our Lady of Apparition) is the patron saint of Brazil. Argentina's sixteenth century icon of *Nuestra Señora de Lujan* (Our Lady of Lujan) is one of the most important pilgrimage sites in Latin America.

- *La Virgen de los Angeles* (*La Negrita*) is the patron saint of Costa Rica.

The Spanish missionaries allowed natives and *mestizos* to worship their indigenous versions of the Holy Mother to hasten their conversion to Christianity, not realizing they would become the dominant religious icons of a new hybrid people and culture. Such icons appeared in most areas of Latin American countries, mixing Catholicism with native religions. The blending of religion and culture is yet another example of selecting the best of both worlds as survival techniques. As it has done with the human species for centuries, natural selection had a major role in determining the evolution of culture. Christianity may have prevailed, but it was indelibly marked with a facade created by indigenous and *mestizo* people.

SEEDS OF DISSENTION

In many areas of the New World *criollos*, indigenous, and *mestizo* groups were forced to pay tribute to Spain's monarchs and comply with traditional laws and customs. Anti-colonialism sentiments grew first among *criollos*, which suffered social, economic and political discrimination at the hands of their European-born peers: the *peninsulares*.

At the same time the indigenous tribes in more remote areas of the continent chose to remain physically, ethnically, and culturally isolated from the invading *gachupines* (from the *Náhuatl* word *cactzopin*, which means he who kicks with "spikes" or "spurs"). The word morphed into *gachupín* in Spanish, a pejorative term used by *criollos*, *mestizos*, and indigenous people when referring to the Spanish ruling class and their sycophants.

It was the educated and disenchanted *criollos*, not the natives or *mestizos*, who fomented the independence movement that led to Mexico's revolt against Spain. In 1810, the *criollo* priest *Miguel Hidalgo y Costilla* called for Mexican independence with his now famous *Grito de Dolores* (shout from the city of Dolores), inciting his fellow *criollo*, indigenous, and *mestizo* followers with his celebrated cry, the *Grito de Dolores* (shout from the city of Dolores): *"¡Muerte a los gachupines! ¡Viva Nuestra Señora de Guadalupe! ¡Viva Mexico!"* (Death to the Spaniards! Long live Our Lady of Guadalupe! Long live Mexico!)

After a long and bloody struggle, independence was won in 1821—eleven years after the call to arms by *Padre Hidalgo y Costilla*. Today he is still revered as the father of Mexico's revolution, which gained independence from Spain. Throughout Mexico, and in many Latino communities across the USA,

Latinos participate in festivities surrounding *El Grito de Dolores* on the eve of *Fiestas Patrias*—Mexican Independence Day—that falls on September 16.

In Mexico City the President starts the ceremony by ringing the actual bell from the church in the town of *Dolores Hidalgo, Guanajuato)* and repeats the call for independence used by *Padre Hidalgo y Costilla*, which culminates at midnight with fireworks and cries of *¡Viva Mexico!* The same celebration is repeated from every *presidencia municipal* (mayor's office) throughout Mexico as part of the annual remembrance.

BEYOND PALE

Despite Mexico's independence from Spain, Spanish rule left indelible marks on Mexico and Latin America. The fair-skinned European "look" remained preferable to the darker shades of skin commonly associated with natives and *mestizos*. It is still common to hear Latino family members gush with pride over the arrival of a *güerito* (pale-skinned baby), while the arrival of swarthier infants is frequently met with sympathetic remarks about the newborn's indigenous heritage.

Discrimination based on skin color has been a phenomenon for centuries in almost all cultures of the world. And in most parts of the world a premium has been placed on the fair-haired. In the modern Americas, light skin is still equated with privilege, power, and wealth. This has led to a large number of indigenous people and their *mestizo* relations being conflicted about their Spanish ancestry, especially when in their own family members may range from *morenos* (dark skinned), to *trigueños* (olive skinned), to *güeros* (fair skinned).

Color differences within the *mestizo* culture are generally viewed as just another of the many distinctive characteristics among siblings and are no greater a concern than being *diestro o zurdo* (right- or left-handed), *alto o chaparro* (tall or short), *delgado o gordo* (thin or fat), and *listo o torpe* (smart or slow).

In a 2008 interview with Dublin-based Independent News & Media, ABC's "Desperate Housewives" star Eva Longoria explained that concept when she addressed the issue of skin color in her response to the question: "At what age did you find happiness in yourself?"

> "Me? Oh, early, early on. It was high school. No, actually younger," Longoria replied, matter-of-factly. "I was the ugly duckling growing up. My sisters were very beautiful and I was the 'ugly dark one,' *la prieta fea*, as a child. I was the only one with black hair. I was the only one with dark skin. So I learned to develop a personality and learned not to rely on my superficial looks, because I didn't have them. It is kind of ironic that [now] I'm on people's lips as 'the most beautiful' or 'the sexiest" (Egan, Barry: *Eva Longoria: Unbelievable*).

It is ironic! For beneath the veneer of Spanish culture there remains strong connections to an indigenous heritage that is an integral element of *mestizos* and their dual identity that still results in internal conflict and confusion related to matters of skin color and race. The clash of cultures that began in the late 1400s continues to this day among Hispanics, Latinos, and *mestizos* in the USA, who now grapple with the challenges associated with acculturation and assimilation into yet another white, Eurocentric society.

Thankfully, it is not a new experience for most Latinos who are often reminded by our elders: The bitterest trials are often blessings in disguise.

History Is
Not Destiny

A veces vivimos sintiendonos encadenados sin saber que tenemos la llave.
Translation: At times we live feeling shackled not knowing we have the key.
Transcreation: They are not free who drag their chains after them.

The proliferation of Latinos in the United States brings to mind the phoenix of Greek and Roman mythology. The fabled bird was said to be able to regenerate when wounded by its attackers, making it impervious to destruction. At the end of its life cycle the phoenix would transform its nest into a funeral pyre and set it ablaze. Once the nest and bird were incinerated, a new phoenix would rise from the ashes to take flight.

Latinos, like the phoenix, continue to regenerate themselves culturally and numerically and appear to be influencing the US like no other ethnic group in our nation's history. Higher birth rates among Latinos, longer life expectancies, and immigration have been major contributors to their growth and cultural reinforcement. Relative to immigration, it is noteworthy that in May 2008 the Census Bureau reported 62 percent of Hispanic population growth was driven by domestic childbirths, contradicting popular belief among many that immigration was the major factor in driving their growth.

The 2010 Census showed that racial and ethnic groups accounted for 91.7 percent of the nation's growth from 2000 to 2010. Over half of the increase (56 percent) was attributable to

Hispanics. White US Americans accounted for only 8.3 percent of growth over the same period. According to demographers, the reason is "total fertility rate"—the number of children the average woman is predicted to have in her lifetime (Passel, *Explaining Why*). There are 1.1 births to every one death among non-Hispanic whites (NHW), while among Latinos there are 8.9 births to every one death. This imbalance will greatly influence the disparity in population numbers between Latinos and non-Hispanics well into the future.

Also, the number of Latinos is increasing in non-traditional geographic areas of the US. What had been historical enclaves for previous generations—Mexicans in the Southwest, Puerto Ricans in the Northeast, and Cubans in the Southeast—are no longer the case. During the post-World War II twentieth century, Latinos transformed themselves from a 90 percent rural population to one that is now over 90 percent urban. They migrated to major US metropolitan centers seeking better employment, education, and housing as they sought out their versions of the American Dream.

Since the "Decade of the Hispanic" (a phrase used to designate the 1980s as the period in which Latinos were supposed to have gained national prominence and recognition as a political, economic, and cultural force), their growth and attendant consumer spending power has transformed them into one of the nation's most attractive consumer markets. Marketing gurus recognized the benefits of reaching-out to this emerging segment of the population because of its potential source of revenue. Yet, one still hears occasional complaints from media and communication practitioners about unsuccessful attempts to communicate with this targeted consumer audience.

Unlike *Hernán Cortés* and his "culturally competent" advisor *Malinche*, some modern professionals (and their clients) felt their outreach efforts had not provided them with an acceptable return on investment (ROI). A major reason for these failed initiatives was that most marketing and advertising professionals simply did not understand how to promote their products and services to this ethnic audience in a culturally relevant manner, other than "literally" translating English-language campaigns into *español*.

THE BIRTH OF 'PANETHNICITY'

Let's review some basic facts about Latinos—the ABCs and *Ñ*, as it were. Most Latinos are descendants of both natives of the pre-Colombian Western Hemisphere and Spanish explorers and crewmembers. They are a confluence of these two distinct geographic and cultural groups who created an ethnic mixture of *mestizos*, a combination of predominantly European Spaniards and indigenous people of the Western Hemisphere that has evolved for over five hundred years throughout the Americas.

By the end of the twentieth century, "Hispanic" and "Latino" were the labels most people in the US associated with the nation's largest, non-European white population. Despite the increased use of these labels, the meaning, etymology, and affinity for these labels were hardly ever explained and understood by mainstream society. Dr. John A. Garcia, the Director of the Resource Center for Minority Data and Interuniversity Consortium for Political and Social Research's (ICPSR) at the University of Michigan, explains that social and political forces over the past fifty years have shaped how Latinos perceive and define themselves in the US. He writes that in the mid-twentieth century "... discussion focused primarily on the labels 'Mexican American' and 'Chicano,' the differences between the terms, and the authenticity of each." He affirms that the composition and distribution of the Hispanic population in the US is drastically different than it was ten, twenty, or thirty years ago (Garcia, *Panethnic Identity*).

In an effort to shed light on the use of labels used to describe this growing segment of our nation's population, this book uses the term "Latino" when referring to community, personal, political, social and other "qualitative" matters; "Hispanic" is used in association with statistics, demographics and other "quantitative" topics. These contemporary labels were used initially to identify people originating from post-Colombian, Spanish-speaking areas of the Western Hemisphere, which to varying degrees have Spanish or other white European bloodlines somewhere in their family trees. Both are used by advocacy and community-based organizations (CBO) and their members to coalesce diverse individuals and communities of the major Spanish-speaking nationalities and cultural groups scattered across the US into a unified voice on issues of common interest.

The word "Hispanic" is a generic term that has been used in recent years to identify those in the US who identify with Spanish bloodlines, language, and cultural heritage. The US Census Bureau adopted the term in 1970 to reflect the growth and diversity of *Hispanos*, Latinos, and *mestizos* and replaced self-identifying ethnic and national-origin categories such as "Mexican-American," "Puerto Rican" and "Cuban-American" in their official census materials and questionnaires. It was the government's attempt to identify individuals who traced their origins to Spain or any of the Spanish-speaking nations of the Western Hemisphere.

For the record, Hispanic and/or Latino origin is based on self-described family ancestry or place of birth in response to a question on the Census Bureau's American Community Survey. Ancestry is not necessarily the same as the place of birth of the respondent, nor is it indicative of immigrant or citizenship status. The Census Bureau classifies all Latinos in the US by using the following criteria, which for some unknown reason omits references to indigenous ancestry:

A. Spanish speakers and/or persons belonging to a single household where Spanish is spoken;

B.   Persons with Spanish heritage by birth location; and

C.   Persons who self-identify as being of Spanish ancestry or bloodlines.

The terms "Hispanic" and "Latino" still overlap and are frequently interchanged. Attempts to make either term universal have been met with varying degrees of acceptance and rejection. Preference for either of the two terms is influenced by a variety of factors, including age, geography, cultural orientation, and degree of assimilation into mainstream society. The label used to address individuals and geographic groups should be determined by the preference of the targeted audience one wishes to reach. It is worth the time and effort to determine such preferences.

It is equally important to note both labels remain specific to the US and are seldom (if ever) used in other Spanish-speaking countries when referring to segments of their populations. It is also important to note that these interchangeable terms are confusing in that they do not denote "race"—members of the Hispanic, Latino, and *mestizo* groups can be of any race or combination of races.

CLASS VS. COLOR

For the sake of clarification, there is also a need to define another racial and ethnic term used in these pages, the term "white." In these essays "white" refers to US residents who claim (or identify with) "white European" ancestry. Historically, the term "Anglo" had been used routinely to describe the original English immigrants to the New World and became generally associated with all whites in the US; but others of white European ancestry did not take kindly to that generic label. Some had political, religious and/or social differences with the British that had existed for centuries.

In recent years, non-Hispanic whites (NHW) in the US have been involuntarily split into two distinct classes: the "haves" and "have-nots." An increasing number of NHWs are finding themselves lacking the most desirable trait of white entitlement: privilege. A May 2008 *Chicago Tribune* article defined the differences between these two poles of the white European ancestry spectrum. In its report about political support among white working-class voters for presidential hopeful Hillary Clinton, it asserted that those who live a life of privilege today act as "… a rarefied club that excludes people based not on their skin color but on their economic status, personal tastes and aesthetic sensibilities," (Daum, *The White vs. Off-White election*).

Generically, the majority of the US population is still referred to as "white," but with the passage of time the term has become more conceptual than literal. Simply put, one no longer has to be of pale skin in order to be "white." The main prerequisites now needed to be part of the *haut monde* are substantial amounts of disposable income or the ability to acquire the material accoutrements symbolic of wealth and success. Of course, to be a member in good standing one must also demonstrate the behaviors and values generally associated with this exclusive club of privilege: pedigree, education, and social standing.

Being white still has its advantages when seeking admission into its many exclusive circles and cliques, but lifestyle and financial wherewithal have become the most critical criteria to gain entrance. Nonetheless, use of the term "white" in this book generally refers to both the "haves" (*haute monde*) and "have-nots" (*hoi polloi*) and it will be up to the reader to determine which is intended in each situation. This is an important distinction, inasmuch as many native- and foreign-born Latinos consider themselves to be white because of their Spanish heritage and/or financial status.

CULTURAL IDENTITY

Now that the waters have been sufficiently muddied, let's continue. Contrary to popular belief not all Hispanics, Latinos, or *mestizos* are "illegal" immigrants. According to the Pew Center, of the estimated ten to twelve million unauthorized immigrants in the US, Mexicans make up 56 percent, while another 22 percent are from other Latin American countries; some 13 percent are from Asia, and 6 percent are from Europe and Canada. Of the fifty million-plus Hispanics counted in the 2010 Census, it is safe to say that over forty-two million are US-born or naturalized citizens. (By the way, that is more than the nearly thirty-four million residents of the USA's northern neighbor Canada.)

A substantial number of today's Latinos point to the fact that their indigenous ancestors were residents of the Western Hemisphere well before the first white Europeans reached the eastern shores of the continent. This fact is not commonly known due to the limited amount of information in US historical accounts and media coverage regarding the presence of indigenous people, Spaniards and *mestizos*, or their contributions to the development of North America.

Focusing on the US-born and naturalized Latinos in terms of cultural and ethnic heritage, by 2011 approximately 65 percent were Mexican, nine percent were Puerto Rican, approximately three percent each were Cuban, Dominican, and Salvadoran; the remainder are a combination of Central and South American, Caribbean and other Spanish-speaking cultures (Motel, *Hispanic Origin Groups*).

Similar to white European immigrants, Latinos also relate culturally to their countries of origin. Self-identification labels are frequently based on regional or national origins and preferred over the generic "Hispanic" or "Latino" labels used commonly in the US.

Reference to country of origin or national heritage is by far the label of choice among most Latinos. *Chileno, colombiano, cubano, dominicano, guatemalteco, hondureño, méjicano, puertorriqueño* and *salvadoreño* are examples of self-identifying labels used in familiar conversation by members of the Latino community when referring to their country of origin—or in the case of US-born citizens, their cultural or national heritage.

Even as assimilation and acculturation occur in regional, social and political enclaves, there are still more specific self-identifying labels of choice to express national, regional, and cultural origins. The terms *Chicano, manito* and *Tejano* (used primarily by the US-born of Mexican heritage) and *boricua* and *nuyorican* (used by Puerto Ricans) are prime examples.

Some immigrants prefer to identify with their home states, regions or cities: *chilangos* from *Mexico City; paisas* from *Medellín, Colombia; regiomontanos* from *Monterrey, Nuevo León, Mexico potosinos* from *San Luís Potosí, Mexico; and salvadoreños* from *San Salvador, El Salvador* are examples of geographic labels. Latinos have so dubbed themselves to distinguish their cultural and nationality groups from the other members of what we in the USA believe is a monolithic, "one size fits all" ethnic population.

CULTURAL SYNTHESIS

The majority of Latinos share a similar indigenous pre- and post-Colombian heritage that developed concurrently throughout the Western Hemisphere. This cultural foundation was in place prior to the arrival of Anglo-Saxons (British) and has influenced many of the common characteristics of *mestizo* culture and the idiosyncratic Spanish spoken by each of the major Latino sub-groups in the US.

Of the two major civilizations that contributed to the creation of the *mestizo*, one was the indigenous people of the pre-

Colombian Western Hemisphere who had populated it for thousands of years. They were descendants of the *Arawak, Ciboney,* and *Taino* from the Greater Antilles islands of *Cuba, Jamaica, Hispaniola,* and *Puerto Rico.* A variety of mainland tribes consist of the *Azteca* from North America, which historians believe consisted of two distinct tribes—the *Tenochca* and/or *Tolteca* and the *Mechica* and/or *Chichimeca*; the *Inca* from South America; and the *Maya* from Central America. These indigenous people were part of the most advanced civilizations of their respective eras and geographic motherlands.

The second distinct group were Spanish explorers, *conquistadores,* and crews. History reminds us the Iberian Peninsula—Spain, Portugal, Andorra, Gibraltar, and a small area of France—had its bloodlines intermingled during nearly eight hundred years of Moorish rule. The Moors were African Muslims (a mixture of Berbers and Arabs) who infused Spain with their non-European genes, culture, and social values. Centuries of Moorish rule resulted in varying degrees of tolerance and acceptance of mixed bloodlines, religions and cultures that resulted in Spain's diverse ethnic, racial, and religious population.

The mixing of "multicultural" Spanish colonizers with indigenous people created the *mestizo* people of the Americas, who continued the ambiguity and contradictions of mixed cultures, especially as it related to race and religion. Despite the obvious evidence of interbreeding there remain individuals from throughout the Americas who continue to profess pure European Spanish ancestry, while others proudly view themselves as descendants of indigenous tribes.

US philosopher Will Durant wrote:

> Civilization is a stream with banks. The stream is sometimes filled with blood from people killing, stealing, shouting, and doing the things historians usually record, while on the banks, unnoticed, people build homes, make love, raise children, sing songs, write poetry and even whittle

statues. The story of civilization is the story of what happened on the banks. Historians…ignore the banks for the
river (Scanlan, *Reporting and Writing: Basics for the 21ˢᵗ
Century*).

For a variety of reasons, Latinos had been "out of sight, out of
mind" for most members of a white Eurocentric society. Their
exploding numbers and projected growth rates now make it
impossible to ignore their presence—or their contributions as
consumers, employees, students, taxpayers, and voters. Increased
knowledge of their history and contributions is one of the keys
to our nation's continued prosperity and the freedom from biases
and prejudices; especially in a country of immigrants who have
proven to themselves and others that our history is not our destiny.

God's Will
Be Done

Cosas a Dios dejadas son bien vengadas.
Translation: Things left to God are best avenged.
Transcreation: The best revenge is to be unlike those who
did you harm.

To understand the rationale behind the concept of God's sanctioning of US American exceptionalism and its influence on generations of white Europeans in the Americas, it is helpful to recognize that the New World was colonized under a principle known as the "Doctrine of Discovery."

In 1095, at the beginning of the Crusades, Pope Urban II issued an edict known as the papal bull *Terra Nullius* (empty land). It gave the royals in Europe the right to "discover" or claim non-Christian lands, wherever in the world they might be. It was extended in 1452 when Pope Nicholas V issued the papal bull *Romanus Pontifex*, declaring war against all non-Christians. These edicts treated non-Christians as uncivilized and subhuman, without rights to land or self-governance. From that point forward, Christians and their sovereign states claimed a God-given right to take control of all lands and used the concept to justify war, colonization, and slavery (*The Doctrine of Discovery and U.S. Expansion*).

The Doctrine of Discovery was a well-established concept in the European Christian world and was used by the major world powers of that time: Spain, Portugal, England, France, and Holland. By the end of the sixteenth century these principles were deeply rooted and led to the conquest of non-Christian lands and people in every part of the world. Even though the United States of America was founded on freedom from such practices, the notion that white European Christians had certain divine rights was etched in the minds of conquerors seeking new worlds to claim for their respective nations.

It may have taken over 900 years, but at a 2012 meeting in Bossey, Switzerland, a committee of the World Council of Churches (WCC) formally denounced the Doctrine of Discovery that had been used to subjugate and colonize indigenous peoples around the world, calling its practices "fundamentally opposed to the gospel of Jesus" (WCC Eeceutive Committee: *Statement on the Doctrine*). The statement rejected the notion held by the doctrine that Christians enjoyed a "moral" and "legal" right, based solely on their religious identity, to invade, seize and control indigenous people and their lands. But the belief in entitlement had already been ingrained in the minds of white Europeans.

PRACTICING WHAT IS PREACHED

The nineteenth century was a major benchmark in the expansion and development of the US; one that was marked by imperialism with religious fervor. The nation's political leadership continued to use the will of God as the rationale for its expansion to the west and south to meet the demands of its increasing population.

The western half of the continent was already home to numerous indigenous tribes and an increasing number of Spanish, Mexican and *mestizo* settlements. Many Latinos even claim ties to the land long before it was "discovered" by European explorers. More than fifty years before the Pilgrims boarded the Mayflower in England, Spanish explorer *Pedro Menéndez de Avilés* and the *Timucua*—natives of modern day Florida—shared a 1565 "Thanksgiving" meal in St. Augustine.

Tejanos celebrated their first "Thanksgiving" in the spring of 1598, after *Juan de Oñate* led more than 400 men, women, and children some four hundred miles across the *Chihuahua* desert to claim the northern *Valle del Rio Grande* for Spain's King Philip II. On the final days of the trip the travelers ran out of food and water, so there was cause for much celebration when they finally reached the *Río Grande*. Annually, on the fourth Saturday in April, people in *San Elizario* (the small town near *El Paso*, settled by members of the *de Oñate* party) people gather for a reenactment and commemoration of Texas' first Thanksgiving.

Later in 1598, *de Oñate* established *San Juan de los Caballeros* in what is now the state of New Mexico. The settlement is located north of *Española* and *Ciudad de la Santa Fe de San Francisco*, known today simply as *Santa Fe*. Spaniards, indigenous people, and *mestizos* had lived in the Southwest for generations and their descendants retained social and cultural values that pre-dated political and cultural borders used to define modern geographic US boundaries. Such historical ties to the land underscore a popular phrase used by many Latinos in the US today: "We didn't cross the border, the border crossed us!"

ALONG CAME JONES

In comparison, the earliest British settlement in the Americas, Jamestown, Virginia, was established in 1607, nearly ten years after *San Juan de los Caballeros* and one hundred years after the founding of *San Juan, Puerto Rico*. Historians refer to the Jamestown settlement—108 Englishmen who began a commercial outpost on the banks of the James River—as the origins of white, Anglo-Saxon, Protestant (WASP) society in the New World. Some 169 years later some of their descendants would become known as the "Founding Fathers," or the framers of the

Constitution of the United States of America, the world's model of democracy, equality, and opportunity.

The early settlers of the thirteen Atlantic colonies and their early attempts at government were influenced by the rights guaranteed to "Englishmen" under the aegis of England's *Magna Carta*, which allowed for all Britishers "...to have and enjoy all liberties, franchises, and immunities to all intents and purposes as if they had been abiding and borne within this our realm of England."

In the early colonies such rights were reserved only for those of British heritage, until Polish immigrants in the Jamestown settlement challenged the exclusivity of those rights during a 1619 meeting of The House of Burgesses, an assembly of elected or appointed officials established by the Virginia Company (founders of the Jamestown settlement) to encourage English craftsmen to settle in the New World. At the time Poles provided the residents of Jamestown both caulking tar (pitch) used for waterproofing boats, ships, and artisan glassworks.

When they learned the rights listed in the *Magna Carta* extended only to "Anglos," they launched the first recorded strike in the colonies and demanded the same privileges granted to the British. Recognizing the critical nature of their skills and products, Anglos extended the coveted "rights of Englishmen" to the Poles. Leveraging their newfound rights, Polish colonists immediately established the first English-Polish bilingual schools to service their community and new Polish immigrants (Seidner, *In Quest of a Cultural Identity*).

The *Magna Carta* also became the source of the USA's most fundamental concepts of law. The US Supreme Court has traced our nation's system of due process—trial by jury of one's peers, speedy and unbiased trials, protection against excessive bail or fines, and the concept of cruel and unusual punishment—to the *Magna Carta*. It was the "rights of Englishmen" that greatly influenced our new nation's laws and Constitution and planted the seeds of white exceptionalism that continues to this day.

THE LAND OF MILK AND HONEY

After invading and taking control of the indigenous people and their lands the Americas prospered, due mainly to the continuing arrival of immigrants that contributed greatly to the New World's growth and progress. Like the pounding waves of the ocean slowly erode the shoreline, waves of immigration altered the social landscape and diversity of the United States of America.

In 1883 Jewish immigrant Emma Lazarus wrote "The Colossus." Its full text is attached to a pedestal of the Statue of Liberty on Ellis Island in New York harbor. It reads:

> "... Give me your tired, your poor, your huddled masses yearning to breathe free, the wretched refuse of your teeming shore. Send these, the homeless, tempest-tost to me, I lift my lamp beside the golden door!"

Words that continue to attract people from every corner of the world.

In 1965, the Immigration and Nationality Act ended immigration policies that gave preference to white European immigrants, resulting in a trend towards a more diverse US population. During the last half of the twentieth century, society placed a greater value on racial and cultural diversity, empowering nonwhites to openly declare and celebrate their cultural and ethnic pride. From 1965 to 2000, over one million immigrants settled in New York City, alone. In Crocheron Park, located in Queens, people from some 150 nations spoke more than 120 different languages, not counting English. This cultural renaissance resulted in a greater number of immigrants' and their children becoming bicultural and bilingual, encouraging other immigrant communities to retain varying degrees of their native cultures and languages.

This resurgence in cultural pride also resulted in ethnic enclaves sprouting-up across the country. The emergence of China towns, Deutsch towns, Korea towns and a spate of Greek, Indian, Italian, Japanese, Polish, and other ethnic neighborhoods is evidence of the ties to distant homelands (and cultures) by an increasingly diverse US population. The newer ethnic enclaves followed precedents established by earlier white European immigrants, who nostalgically named areas and territories after those in their respective countries of origin: New Amsterdam, New Haven, New Jersey, New London, New Orleans, New York, etc.

The continuing waves of immigrants arriving in the US stopped in such immigrant-friendly enclaves to get their bearings before moving to other parts of the country, taking with them a commitment to adopt the USA's white Eurocentric culture and English language. Most European trappings disappeared within a generation or two, leaving diluted, and fewer unadulterated, versions, of Old World enclaves, customs, celebrations and cultures.

CREEPING INCREMENTALISM

For Hispanics, Latinos, and *mestizos*, their presence in the Americas has been substantially different. In contrast to white Europeans, they were not "tempest-tost" like those who crossed oceans in their quest for freedom or new opportunities.

Due to the close proximity of Mexico, Puerto Rico, and Cuba, most Latinos did not make such long-distance sea voyages. The US figuratively delivered itself to their doorsteps through military force in efforts to expand its geographic and political boundaries in a relatively short period of time: 1846 to 1898.

Imperialism is defined as the policy of extending the rule or authority of an empire or nation over foreign countries, or of acquiring and holding colonies and dependencies. Usually it occurs when a larger, economically or militarily powerful group forces its will on a smaller, less powerful one; the territorial expansion of the USA into Mexico, Puerto Rico and Cuba is a prime example.

In 1819 Spain settled a long-standing dispute with the USA over its southern border; in return for Florida and the Gulf Coast territories east of the Mississippi River, the US ceded its claims to the Texas territory. Soon thereafter Mexico's War of Independence resulted in the end of Spain's rule over Mexico.

The newly created Mexican Republic began granting tracts of land to US citizens and European immigrants on the condition they improve the land, convert to Catholicism, learn Spanish, and become Mexican citizens. In response to the offer of free land, hundreds of US citizens and immigrants came to *Tejas* in the 1820s. Most white Europeans immigrants were farmers and came to Texas as independent single families. These settlers soon self-identified as "Texians" and adapted to their Mexican surroundings; but few complied with the Mexican government's conditions of immigration.

About the same time, *Tejanos*—residents of Mexico's then northeasternmost territory—were becoming increasingly disenchanted with the philosophy of a strong central government seated in Mexico City being espoused by President *Antonio López de Santa Anna*. Ultimately tensions arose between the Mexican government and the residents of *Tejas*, as well as by the growing number of Texians concerned with Mexico's opposition to slavery, lack of government services, and immigrant settlement requirements. The Mexican government responded by further restricting immigration inducements and making it "illegal" for US citizens to settle in the Mexican territory of *Tejas*.

Similar to the current anti-immigration controversy taking place in the USA—only in reverse—white settlers, farmers, ranchers, merchants, and mercenaries kept coming to *Tejas* and ignored Mexican laws related to immigration. Mexico's subsequent ban of slavery further infuriated Texians wanting to expand the cotton industry. Mexico's anti-slavery stance fueled the flames of rebellion that coincided with a call to arms by *Tejanos* for an independent state. US and European immigrants, who had previously accepted Mexico's invitation to take up residency in its northernmost territory, supported the insurrection.

In December of 1835 a declaration of independence was ratified and established the Republic of Texas. It was signed by Mexican citizens and Texian immigrants and enacted March 2, 1836. By 1836 there were 38,000 settlers in Texas (most of them of white European stock) who took up arms against the Mexican government. Four days later, March 6, 1836, the thirteen-day siege of the *San Antonio de Valero* mission—the Alamo—ended as Mexican military forces overran the Catholic mission, turned fortress.

Many of the Texians who perished in the Alamo were in *Tejas* to acquire land Mexico had doled-out by the hectare (equal to 2,471 US acres) to US citizens and European immigrants as incentives to settle and develop *Tejas*. *Tejano* combatants defending the Alamo were so committed to "local rule," that they rejected offers from the Mexican army to vacate the Alamo before the battle began. They chose to remain and fight alongside immigrants Davy Crockett, William Bowie, Jim Travis, and a substantial number of *filibusteros*—mercenaries who engaged in unauthorized military expeditions into a foreign country to foment or support revolutions. Today the term "filibuster" is associated with a parliamentary procedure used to obstruct a vote, but in Spanish it still refers to a pirate or plunderer.

The romanticism of the Alamo and the "grit" attributed to US immigrant settlers is a strong lure for many. British rock star Phil Collins has ventured forth in chronicling the history of the Alamo. He is the owner of a major collection of artifacts related to the battle of 1836 and has authored a book about his interest in the Alamo and the history of the Texas Revolution based on artifacts and documents from his private collection. He told *Rolling Stone*, "I'm very proud of myself for writing it and getting all the history accurate" (Collins, *The Alamo and Beyond*).

Latinos, *Tejanos* in particular, have harbored their own perspectives of the Alamo and its role in Texas history. This point of view is a result of *Tejanos* repeatedly having their civic and historical contributions omitted or minimized in US history textbooks and entertainment media accounts; first as citizens of Mexico, then as citizens of the independent republic of Texas, and more recently as US citizens after Texas was admitted into the Union.

Of the nearly two hundred men who died defending the *Alamo*, only nine were Mexicans, or *Tejanos*. Few people outside of their immediate family members, descendants and members of their community ever associated the names of *Juán Abamillo, Juán A. Batillo, Carlos Espalier, Antonio Fuentes, José María Guerrero, Dámacio Jímenes, Tóribio Losoya, Andrés Nava,* and *Gregorio Esparza* with the historic battle at the *Alamo*. Esparza's story is noteworthy because he not only fought for the independence of *Tejas*, he fought against his brother, *Francisco*, a Mexican soldier stationed at the Alamo.

US history, textbooks, and countless media interpretations of the Alamo (and its influence on Texas history) continue to focus on the exploits of white European citizens and immigrants, while routinely omitting the role Spaniards, Mexicans, *mestizos,* and *Tejanos* played in the growth and development of Texas.

Norteamericanos were attracted by affordable (and unprotected) land and since the overwhelming majority was from the agricultural South, they were familiar with tending the land. In a matter of a few years legal, educational, and religious institutions patterned after those in the USA took root and grew. Texians also took control of the social, political, legal and economic affairs of the territory. It was quite easy to claim title to *Tejanos'* lands and personal property in the courts and have such judgments enforced—and defended—by the law enforcement agencies established by the Texians.

SAME DIFFERENCE

Expansion into and occupation of the coveted territory and the accompanying armed conflict were often justified with claims of US American exceptionalism. In his book *Race and Manifest Destiny: The Origins of American Racial Anglo-Saxonism*, US author Reginald Horsman wrote about the commander-in-chief of the Texas militia Sam Houston, who saw the struggle for Texian independence "… as one between a glorious Anglo-Saxon race and an inferior Mexican rabble."

By the mid-1800s the concept of the US as a nation of "God's people" underwent a major transformation. Horsman argued that in the US, by the mid-eighteen century, the concept of a "chosen people" underwent a radical transformation. Whereas US Americans in the previous century saw themselves as a people imbued with a spirit of egalitarianism, by the mid-eighteenth century they had begun to justify slavery, the extermination of indigenous people, and the displacement of Mexican and *mestizo* people from their lands.

Horsman wrote: "… by 1850 the emphasis was on American Anglo–Saxons as a separate superior people who were destined to bring good government, commercial prosperity, and Christianity to American continents of the world." This racial group was superior and "inferior races" were in peril as the US casts its foreign and domestic polices within the parameters of race (Horsman, *Race and Manifest Destiny*).

The fostering of this "superiority complex" was also evident during debates in 1845 related to the annexation of Texas. Secretary of State James Buchanan (who twelve years later would become the fifteenth president of the US) declared, "Our race of men can never be subjected to the imbecile and indolent Mexican race" (McCullough, *Regions of Identity*). It doesn't require a quantum leap to conclude that the seeds of racial discrimination were sown and openly supported as a just cause by individuals occupying the highest and most respected offices of political and military influence in the nation.

Prior to the Mexican-American War in 1846, US westward expansion had not extended much beyond the Mississippi River. Then in 1845, an essay entitled "Annexation," written by John L. O'Sullivan (1813-1895), gave birth to the term "Manifest Destiny." The author claimed:

> ".... the right of our manifest destiny to over spread and to possess the whole of the continent which Providence has given us for the development of the great experiment of liberty... is right such as that of the tree to the space of air and the earth suitable for the full expansion of its principle and destiny of growth" (O'Sullivan, *Annexation*).

O'Sullivan predicted the US would acquire California in the same way it had just acquired Texas: pioneers would venture to California, eclipse Mexicans and Native Americans, win independence, and then seek admission to the Union. Regardless of what the concept was called—Doctrine of Discovery or Manifest Destiny—the principles espoused in O'Sullivan's essay would justify the USA's hunger for land and power. Needless to say, it proved disastrous for indigenous and other non-whites who lost life, liberty, and property as the result of "God's will."

The "divine" mandate associated with Manifest Destiny captured the imagination of politicians, settlers, and commercial interests alike. It was used frequently to rationalize unchecked immigration and expansion into the western territories by US Americans and European immigrants and ultimately led to war with Mexico. US and Texas history books, as well as myths and folklore, would lead most people to believe the Mexican-

American War was fought over basic freedoms and democratic principles. In retrospect it appears US territorial expansion, support of slavery, and personal gain motivated the invasion and taking of Texas.

Early US military victories in Texas prompted calls for the annexation of the entire country of Mexico. Many US politicians contended that bringing Mexico into the Union was the best way to ensure peace during the nation's westward expansion. The idea of appropriating the entire country created considerable controversy. Advocates of Manifest Destiny maintained US laws should not be imposed on people against their will, and the complete annexation of Mexico would be a violation of such religion-based principles. It also meant extending citizenship to millions of Mexicans.

John C. Calhoun—the former US Vice President (1825-1832), US Senator from South Carolina (1832-1843 and 1845-1850) and US Secretary of State (1844-1845)—had supported the annexation of Texas, but opposed a full overthrow of Mexico for racial reasons. In a now famous speech to Congress on January 4, 1848, he made his views quite clear:

> "I know Sir, that we have never dreamt of incorporating into our Union any but the Caucasian race, the free white race. To incorporate Mexico, would be the very first instance of the kind, of incorporating an Indian race, for more than half of the Mexicans are Indians, and the other is composed chiefly of mixed tribes....I protest against such a union as that!...Ours, sir, is the Government of a white race" (Rodriguez, Mongrels, Bastards, Orphans, and Vagabonds).

The debates that followed brought to the forefront major contradictions of Manifest Destiny principles. While the racial superiority theme inherent in the concept suggested that Mexicans were a lesser race and not worthy to become "equal" citizens of the US, the noble "mission of spreading democracy" implied Mexicans would be improved by being exposed to the practices of US democracy. To many historians Manifest Destiny became more of a rationale than public policy, used primarily to condone the confiscation of large tracts of land, among them the territories of Louisiana, Texas, Oregon, and northwest Mexico—today's US Southwest.

Even among US soldiers who participated in the US-Mexico War there was considerable disagreement over the religious rationale for the war. At that time some 40 percent of the US military forces consisted of immigrants, many of who had opted for military service as a way to gain US citizenship due to the fact that gainful employment was not readily available to people of certain nationalities.

Those discriminatory practices, economic, moral and religious biases drove one group of US soldiers to desert and fight on the Mexican side. They were a mostly Irish unit known as the *Batallón de San Patricio* (St. Patrick's Battalion). The Mexicans also referred to them as *San Patricios* and *los colorados* (the red ones) because of their reddish hair and ruddy, sunburned complexions.

> "The *San Patricios* were alienated both from American society, as well as the US Army," says Professor Kirby Miller of the University of Missouri, an expert on Irish immigration in the US. "They realized that the army was not fighting a war of liberty, but one of conquest against fellow Catholics such as themselves." (Brennan, *Ode to the Irish: The Story of St. Patrick's Battalion*)

As a result of their battlefield bravery, the *San Patricios* gained high levels of respect from members of the Mexican army. They left an indelible mark on Mexico and continue to be honored and memorialized as heroes on two separate dates: September 12, which is the generally accepted anniversary of the executions of those convicted by the US Army for desertion in time of war, and March 17, Saint Patrick's Day. Schools, churches, and other landmarks throughout Mexico take their names from these *Mártires Irlandeses* (Irish martyrs). Their story serves to further illustrate the negative attitudes on the part of Anglo-Americans towards other white European immigrant groups during the nineteenth century, especially those who practiced Catholicism.

BACK TO SQUARE ONE

By the end of the US-Mexico War in 1848, Mexicans, indigenous tribes and *mestizos* in the Southwest found they were relegated to yet another type of caste system, similar to the one faced by past generations under Spain's rule. Fair-skinned *criollos* and *mestizos*—considered to be socially, economically or otherwise acceptable—were allowed access to US white Euroentric society, alongside other immigrants who had chosen to shed their foreign cultures and languages in order to assimilate into the USA's "melting pot."

Next to the War of Independence and the Civil War, the US-Mexico War was perhaps one of the most important conflicts in establishing the foundation of the USA as a modern world power. The war was controversial at the time and the political maneuvering surrounding it are echoed in many modern debates over two critical federal government issues: immigration policy and presidential war powers.

Nonetheless, what was once a considerable part of Mexico's national footprint (one with a common culture, language, economy, and political systems) had been absorbed by the United States. The appropriated territory, along with the discovery of gold in California in 1849, heightened the attraction of the western frontier among US citizens and white European immigrants looking for opportunities in the newly acquired Mexican territory.

Waves of immigrants, settlers, and businessmen had used Manifest Destiny as a lever to pry ownership—along with political and economic control of the land—from Mexico and North America's indigenous people. Life under the stars and stripes in the Southwest proved to be the beginnings of yet another clash of cultures; this one between Spaniards, Mexicans, and *mestizos* on one side and the increasing flow of white US citizens and immigrants on the other. It is obvious that racism and its related discriminatory practices are part of our nation's social and religious fabric that have been handed down from generation to generation for so long, that many Americans consider it an entitlement.

If westward expansion of the US was indeed a function of God's will—as it is commonly rationalized under the auspices of the Doctrine of Discovery and Manifest Destiny—then people who profess to believe in Divine Intervention must also consider the possibility of the Biblical proverb: "The Lord giveth, and the Lord taketh away."

Toppling
the Dominoes

Las desgracias nunca vienen solas.
Translation: Misfortunes never arrive alone.
Transcreation: When it rains, it pours.

During his second tour of the New World *Cristóbal Colón* landed on an island inhabited by *Taino* natives who called the island *Borikén*. The Spaniards pronounced it *Borinquen* and referred to the natives as *boricuas*. They also renamed the island *San Juan Bautista*, which was changed to *Puerto Rico*, but its capital city retained the name of *San Juan*.

In 1508, *Juan Ponce de León* was named the island's first governor, enabling him to institute a sequence of events similar to Spanish conquests of other New World territories. The indigenous *Taínos* were expected to pay homage to the king of Spain with tributes of gold, labor and provisions for the Spaniards, while observing Christian ways. The *Taínos* rebelled in 1511, when several *caciques* (tribal leaders) conspired with their traditional enemies, the *Caribs*, to oust the Spanish. Their rudimentary weapons proved to be no match against the Spaniards' horsemen and firearms and they were quickly dispatched. By the latter half of the sixteenth century harsh working conditions and diseases introduced by the Spaniards had eradicated most *Tainos*. African slaves were imported to the island to replace the depleted native inhabitants.

Puerto Rico flourished and became an important Spanish military outpost, as well as a commercial port. But by the late

1600s and early 1700s Spain's colonial emphasis had focused on the more prosperous mainland territories of New Spain, leaving the island relatively unsettled. To protect the island from its enemies, Spain built military installations on its shores, among them *La Fortaleza, El Castillo San Felipe del Morro* and *El Castillo de San Cristóbal.*

THE ENCHANTED ISLAND

By the end of the 1800s, *Puerto Rico* was in its heyday. It had established musical, literary, and cultural traditions and was home to a respected university whose degrees were recognized across the Atlantic in Spain and Europe. Its coat of arms dated back to 1511, 96 years before the founding of Jamestown, Virginia, and 109 years before the landing of the Mayflower on Plymouth Rock. *Puerto Rico* had established a highly evolved political system that also created a thirst for independence from Spain among the island's residents. After four hundred years of colonial rule, *Puerto Rico* finally negotiated a Charter of Autonomy with the Spanish government in 1897, only to be invaded the following year by the US.

In only four months (April to August) Spain sued for peace and under conditions of the Treaty of Paris ceded the islands of Cuba, Puerto Rico, the Philippines, Guam, and the Caroline Islands (modern Micronesia and Palau). On July 25, 1898, the US began the annexation process of *Puerto Rico*, which was immediately colonized and began the twentieth century under US military rule, with its governor serving at the pleasure of the President. Puerto Rico had been transformed from a self-sustaining Spanish territory, into one that was politically, socially, and economically dependent on the US.

Under political control of the US government, the Commonwealth of Puerto Rico experienced less political and economic autonomy than under the Charter of Autonomy it had negotiated with Spain. It lost the right to elect voting representatives to its Congress, to participate in negotiations between Spain and other countries affecting the island's commerce, to ratify or reject commercial treaties affecting Puerto Rico, and to frame tariffs and fix customs on imports and exports. None of these rights were retained under US rule.

Upon becoming a US territory, residents of the annexed island were soon providing much of the East Coast and Midwest with a low-cost workforce and filling labor shortages in critical mainland US jobs—particularly in manufacturing industries and the steel mills and foundries. In 1917 Puerto Rico's residents were granted US citizenship, which happened to coincide with the start of World War I and the initiation of conscription into the US armed forces. Puerto Rico had many of its sons and daughters serve honorably and heroically in every US war since; yet as of 2012 they are still not allowed to vote for the nation's Commander in Chief, or elect representatives to the US Congress.

In our nation's progress toward "a more perfect union" the goal of universal suffrage remains unfulfilled for a substantial number of US citizens. Today the residents of the Commonwealth of Puerto Rico remain disenfranchised. They still live under political conditions that in the past kept non-Protestant whites, non-landowners, women, and blacks from exercising their vote.

A ROSE BY ANY OTHER NAME

Today, the state of New York has the highest concentration of Puerto Ricans. There they are known as *Boricuas, Nuyoricans,* "stateside" or "mainland" Puerto Ricans, and *puertorriqueño americanos;* but "all" are US citizens. New York City continues to be home to the largest Puerto Rican population outside the Commonwealth of Puerto Rico, but they are also represented in all fifty of the nation's states and territories, with substantial numbers in Connecticut, Florida, Massachusetts, Illinois, New Jersey, Ohio, Pennsylvania and Texas. They also have a presence in Arizona, California, and Hawaii due to migration to these states during the early 1900s to seek employment in the agricultural industries.

In 2003, the number of Puerto Ricans born in the US surpassed the population of those on the island; but regardless of their residency, culturally they remain *puertoriqueños*. There are now over four million in the US, with which the island's government maintains strong ties and relations. A telephonic survey conducted by Bendixen & Associates for the Puerto Rico Federal Affairs Administration at the start of the new millennium found a number of indicators of what was termed a strong "dual identity" among stateside Puerto Ricans. The survey found:

A. Over two-thirds (68 percent) say that most of their children's friends are Latino or Puerto Rican.

B. Nearly two-thirds (63 percent) attend celebrations like the Puerto Rican Day parade.

C. Over half (54 percent) are very connected to their families on the island.

Another indicator of the strong identification by Puerto Ricans with the Island is their continued use of the Spanish language; Puerto Ricans are New York City's largest bilingual population. Factors that contribute to the strength of their Puerto Rican identity are similar to those found among the other two major Latino nationality groups, Mexicans and Cubans, which include:

A. The continuous interaction and/or concern with their motherland.

B. A tradition of maintaining motherland cultures in the US.

C. Experiencing racial-ethnic prejudice and discrimination in the US.

D. The continuation of residential and school segregation in the US; among Latinos, Puerto Ricans remain the most residentially segregated.

Combining island and stateside populations, Puerto Ricans represent approximately eight million of the total US Hispanic population of fifty million-plus. The majority of Puerto Ricans remains geographical located in the northeastern US and at the turn of the century were the most urbanized ethnic group in the nation, with 55.8 percent living in metropolitan areas. This is more than double the concentration by non-Latinos (25 percent) and higher than that of Central and South Americans (47.9), Mexican-Americans (43.1) and Cuban-Americans (22.3).

'I WANT TO LIVE IN AMERICA'

Concentration of Puerto Ricans in urban areas such as New York City may have contributed to yet another example of Latino stereotyping. The 1957 Broadway musical "West Side Story" introduced theater crowds to the Puerto Rican segment of the nation's Latino population. In the classic musical Puerto Ricans were portrayed as violence-prone gang members, criminals, and indolent welfare recipients. There were mixed emotions about being the focus of a Broadway play; some Puerto Ricans and other Latinos were pleased with the attention given to their traditionally overlooked community, while others questioned the focus on negative stereotypes generally associated with Latinos.

The play was made into a motion picture in 1961, which further spread images of Puerto Ricans to a broader swath of white Eurocentric Americans. Despite arguments made by its producers that the movie version of the play was intended to be "a fun musical with good music and good dancers," it was for many US Americans the only images of Puerto Ricans to which they had ever been exposed (Salinas, *West Side Story Stereotypes*).

Despite its premise of "white versus brown" street gangs, the film had only one Latina in a major role; Puerto Rican actress *Rita Moreno* was cast in the supporting role of *Anita*. The late Natalie Wood played the lead female role of *María* and had her skin cosmetically darkened to make her appear "more Puerto Rican," Hollywood code for "darker." (A similar fate was visited on *Jossie de Guzmán*, a native Puerto Rican depicting *María* in the 1980 Broadway production, who also had to have her skin darkened to make her look "more Puerto Rican.") Apparently, there were preconceived notions about what Puerto Rican skin color was supposed to be, and to fit those notions, "black face" gave way to "brown face."

The dialogue and music lyrics were filled with racist references that persist to this day:

> "Yeah, but these PRs are different. They multiply. They keep comin'. Like cockroaches. Close the windows. Shut the doors. They're eatin' our food. They're breathin' all the air. The end to free enterprise..."

> "Boy, what you Puerto Ricans have done to this neighborhood."

> "All right, Bernardo, get your trash outta here."

Defenders of "West Side Story" argued that the Puerto Rican community had made a "mountain out of a molehill"—basically ignoring the racism and discrimination Puerto Ricans faced as a result of negative stereotypes perpetrated by the entertainment industry. Like the objectionable advertising campaigns that depicted Latinos in less than positive roles, the producers maintained their "artistic" efforts were never intended to be stereotypic or injurious to Puerto Ricans.

Even today Puerto Ricans are still not recognized by some segments of our society as citizens. A recent example of this display of ignorance and prejudice was exhibited during a nationally televised Kansas State University vs. Southern Mississippi University 2012 NCAA basketball tournament game played March 15, 2012. A chant, "Where's your green card?"—a reference to immigrant status—was directed at K-State player Angel Rodriguez by members of the Southern Miss band. Ironically, Rodriguez was born in Puerto Rico, which makes him a US citizen, a fact most high school and college students should have already learned.

CUBA LIBRE, ANYONE?

A series of events in which one causes or influences the next is often referred to as a "domino effect." The Spanish-American War, which prompted the invasion of Puerto Rico in 1898, was the result of US intervention in Cuba's War of Independence from Spain—the lynchpin in a series of events that resulted in the toppling of a third major Spanish-speaking territory.

Having economic and strategic interests in Cuba, some politicians and business interests argued in favor of the US taking Cuba from Spain (along with Hawaii, the Philippine Islands, Puerto Rico and other Caribbean islands) because "great powers" needed strategically located colonies. The winds of war were blowing and were unfurling economic and strategic interests for the world to see.

The relationship between the USA and Cuba differed from those with Mexico and Puerto Rico. Trade agreements between Cuba and the US colonies had flourished as a result of attempts by commercial interests in the thirteen colonies to avoid paying import taxes to England. At that time Cuba was a Spanish colony and the center of tobacco and sugar production in the western hemisphere. It had become a major trading partner for the soon-to-be "independent" US colonies and by 1818, trade relations between Cuba and the US had begun to surpass those between Spain and the USA.

As the first Territorial Governor of Florida (c. 1821), Andrew Jackson reportedly asserted that Cuba was "the most interesting addition that could ever be made to our system of States." As US President (1829-1837), he is reported to have said to his Vice President John C. Calhoun that the US "ought, at the first possible opportunity, to take Cuba." For years to follow, that idea circulated among high-ranking US government officials wishing to add Cuba to the Union (Thomas, *Cuba*).

In 1823, discussion had begun at the highest political levels about the US expanding the Union to include Cuba. In a letter to President James Monroe dated October 24, 1823, Thomas Jefferson wrote, "I candidly confess that I have ever looked on Cuba as the most interesting addition that could ever be made to our system of states" (Leypoldt, *The Publisher's Weekly*).

Finally, in 1884, US diplomats meeting in Ostend, Belgium hatched a plot that came to be known as the Ostend Manifesto. It proposed the purchase of Cuba from Spain for $130 million. The Ostend narrative declared in true Manifest Destiny bravado, "... Cuba is as necessary to the North American republic as any of its present members, and that it belongs naturally to that great family of states of which the Union is the Providential Nursery" (Aix-la-Chapelle: *Full Text*). After the plot was made public, it was quickly abandoned due to opposition from anti-slavery supporters who believed Cuba would become a slave state.

By 1877, the US was consuming over 80 percent of Cuba's exports, thereby controlling the island's commercial endeavors, prices, and production levels. Cuba's business sector was essentially in the hands of the *yanquis* (Yanks), who were migrating to Cuba in unprecedented numbers, making the islands northern shore look more like the US coastline. The long-established relationships between Cuba and the USA facilitated the integration of Cuban commerce into the US economy; the strengthening of businesses ties further undermined the nation island's relationship with Spain.

Concurrently, many religious zealots in the US wanted to Christianize the world around them according to their prevailing views of religion. Traditionally, religion in Cuba had been mainly Catholic (estimated at almost two-thirds of the population), and influenced by *Santería*, which blended elements of West African beliefs with Roman Catholic and indigenous traditions. *Santería* made it possible for Africans to retain their traditional beliefs while appearing to adapt to Catholicism.

Like Mexicans and Puerto Ricans, Cubans maintained ties to Roman Catholicism and its icons. *La Virgen de la Caridad del Cobre* (Our Lady of Charity of El Cobre) is the religious patroness of Cuba and is greatly revered and seen as a symbol of Cuba. In *Santería, La Virgen de la Caridad* was syncretized with the goddess *Ochún* and is celebrated annually on September 8. Protestants did not consider Roman Catholics or the practice of *Santería* to be acceptable and wanted to invade Cuba in order to convert the "pagans." President McKinley, a devout Christian, claimed to have been commanded in a dream to send the country to war, which coincided perfectly with the various political pressures forced on him to take military action against Spain.

In spite of the religious rationale for military intervention in Cuba, Protestantism—which today includes Baptists, Pentecostals, Jehovah's Witnesses, Seventh-day Adventists, Presbyterians, Anglicans, Episcopalians, Methodists, Quakers and Lutherans—remains less than five percent of the island's religious population.

FAIR AND BALANCED

Another major influence in US military involvement in Cuba was the US news media. Two of the nation's top publishers in the late

1800s, William Randolph Hearst of the *New York Journal* and Joseph Pulitzer of *The World*, stood out among key "war hawks" that supported a war to liberate Cuba. As one of few sources of public information, newspapers had become influential in forming public opinion.

Both publishers saw a war with a world power like Spain as an opportunity to increase circulation (and advertising sales revenues) at their respective newspapers. They were both determined to reach a daily circulation of a million readers and didn't mind making up (or embellishing) stories in order to attain their objectives. Parlaying the growing spirit of US nationalism, these future media moguls distributed competing sensationalized, and sometimes manufactured, anti-Spain articles, which gave birth to the term "yellow journalism."

Together Hearst and Pulitzer created a patriotic frenzy in the US by printing news articles designed to stir emotions and foment bellicose sentiments against Spain. By the time the USS Maine exploded in Havana's harbor on February 15, 1898, the US print media had aroused national sentiment to the point that President McKinley feared his political party would suffer if he did not declare war against Spain. The sinking of the USS Maine was used as additional rationale for the Spanish-American War and popularized the phrase: "Remember the Maine, to Hell with Spain!"

The US press had no doubts as to who was responsible for the disaster; it was the "cowardly Spanish" they reported. The *New York Journal* even published graphic representations of how Spanish saboteurs had fastened an underwater mine to the ship and remotely detonated it from ashore. The explosion became a subject of much speculation: "Was the sinking of the battleship due to an internal explosion or an external mine?" To this date the real cause remains an unsolved mystery. However the seeds of distrust of the Spanish had been planted in the minds of US citizens and the "press" became a dominant political influence that is true to this day.

Although Cuban independence from Spain was granted in 1898, US military forces took control of the island. The interim military government limited local Cuban involvement in the island's governance and disbanded the Cuban army. Similar to its oversight of Puerto Rico, the US reserved the right to oversee Cuba's international pacts and agreements, its economic and internal affairs, and including the right to establish a military naval station at Guantanamo Bay. Most of these early provisions were repealed by 1934, but the naval base remains under the control of the US and as of 2012 was still mired in controversy as a "holding facility" for alleged and suspected terrorist prisoners.

Cuba's economy continued to be driven by sugar, which accounted for as much as 80 percent of its export revenues. Located only ninety miles off the coast of Florida, it was supported by a strong tourist industry that relied on Havana's hotels, gambling casinos, and brothels. The control of Cuba and its economy proved to be a major benefit of the Spanish American War as it ensured protection for thriving US-Cuban commercial efforts, which dated back to pre-1776 colonies.

By the end of the 1950s, Cuba had developed into one of the leading economies in Latin America, yet economic disparities among its residents increased. US and other foreign investors managed Cuba's economy and together controlled about three-fourths of all agricultural properties and 40 percent of sugar production. Dictator *General Fulgencio Batista* exercised absolute control over the political system until 1959, when Fidel Castro and his revolutionary forces overthrew Bautista and evicted all external interests from the island, including the US.

YEARNING TO BREATHE FREE

Since then US policies related to immigrant Cubans have been positive, for the most part. With the arrival of some 500,000 Cuban refugees in the 1960s (mainly from the upper- and middle-classes), federal programs were established for job training, business loans, education subsidies and home purchases. These programs provided substantial advantages to Cuban immigrants in their relocation efforts to Florida and other parts of the US. Unlike other Latin Americans, Cubans did not have to go through a lengthy immigration process; once they set foot in the US they were legal.

Of the three major Latino groups, Cubans have had the greatest amount of success in assimilating into the USA's white Eurocentric economic, political, and social mainstreams. There are some who say it was due to social and economic compatibility, as most of the early refugees from Cuba were well-educated professionals and successful entrepreneurs of Spanish heritage, whose middle- and upper-class and political values closely approximated those of conservative US white European Americans.

Between 1962 and 1979, hundreds of thousands of Cubans entered the country, but Cuba's favored nation status may have come to an abrupt end with the Mariel Boatlift of the 1980s. In response to some ten thousand Cubans seeking asylum at the Peruvian Consulate in Havana, President Jimmy Carter authorized sanctuary for 3,500. Top priority was to be extended to political prisoners, followed by relatives of families already established in the US and lastly to refugees seeking political asylum. However Cuba sent whomever it wished, including imprisoned criminals and institutionalized mentally ill patients. The Castro regime promoted the notion that everyone was free to leave the island. US officials were surprised when refugees started arriving on Florida's shores on April 21 1980; the number of anticipated Cubans had ballooned from the initially authorized 3,500 to nearly 125,000.

Cuban "boat people" arrivals continued over the years and rose from several hundred in 1989 to a few thousand in 1993. After a series of Castro speeches in 1994, riots ensued in Havana, and the Cuban exodus by boat escalated. The US Coast Guard and US Border Patrol intercepted almost forty thousand Cubans in 1994, the highest numbers since the Mariel Boatlifts of 1980. Immigration patterns have changed since the mid-1990s. Many began leaving from Cuba's southern and western coasts to Mexico's *Yucatán* peninsula; from there, they traveled to the US border, crossing into Texas to seek asylum.

Many without family ties in Florida settled in the Houston area. The term "dusty foot" (a reference to the "wet foot, dry foot" immigration policy) is used to identify Cubans coming to the US via Mexico. Regardless of their routes this group of immigrants had caught the public's attention and Cuban refugees became part of the undesirable Latino immigrants coming to the US.

In 1995, the US gave Cuban immigrants treatment that no other group of refugees or immigrants received: the "wet-foot, dry-foot policy" allows Cubans who reach US soil a fast track to permanent residency. The government amended the 1966 Cuban Adjustment Act during Cold War tensions between the US and the island nation. Under the policy, when Cuban nationals are apprehended in the water between the two countries, they are considered to have "wet feet" and denied entry into the USA; those who make it to shore are considered to have "dry feet" and qualify for legal permanent resident status and US citizenship. The law does make exceptions for Cubans caught at sea who can prove they are vulnerable to persecution if sent back. The evidence has to be clear and convincing for the government to grant asylum, however (Morley, *U.S.-Cuba Migration Policy*).

THERE'S NO ESCAPING IT

Many Americans were already aware of renowned Cubans like *Desi Arnaz, Celia Cruz, Xavier Cugat, La Lupé, Benny Moré, Damaso "Prez" Prado, Mongo Santamaría* and other world-class Cuban entertainers. Premium cigars and rums notwithstanding, they were some of the most recognizable *cubanos* in the USA.

Yet the motion picture industry could not resist presenting mainstream America with the latest in a line of Latino stereotypes. The 1983 movie "Scarface" was an example of how even a successful, highly educated, politically-conservative group like Cuban émigrés could not escape the stereotyping previously visited on other Latinos.

Al Pacino played the role of Tony Montana, a Cuban beneficiary of the Mariel Boatlift, who becomes a violent, cocaine-dealing hoodlum obsessed with traditional symbols of success: power, material wealth, and the gratuitous "eye candy" (played by Michelle Pfeiffer). In one of his tirades, Montana (in a thick theatrical Spanish accent) espouses his perception of success in the US. "In this country, you gotta make the money first. Then when you get the money, you get the power. Then when you get the power, then you get the women."

The film's emphasis on the influx of Cuban "undesirables"—along with little attention paid to the political reasons for the mass exodus from Castro's communist government—resulted in criticism and opposition to the film's production by the Cuban-American community. Response to the finished film was also mixed and openly lambasted for its criminality, violence, and profanity—similar to previous negative stereotypes and fear-inducing portrayals used by news and entertainment media to project Latinos to mainstream US America.

TAKES A LICKIN', KEEPS ON TICKIN'

Despite the barriers and obstacles placed before them, Latinos in the US continue to compete and persevere in order to obtain their "piece of the pie" in a society historically concerned with cultural, racial, and class differences. There is no doubt Latinos have contributed to the growth and prosperity of this country, which has become their economic and political "fatherland." However, many US-born and immigrant Latinos from throughout the Americas are now circling the wagons around the cultures and customs of their motherlands and attempting to balance the best of two cultures—unlike previous generations who jettisoned theirs in an attempt to blend into the homogenizing "melting pot."

Common languages and similar cultures—along with their experiences with prejudice and discrimination—binds Latinos together as the nation's largest ethnic group that continues to grow in size, influence, and power. Whereas most immigrants left faraway countries to start anew in a foreign land, Latinos literally had the US come to them, allowing proximity to their native cultures, language, and geographic origins—be they the Caribbean Islands, Central and South America, or the modern Southwest. By understanding these ties to motherlands that have existed for millennia, one can understand why their cultures continue to evolve in a country that is only 230 years old.

In a span of fifty years the US toppled the societies of the three major Spanish-speaking homelands of modern Latinos. Yes, Mexicans, Puerto Ricans, and Cubans suffered defeats at the hands of a superior economic, military, and political power. Yes, when it rains, it pours. And yes, what doesn't kill you makes you stronger.

To Protect
and Serve

Más vale la seguridad que la policía.
Translation: One's security is more valuable than the
police themselves.
Transcreation: Tyranny often hides behind the badge of
authority.

Latinos remain skeptical about their interaction with law
enforcement and the criminal justice systems in the United
States, especially with immigration enforcement practices being
placed in the hands of local law enforcement personnel. Why?
Basically they are dubious about how such enforcement will
be implemented.

According to *NBC Latino News,* a poll conducted by Latino
Decisions for the National Hispanic Media Coalition found
nearly one-third of non-Hispanics believe over 50 percent of all
Hispanics in the United States are undocumented immigrants
(Lilley, *Poll*). Of the more than fifty million Latinos in the US,
approximately 80 percent of them are native-born or naturalized
citizens. That translates into the possibility of forty million US
citizens being suspected of being "illegal" immigrants, too often
solely on the basis of appearance, accent, and/or surname.

Proponents of increased enforcement say, "If you haven't done
anything wrong, you have nothing to fear!" Let me remind "law
and order" types that since the end of the Mexican-American
War in 1848, Latinos in the US have experienced abuse and disrespect at the hands of law enforcement personnel, while many
more have been denied due process by the criminal justice system.

There are Latino immigrants who live, reside, and work in the US without the proper or up-to-date documentation, but historically there has been a distinct difference in how law enforcement officials mete out their versions of "protect and serve" when it comes to US-born Latino citizens and authorized immigrants.

For generations, relations between Latinos and law enforcement agencies have suffered because of misconceptions, misunderstandings and distrust between white Eurocentric US Americans and Latinos. Much of the apprehension on the part of Latinos, especially in the Southwestern states, stems from accounts beginning with the years immediately before, during and following the Texas Revolution in 1836. It continued well beyond the end of the Mexican-American War in 1848, when border states' police, sheriffs, judges and other legal systems were used as tools for special interests to enforce property dispossessions causing Mexican and *mestizo* owners to lose their homes, livelihoods and personal property.

The Treaty of Guadalupe Hidalgo, which brought an end of the Mexican-American War, also ceded a large portion of Mexico to the US in exchange for $15 million and relief from debt. The treaty was supposed to protect the existing civil rights and land claims and provide full US citizenship to Mexicans who remained in the ceded territories. In ratifying the treaty the US Senate eliminated one important article that ensured the US government would honor and guarantee all *mercedes* (land grants) awarded by Spain and Mexico in the territories ceded to the USA—with the condition that all land grants be "legally" proven. In 1851, Congress passed the first laws regarding property protection provisions under the Treaty of Guadalupe Hidalgo, but it was limited only to Spanish and Mexican *mercedes* in California.

In 1854, Congress established the office of the Surveyor General of New Mexico to ascertain "the origin, nature, character, and extent to all claims to lands under the laws, usages, and customs of Spain and Mexico." Treaty obligations, as well as accepted principles of International Law, required the US to respect valid land grants located in the territories ceded to the US by Mexico in 1848 and 1853. Some six years elapsed before a procedure was established to adjudicate the validity of private land claims brought by Mexican owners. A Committee on Private Land Claims was established and seats on the panel were handed out as political perquisites. Due to the subsequent amount of corruption in determining claims based on political rather than legal factors, Congress was forced to abolish the Committee. Congress created the Court of Private Land Claims in 1891 that consisted of five justices, which was to exist for only 4 four years, but lasted nine (Bowden, *Bowden Book I*, Chapter Six).

The court was responsible for deciding land claims in the territories of New Mexico, Arizona, and Utah—and the states of Nevada, Colorado, and Wyoming. It heard over three hundred cases involving more than thirty-six million acres of land and confirmed only 87 land grants, for a total of three million acres—less than 10 percent of the land grants in question. Many of the confirmed grants were even further reduced in size from what was actually claimed. In all, over thirty-three million acres of land belonging to Mexican families were lost as a result of judicial bureaucracy and malfeasance.

The court attributed the reasons for the reductions to the Spanish system of apportionment measures and boundary definitions to centuries-old landmarks that were hard to find; *varas*, the standards or criteria for measurements varied depending on when the grant was made; or the grant might be to the *faldas* (skirts of the mountains), which could be anywhere from the edge of the foothills to the timberline. These "legal" strokes of a pen created new, and reinforced past, attitudes that contributed to strained relations between Americans of Mexican descent and US law and justice systems that would continue for generations.

TO PROTECT AND SERVE

Apprehension on the part of Latinos toward US law enforcement and the courts is based on generations of personal, family, and community experiences with prejudice, violence, and discrimination at the hands of vigilantes, police and the justice systems. Even today members of the Latino community say they, or someone they know, has encountered violations of their civil rights with unwarranted search and seizure, brutality, disrespect, and profiling practices due solely to being—or appearing to be—Latino.

Among such violations are atrocities committed by Texas Rangers—or *rinches* as they were called by Spanish-speakers—against *Tejanos* and *Méjicanos* that have been handed down for generations in a variety of forms: *cuentos* (folk stories), *corridos* (musical ballads of folk heroes and injustices), word of mouth, and articles in Spanish-language newspapers.

One such case in the early twentieth century alleged Mexican revolutionaries plotted an uprising against new white landowners in Texas that was never fully carried out, but there were alleged raids that resulted in property thefts and the deaths of some white settlers. The Texas Rangers were called in and protection quickly turned into retaliation. The vaunted lawmen were credited with the 1918 massacre of the entire male population—fifteen Mexican men and boys ranging from 16 to 72 years of age—of Porvenir in western Presidio County (Webb, *The Texas Rangers*).

Investigations by the Texas Legislature in 1919, found that in the years 1910-1919 as few as three hundred and as many as five thousand Mexicans were estimated to have been killed by Texas Rangers. The investigations found the state police force had been involved in innumerable acts of brutality and injustice.

One such atrocity led to the 1975 production of a documentary film, "Border Bandits," which focused on Roland Warnock, then a 19-year-old working at the McAllen Ranch in South Texas. He claimed to have witnessed a team of Texas Rangers shoot and kill 67 year-old *Jesús Bazán* and his son-in-law *Antonio Longoria* in 1915. Warnock's recollection and ensuing investigation into the facts surrounding the murders were the basis of the film which was directed by Roland's grandson Kirby Warnock, who remembered hearing the story when he was a child.

"The thought of the Texas Rangers shooting an unarmed man in the back was unbelievable, but also unthinkable," Kirby Warnock said about his reaction to his grandfather's story. In the film, he comments how "most Texans" shared his initial reaction and refused to believe the storied lawmen were capable of such unlawful acts. The documentary was a counterpoint to the heroic and "larger than life" accounts of the Texas Rangers proudly promoted in films, print, media, as well as folklore. The film challenged the mythical exploits of this "elite" cadre of lawmen by exposing their use of state-sanctioned terrorism. It also uncovered the racial hierarchy of "white over brown," particularly as it related to illegal land acquisition, forceful repression and racial discrimination.

Initially Warnock's investigation focused on the deaths of *Bazán* and *Longoria* as if the murders were an isolated incident. Their killing didn't even warrant death certificates and were viewed as two more dead Mexicans of the unreported number who lost their lives during this time period: men, women, and children whose only crime was being "brown" in an increasingly "white" Texas.

Among the numerous historical texts written about the violent period of the early twentieth century is William D. Carrigan's, *The Making of a Lynching Culture*. According to the author— a professor of history at Rowan University in New Jersey—the Rangers responded to suspect Mexican behaviors:

> "with brutality, with assassinations, murders, lynchings and massacres...Thousands of Mexicans fled the region, were killed without trial, taken out of jail and executed... It was a terrible, bloody period of violence even defenders

of Texas Rangers (write about)" (Carrigan, *The Making of a Lynching Culture*).

Similar stories of confrontation between the vaunted state police and Latino citizens continued into the 1960s and 1970s when Texas Rangers were called in to break up labor strikes organized by Latino civil rights activists. Such accounts were "salt in the wound" for some who bristle at the mention of *los rinches*. Latino sentiment towards the Texas Rangers is another example of why an accurate chronicling of history is critical in an increasingly multi-cultural society.

OLD HABITS DIE HARD

Now let's turn the calendar pages forward to August 2, 1942, in Southern California for another example of why Latinos became wary of white Eurocentric law enforcement and justice. This particular episode revolved around the so-called "Sleepy Lagoon murder," which was set in an environment of ethnic and racial paranoia that permeated Southern California in the early 1940s. Following a fight between young Mexican Americans from neighboring *barrios* (neighborhoods) in Maywood, CA, which was believed to have resulted in the death of one of the participants, the Los Angeles Police Department (LAPD) arrested some two dozen members of what local media had dubbed the "Thirty-Eighth Street Gang" and charged all of them with murder. The media reported on the death of a single youth as proof of a "Mexican crime wave" (Larralde, pp. 17-160).

Testimony began on October 19, 1942, and the typecasting of the defendants continued. An example of the bias was the testimony of prosecution witness Lieutenant Edward Duran Ayres of the Los Angeles Sheriff's Office:

"Mexican Americans are essentially Indians and therefore Orientals or Asians. Throughout history Orientals have shown less regard for human life than have the Europeans. Further, Mexican Americans had inherited their 'naturally violent' tendencies from the 'bloodthirsty Aztecs' of Mexico, who were said to have practiced human sacrifice centuries ago" (Smith, *Great American Trials*).

On January 12, 1943, all but five of the Sleepy Lagoon defendants were convicted of murder or assault. Their trial ended on January 13, 1943, under the supervision of Judge Charles W. Fricke. Nine of the defendants were convicted of second-degree murder and sentenced to time in San Quentin Prison. The rest of the suspects were charged with lesser offences and incarcerated in the Los Angeles County Jail (Larralde, 117-160).

The convictions were subsequently reversed on appeal in 1944. However confidence and trust in the US law enforcement and justice systems had suffered another blow within the Mexican-American community. Many wary Latinos in Los Angeles believed the same sentiments on the part of the majority community that led to the Sleepy Lagoon trial resulted in the "Zoot Suit Riots" of 1943.

The Zoot Suit riots were a series of street melees during World War II that took place between white servicemen stationed throughout Southern California and Mexican-American, African-American, and Filipino-American youth, who wore the trendy outfits, considered by the general population as unpatriotic and extravagant use of fabric during war time (Jamieson & Romer, *The Changing Portrayal of Adolescents in the Media Since 1950*).

Led by media portrayals, a public outcry for justice and vengeance against the Zoot Suit wearing youths motivated the LAPD to conduct a round-up of "suspicious looking" individuals on the nights of August 10 and 11, 1943—with the help of "unofficially deputized" white servicemen, who were unleashed throughout

Los Angeles to attack, strip, and beat young non-white males "at will." In all, over six hundred individuals were attacked and arrested on suspicion of assault and armed robbery—175 were held on those charges. Of those arrested during the round-ups, everyone was Mexican-American.

Historian and author Carey McWilliams witnessed the attacks and wrote:

> Marching through the streets of downtown Los Angeles, a mob of several thousand soldiers, sailors, and civilians, proceeded to beat up every zoot-suiter they could find... Streetcars were halted while Mexicans, and some Filipinos and Negroes, were jerked out of their seats, pushed into the streets and beaten with sadistic frenzy (McWilliams, *North from Mexico: The Spanish-Speaking People of the United States*).

According to retired Deputy Sheriff Don McFadden, who was quoted in a book by oral historian and Pulitzer Prize winner Studs Terkel:

> Servicemen would go into theaters in downtown L.A. They'd go up and make the projectionist shut-off the movie, right? Turn the lights on. They'd go down both aisles. Any Zoot-Suiters they saw (he laughs), they'd drag him right out by his seat and (claps hands) beat him, tear his clothes up, what have you. They were mostly sailors and marines. They came from San Diego (Terkel, *The Good War: An Oral History of World War II*).

In the aftermath of the attacks, the LAPD ignored the white attackers and arrested only zoot-suiters. Los Angeles area media and newspapers, including the Times, Examiner, and Daily News, lauded the servicemen's patriotism while taking an inflammatory tone directed squarely at Mexican-Americans in their reporting—during and after the riots. The media vilified zoot-suiters to the point of portraying them as members of murderous and dangerous gangs; traits that were quickly adopted as movie themes by nearby Hollywood studios, resulting in stereotypes associated with Latinos that remain in effect to this day.

However, local community activism and organizing raised awareness and funds for the defense of those arrested, resulting in their release and their eventual acquittal. Despite the rampant paranoia over a Mexican crime wave, in October 1944, the Second District Court of Appeals reversed the murder convictions of those charged. Other attacks on zoot suit-wearing youths took place in Beaumont, TX; Chicago, IL; San Diego, CA; Detroit, MI; Evansville, IL; Philadelphia, PA and New York, NY. The seeds of distrust of law enforcement within the Latino community had once again been validated (Novas, *Everything You Need to Know about Latino History*).

TAKE IT FROM THE TOP!

Some law enforcement proponents defend the Texas Rangers' atrocities, the Sleepy Lagoon murder and Zoot Suit attacks as justified or isolated events, but these types of behaviors on the part of law enforcement toward the Latino community continued. On August 29, 1970, more than twenty thousand Latinos and supporters gathered to take part in the National Chicano Moratorium Committee's East Los Angeles protest against the war in Vietnam, as well as the disproportionately high casualty rate of Latino military personnel serving on the front lines. Among all US soldiers from the Southwest, nearly 20 percent of the war casualties were Latinos—nearly twice their percentage of the US population at that time (Johnson, *Remembering the Chicano Moratorium*).

Demonstrators took advantage of the event to protest the absence of equal employment, housing, and other civil rights afforded to US citizens. The peaceful rally at Laguna Park (now Ruben F. Salazar Park) in East Los Angeles was disrupted when 1,500 LAPD officers and L.A. Sheriff's deputies attempted to disperse the marchers by shooting tear-gas canisters into the crowd. Four people were killed and hundreds were arrested. Among the victims was the renowned *Los Angeles Times* reporter-columnist Rúben Salazar—killed by an armor piercing tear-gas projectile fired into the Silver Dollar Cafe, where he and others had sought shelter.

Salazar had previously brought considerable attention to abuse of Latinos by the LAPD, which had become a frequent target of his investigative reports. He had repeatedly written about the high Latino casualty rates in the Vietnam War. As a result of his reporting and commentaries, Salazar was under investigation by the LAPD and the Federal Bureau of Investigation (FBI).

Due to his media popularity and recognition as a role model, his death had far-reaching consequences and led many community activists to continue their focus on police brutality and inequality. While an inquest found that his death was a homicide, the deputy sheriff who fired the shell was never charged or prosecuted.

Historically, Latino communities had experienced a greater share of police mistreatment and harsher penalties in the criminal justice system. Demonstrations related to law enforcement abuse, profiling and variances in sentencing between whites and non-whites convicted of similar offenses had become commonplace in Latino communities across the nation.

On May 1, 2007, the LAPD again used unwarranted physical force against the Latino community; this time law enforcement officers attempted to disperse a crowd at an immigration-rights rally. Police wielded batons and fired 240 "less-than-lethal" rounds at demonstrators and news media personnel covering the event. The police actions injured at least ten people—including seven news reporters—and raised questions about overly aggressive tactics to disperse a largely peaceful crowd that had obtained a legal permit to stage the rally. Even the LAPD police chief labeled some of the officers' actions "inappropriate" (Reston and Rubin, Los Angeles to pay $13 million to settle May Day melee lawsuits).

The advent of community oriented policing practices, along with the diversification of police staffing to include bilingual/bicultural officers—have improved relations between law enforcement and the Latino community. Many in the public sector recognize increasing Latino population numbers and attendant growing influence as taxpayers and voters is also changing attitudes and behaviors on the part of public policy makers and law enforcement personnel. By gaining influence within municipalities, counties, states, federal and other governmental entities, Latinos are helping to promote the notion that law enforcement and criminal justice systems in the US are about protecting and serving all members of the community, regardless of appearance, language spoken or place of birth.

The Power of Self-Determination

Ser independiente es el privilegio de los fuertes.
Translation: Independence is a privilege of the strong.
Transcreation: A strong, positive self-image is the best preparation for success.

During the middle of the twentieth century, demographers began publicizing the high rate of growth among Latinos in the United States of America. Aware of their growing numbers, potential consumer power and latent political influence gave rise to the term "Sleeping Giant" when referring to Latinos. Demographers concluded the projected growth rate of Hispanics would greatly affect the economic, political and cultural balance of our nation. Reference by social scientists to a sleeping giant connoted a degree of dormancy (not requiring immediate attention) and numerical growth (that could not be ignored). What may have been underestimated was that this particular giant was still in its infancy and would continue its incredible rate of growth that is projected to reach 25 percent of the total US population by 2050.

It is said that a generation that ignores its history has no past or future. It is essential that the history of Latinos in the US be shared so we can begin to understand how they may further influence the future of our nation. Latinos represent a wide range of ancestral backgrounds, from Spanish explorers to indigenous tribes from throughout the Western Hemisphere. The majority of Latinos are *mestizos*—the offspring of indigenous people and Spanish conquerors—who proudly (and some defiantly) refer to their *Azteca, Chibcha, Inca, Maya, Mechica, Quechua, Quisqueyano, Taino, Tolteca, Yaquí* and other indigenous origins at the expense of their Spanish ancestry. These indigenous populations consisted of culturally distinct groups from most areas of what is now North, Central and South America. There are many more indigenous groups, but attempts to list all of the genealogical roots would be a daunting task.

A critical factor to consider is the survival of the Spanish language and the simultaneous evolution of *mestizos* and their culture; the result of combining two distinct civilizations: the Spanish and the indigenous people of the Western Hemisphere. It is these ties to their pre-Colombian heritage that help to explain the attachment many Latinos feel toward geographic regions of the Americas. That attachment is reinforced by those who take exception to Eurocentric references associated with the term Hispanic and Latino; instead they promote the indigenous, pre-Colombian concept of *Nican Tlaca* (*Náhuatl* for "We the people here") as an alternative.

Many Latinos do not identify with the label "Indian" because they feel that term describes people from India. They also reject the term "Native American" because the indigenous inhabitants of the continent were not related to *Amerigo Vespucci*, the Italian explorer, financier, navigator, and cartographer for whom the Western Hemisphere was named. Some advocates of *Nican Tlaca* feel the *Azteca* civilization—the combination of *Mechica* and *Tolteca* tribes—contain historic, cultural, linguistic, and hereditary characteristics that are the foundation of a single nation, which includes a substantial number of the people and cultures of the continent.

Conversely, there are also those who steadfastly hold on to their Spanish ancestry, often rejecting any connection to indigenous bloodlines. They claim "pure" Spanish (*Hispano*) bloodlines and connections to ancestors who built the Spanish cities of *San Agustín* in *Florida* and *San Juan* in *Puerto Rico*, or searched for the fabled "Seven Cities of Gold" throughout the present Southwest region of the USA. *Hispanos* have resided in enclaves that pre-date US westward expansion throughout modern-day California, Colorado, New Mexico, and Texas. Some have practiced local customs and lifestyles for more years than the existence of today's political borders that define the areas in which their ancestors lived for hundreds of years.

Relatively speaking, *indigenismo* (nativism) has experienced a renaissance of sorts. It was a component of nationalist ideology that became influential in Mexico during and after its revolutionary period, circa 1910-1920. It was also a cultural movement supported by artists and writers exploring Mexico's national heritage, for up to that point the country's history was missing much of its pre-Colombian past. On a broader scale it defined Mexico and its people as products of the mixing of European and indigenous bloodlines, emphasizing the concept of a *mestizo* people.

The creative minds of this cultural movement incorporated indigenous imagery and concepts to design and underscore social messages to society. These efforts became the basis for much of Mexico's greatest works of art, which remain the subjects of painted walls (*murales*), paper, canvas and other media that capture the indigenous legacy that can be seen today in Mexico and in *barrios* throughout the United States.

AZTLÁN: MYTH OR FACT?

The concept of *indigenismo* also flourished in the US Southwest, which became a hotbed of spiritual, social, and political reverence among US Americans of Mexican and indigenous descent, especially as it related to cultural, educational, and social issues. Those who wished to emphasize their indigenous heritage refer to *Aztlán* as the place of origin and ancestral home of the *Azteca*, who are said to have originated in the semi-arid environments of

northern Mexico as one of the *Chichimeca* tribes. In the indigenous *Náhuatl* language the word *Aztlán* is believed to be the
combination of *aztatl* (heron) and *tlan* (place of).

References to *Aztlán* among indigenous and *mestizo* peoples in
North America are very similar to those of real or mythical—yet
equally venerated—sites from around the world, which include:

- Asgard, home to Valhalla of Norse mythology
- Avalon, the island home of Camelot of early Arthurian
  literature
- Mount Olympus, mythical home of the Greek gods
- Shangri-La, the land of bliss located high in the mountains
  of Tibet.

There remain conflicting opinions on whether *Aztlán* is real or
mythical; but most involved in the discussions agree that it actually refers to a place somewhere North of modern day Mexico
City. Although its exact geographic location remains in question,
it is considered by some historians to be in the general area of
today's Southwestern US.

Some Chicana/o and Mexican scholars describe *Aztlán* as the
originating point in the search by the *Azteca* for *Tenochitlán*, a
place where they would create agricultural and densely populated
ceremonial, political, and religious centers. They founded their
ancient capital circa 1320 in the marshlands of *Lago Texcoco* and
established one of the most complex, advanced civilizations in
the Western Hemisphere. The Spaniards destroyed it in 1521,
and proceeded to rebuild Mexico City on the same site.

Pre-Colombian civilizations from the *Anahuac* (Valley of
Mexico) area developed socio-political infrastructure, written
languages, advanced technological, scientific, engineering and
mathematical skills. Like their predecessors the *Maya*, who are
credited with introducing the concept of zero (c.350 Ad/Ce),

the *Azteca* designed and traveled via long-distance trade routes and waterways resulting in the proliferation of their culture throughout what is now Central and North America. Their sun calendar accurately measured days, months, and cosmic cycles and is evidence of their advanced knowledge of astronomy and mathematics.

In the case of the *Mechica*, their tribal name morphed into modern descriptions of the country and the people who rose from their civilization: *México* and *méjicanos*. There are many who believe it is from the word *Mechica* (or more precisely *mechicanos*) that the term "chicano" evolved and was adopted by social and political activists of Mexican ancestry in the US wishing to connect with the culture and history of their ancestral homelands.

Despite their accomplishments and contributions, these early civilizations were downplayed and nearly eradicated from recorded history in the Americas by the advent of Spanish and English colonization and their respective interpretations and revisions of history. Over time the indelible marks left on the continent by the early indigenous people have resurfaced and are openly and increasingly recognized and celebrated.

Due to a history of limited access and barriers to education, employment, housing and civil rights in the US many Chicana/o and Mexican American authors, poets, community advocates, and political activists adopted *Aztlán* as their "spiritual" and "cultural" homeland in the Southwestern US. It became the basis of community empowerment initiatives, which in turn became the foundation of self-determination movements by community activists and students in high schools and college campuses with substantial Latino enrollments.

A SEARCH FOR THE PAST

Despite numerous examples of a Latino presence prior to the waves of white European immigration into the Southwest, English-language US History and reference books reveal little related to the southwest region's Mexican and *mestizo* presence, much less their contributions to the Americas. This lack of historical information prompted Latinos in the US (and others interested in the history of the region) to search for information from alternative sources. Such sources included Mexico and other Latin American countries.

The works of several authors—from colonial to contemporary periods—became the fountains of information for many scholars thirsting for knowledge about the Mexican and *mestizo* experiences and other intellectual perspectives. Among these authors was Mexican philosopher *Antonio Caso Andrade*, who in 1918, substituted the October 12 celebration of Columbus Day to praise the *mestizo* people and coined the term *"la raza"* to describe the rich mixture of Spanish and the indigenous cultures of the Americas. He was among the first to use the term *"raza"* to refer to specifically to *mestizos*. Ten years later Mexico declared *Día de La Raza* (day of the *mestizo* people) a national holiday. It was subsequently adopted by the other Spanish-speaking nations throughout the Americas.

Another respected writer was Mexican philosopher *José Vasconcelos Calderón* (1882-1959), Mexico's first Secretary of Public Education (1921-24) and a 1929 presidential candidate. He and a small circle of contemporaries were considered by many of the world's intellectuals of that era to be among the most influential individuals in the development of modern Mexico. In a 1925 essay *"La Raza Cósmica"* *Vascocelos Calderón* promoted the concept of a future "fifth race" in the Americas: a confluence of all the world's then defined racial groups, without concern for geographic origin to create a new civilization: *Universópolis* (Vasconcelos Calderón, *La Raza Cósmica*).

Regarding his concept of a fifth race, *Vascocelos Calderón* hypothesized that traditional, exclusive concepts of race and nationality could be transcended in the name of humanity's common destiny. He opined that Latin Americans had the bloodlines of the four major races then known to the "Old World" based on color: red (the indigenous of the Americas), yellow (Asians and Pacific Islanders), white (Caucasians) and black (Africans). It is believed by many that he referred to this confluence of races when he coined the motto for Mexico's National Autonomous University: "*Por mi raza hablará el espíritu*"—the spirit shall speak for my people.

Vascocelos Calderón also coined the phrase *la raza de bronce* (the bronze people) to refer to the new synthesized and recombinant race of people. This concept attracted a number of supporters, especially among US *Chicanos* who were promoting self-determination and civil rights and envisioned the positive effects their culture could have in the US. In its modern form the label *la raza* is routinely used by Latinos to refer to the mixed race people of the Americas: *mestizos, mulattos, zambos,* and other manifestations, regardless of race or ethnicity.

Another literary influence was *Octavio Paz Lozano* (1914–1998), a Mexican writer, poet, diplomat, and winner of the 1990 Nobel Prize for Literature. One of his most notable works, *El Laberinto de la Soledad* (The Labyrinth of Solitude)—a collection of nine essays: "The *Pachuco* and other extremes," "Mexican Mask," "The Day of the Dead," "The Sons of La Malinche," "The Conquest and Colonialism," "From Independence to the Revolution," "The Mexican Intelligence," "The Present Day," and "The Dialectic of Solitude"—focuses on *mestizo* identity and demonstrates how at the end of the existential labyrinth there is a profound feeling of solitude (Paz Lozano, *The Labyrinth of Solitude*).

Paz Lozano wrote that solitude is responsible for the Mexican perspectives on *muerte* (death), *fiesta* (celebration), and *identidad* (identity). Death is seen as an event to be celebrated, but also repelled because of the uncertainty it represents; celebration expresses a sense of communality, essentially emphasizing the idea of not being alone; and how the true Mexican identity is achieved through socializing.

Collectively, his themes address the way in which Mexicans (and perhaps other Spanish-speaking nationalities) inherited two distinct cultures, the indigenous and the Spanish, but by denying either of them *mestizos* become stuck in a world of solitude. *Paz Lozano* and his essays resonated greatly with those who sought insights into the Chicano/a, Mexican-American, Latino/a and Hispanic psyches.

José Vasconcelos Calderón, Antonio Caso Andrade, Octavio Paz Lozano, and other Latin-American *literati* provided Latinos with a missing link to their history, culture, and philosophy. Armed with this sense of self and renewed commitment to connect with their heritage and history, Mexican-Americans in the United States experienced an increase in their collective sense of "historical" pride.

COMMUNITY ORGANIZING

In addition to established advocacy and civil rights organizations like the League of United Latin American Citizens (LULAC), The American G.I. Forum, the Mexican American Political Association (MAPA), there were numerous Chicano/a groups that emerged during the 1960s and 70s, many of them focused on community organizing efforts to address unacceptable economic, educational, and political practices affecting the residents of their communities and their collective quality of life.

An example of such community oriented efforts was a 1966 Chicano/a student conference in Los Angeles, where a group of high school students came together to discuss a variety of issues affecting their education and communities. The participants at this event formed an organization called Young Chicanos for Community Action (YCCA) in 1967 to support the campaign of Dr. Julian Nava for a seat on the Los Angeles Unified School District Board of Education. As a result of these efforts, Dr. Nava became the first Mexican American elected to the LAUSD board in an "at-large" election. He received more than two million votes—the most votes ever received by a victorious Latino candidate for elected office in the US at the time of his victory.

Both male and female members of YCCA wore brown berets as a symbol of unity, cultural pride, and their opposition to historical examples of educational discrimination against Mexican Americans and Chicanos/as. They came to be recognized by their headwear and were referred to as the "Brown Berets." Their agenda was to address inadequacies in public-supported services for the Chicano/a community; especially in matters related to criminal justice, law enforcement, public education, health care, job opportunities, political representation—as well as US involvement in the Vietnam War.

Variations of the Brown Berets soon followed throughout California, Texas, New Mexico, New York, Florida, Illinois, and serveral cities with large or substantial Latino populations in other states. These young voices exemplified a renewed commitment to community organization efforts and non-violent civil protest on the part of activists. Farmworkers' union organizer Cesár E. Chavéz, may have best captured the importance of youth and student involvement in community organizing efforts when he said, "We need to help students and parents cherish and preserve the ethnic and cultural diversity that nourishes and strengthens this community—and this nation" (Chavez, *Education*).

BRIDGING THE GAP BETWEEN TOWN AND GOWN

The cultural renaissance movement spread and resulted in the creation of numerous educational initiatives. One of those was "*El Plan de Santa Barbara*: A Chicano Plan for Higher Education." The document developed proposals for a curriculum emphasizing Chicano studies, the role of community involvement in education, and the necessity of Chicano/a political independence (Chicano Coordinating Council on Higher Education, *El Plan de Santa Barbara*).

El Plan de Santa Barbara was adopted at a meeting of college and university professors, college and high school students and community activists at the University of California, Santa Barbara in April 1969. The conference brought together independent and unconnected Chicano/a groups from throughout the Southwest to form the *Movimiento Estudiantíl Chicano de Aztlán* (Chicano Student Movement of *Aztlán*)—a network of unified, community-based, student organizations that came to be known by its acronym: MEChA.

The college campus groups proposed two fundamental goals for the Chicano/a student movement. The first was that MEChA was to become involved in the social and political activities in Latino communities located near their school campuses with the common aim of helping to develop local sustainable communities; the second called for MEChA to become a permanent campus voice for redirecting university attention and resources to the educational needs of Chicano/a students in the surrounding communities.

According to the plan, such goals would redefine the concept of "town and gown" as meaningful relationships between Latino communities and its public and private institutions of higher learning. The plan reflected MEChA's expectation that part of its on-campus empowerment would result from local community support. The thinking was, "if political and educational changes were to be won on campus, the communities surrounding those campuses would have to be engaged and supportive."

MEChA's strategy was to establish itself as both a creditable campus student group and a viable community-based resource. It came to symbolize the emergence of a new generation of college-educated, culturally competent, community oriented leaders. It encouraged Latino students to see themselves as a part of a new cultural and political movement committed to combating discrimination in a an educational system that had limited the participation of Latinos in higher education—and disregarded much of their indigenous and *mestizo* history, culture and heritage from US history curricula.

The need to raise community consciousness was not limited to those inside the institutions of higher learning, but included community leaders and residents as well. The MEChA student movement helped to redefine the relationships between institutions of higher learning and the Latino community and greatly enhanced the role of Latinos as stakeholders in higher education.

A LINE IN THE SAND

Community organizing and advocacy initiatives were simultaneously undertaken in other areas of the country. In response to the June 12, 1966, shooting by a white Chicago police officer of Arcelis Cruz, an unarmed 20-year-old, the West Town community erupted into an open display of civil disobedience, which came to be called the "Division Street Riots." It was the latest incident in a series of police shootings of Puerto Rican residents.

The violent outbreak lasted three days. At its conclusion, sixteen people were injured, forty-nine were arrested, and over fifty buildings had been destroyed. These acts of civil disobedience served as a turning point for Chicago's Puerto Rican community that became more active in confronting the city's political leadership about their concerns over public service issues.

The Cruz shooting—and its resulting unification of the Puerto Rican community in Chicago—led to the creation of several service organizations that would grow to play an important role in the future of Puerto Ricans across the US. Among them were the Spanish Action Committee of Chicago and the Latin American Defense Organization, which in turn paved the way for the expansion of other existing community groups such as *ASPIRA* (a New York drop-out prevention and education organization that now reaches out to include all Latinos—and a significant group of non-Latinos—throughout the US) and the creation of others, such as the *Segundo Ruiz Belvis* Cultural Center (founded in 1971 to preserve and promote appreciation of the culture and arts of Puerto Rico, specifically its African heritage).

This instance of civil disobedience, similar to what had already occurred in black communities across the US, contributed to the transformation of a *barrio* social club into a regional and national leadership development, political action, and social change movement. It also led to the formation of the Young Lords Organization (YLO) by José "Cha Cha" Jiménez in 1968 and soon added chapters in other areas of the country, including: Boston, MA; Bridgeport and New Haven, CT; Newark, NJ; New York, NY; Philadelphia, PA; and the Commonwealth of Puerto Rico.

Initially a Puerto Rican organization, other Latino and black groups were invited to join as the organization matured into a political group. Puerto Ricans had shared a common heritage and historical background with African Americans; both having experienced segregation and discrimination based on color. The invitation to blacks according to Young Lords Party member *Pablo Guzmán* of New York was simple, due to a common experience with racism by blacks and Puerto Ricans—as well as the color consciousness among Puerto Ricans themselves—it was an obvious coalition. *Guzmán* matter-of-factly explained why blacks were invited to join the YLO Party, "Because before people called me a spic, they called me a nigger. So that was, like, one reason as to why we felt the Young Lords party should exist" (Santiago, *Boricuas*).

Although they were relatively small in numbers, their influence was felt. They proved that an organization does not have to be large in size in order to be effective. Through community organization initiatives they had instilled a sense of determination and pride among Puerto Ricans, young and old. Their "purple berets" also became a symbol of change in many Puerto Rican communities. The groundwork had been established for a new generation of *boricuas* concerned with substantive changes for the residents of their *barrios*.

The YLO movement was a community-oriented initiative on the part of vocal US citizens interested in appropriate responses from their tax-supported public agencies and officials. Vestiges of their militancy and political activism are still felt and periodically surface in response to inattention to issues important to Latinos in general, and to *puertorriqueños* in particular.

STRENGTH IN NUMBERS

Latinos had begun to take active roles in determining their individual and community destinies. This new era of community empowerment spawned a number of today's most renowned and respected local, state and national advocacy organizations and community leaders. Many of these giants, on whose shoulders today's Latino/a leaders stand, promoted inclusion of Latinos in all facets of our nation's economic, educational, political and social arenas. This type of community organizing and advocacy opened the doors for many and continues to play a major role in the lives of Latinos in business, community and political activities to this day. They include such innovations as equal opportunities in key areas like education, employment and vendor/supplier contracting opportunities in both private and public arenas.

Concerns over these common issues resulted in the formation of communication networks among Latinos from all parts of the nation. Despite the fact that geographic factors had historically hampered national unification efforts among the various Latino groups, common goals, language, similar cultures and shared discrimination experiences provided the catalyst for geographically diverse Latinos to create a unified "critical mass" around a number of social and political issues.

As a result of their inaccessibility to equitable public services, especially in areas of education, criminal justice, employment opportunities, and housing, an increasing number of civic-minded Latinos and community-based advocacy groups began initiatives that raised expectations among more Latino citizens. The call to challenge injustices was not lost on community leaders who understood that the growing number of consumers, taxpayers, and voters represented "power" at the cash register and the ballot box. Ironically, the coalescing of culturally and geographically distinct groups under a single, generic "Hispanic" label used by government agencies and news media helped to accelerate the formation of a national identity, agenda, and network for the nation's Latinos.

Many non-Hispanics wonder why such extreme political and social movements were necessary. "After all, aren't we all Americans?" some ask. Others comment, "We don't have special programs for other groups, why should we have them for 'Latinos?'" The least tactful use a variety of bumper sticker clichés. "If you don't like it here, go back to where you come from!" or "America, love it or leave it!" Apparently, the lack of historical facts makes it difficult for many non-Hispanics to grasp the concept that many Latinos in the USA never left "where they were from." In fact, some have been residents of this land since before the landing of the Pilgrims on Plymouth Rock.

Regardless of one's perspective, there is little doubt Latinos were (and remain) the object of bias, racism and discrimination, especially among those fearing they are part of a shrinking white Eurocentric majority. There is no logical explanation for this behavior; however, in order to overcome the barriers to positive relationships we must first recognize that such fear-based apprehension and prejudice exists.

INSTITUTIONALIZED RACISM

A common definition of discrimination is the treatment or consideration of, or making a distinction in favor of or against, a person or thing based on the group, class, or category to which that person or thing belongs rather than on individual merit. Examples of efforts to prevent equal access include government-sponsored legislation enacted during the most productive and wealth-building periods in our nation's history. The most blatant illustrations of such legislation included the following:

- **The 1934 National Housing Act** established the Federal Housing Administration (FHA) and its programs of the 1930s and 1940s that subsidized low cost loans and provided homeownership assistance to millions of working-class US citizens. Government underwriters introduced a "national appraisal" system that tied property value and loan eligibility to "race" and/or color of applicants. Non-white and mixed-race neighborhoods received the lowest ratings and were denied access to these "publicly funded" loans. Of the $120 billion of new housing subsidized by the federal government between 1934 and 1962, less than 2 percent went to non-whites. People of color were statutorily excluded from "public subsidized" homeownership—a public benefit that is considered a major factor in the creation of family wealth in the USA.

- **The 1935 Social Security Act** guaranteed an income for millions of US workers upon retirement. The act specifically excluded domestic and agricultural workers (mainly Latinos, African Americans and Asian Americans), who paid into the system, had the least opportunity to save, were least likely to have pensions and were the most vulnerable to economic recession. This legislation systematically excluded non-whites from the protection and benefits legally granted to white European American citizens.

- **The 1935 Wagner Act** helped establish another financial benefit for US citizens: the right to unionize. The Act's original version prohibited racial discrimination, but the American Federation of Labor (AFL) fought against the inclusion of "minorities" and prevailed; the enacted version of the law allowed unions to exclude non-whites from membership , who were not only excluded from higher-paying jobs, but were also denied union protection and benefits (medical care, full employment, and job security). The legislation legally barred non-whites from challenging their exclusion. Although the laws were revised in the late 1950s, many craft unions remained predominantly "white" well into the 1970s due to deeply imbedded legacy (family preference) practices and other "unwritten" membership criteria.

A CLASS APART

After gaining US citizenship following the end of the Mexican-American War in 1848, many Americans of Mexican birth lost their land due to newly enacted US property and real estate laws. With the loss of their land came other losses and in only a few generations, Spanish, Mexican and *mestizo* land owners became the hired hands at their former family ranches and farms. Following the Civil War, great numbers of Southern whites migrated into southern Texas looking for new beginnings and agricultural lands, bringing with them traditional racial biases and attitudes.

In 1896, the US Supreme Court had ruled "separate but equal" laws for blacks were legal (*Plessy v Ferguson*), which were readily applied to Spaniards, Mexicans and *mestizos*. Despite "legal" government sanctioned barriers and overt efforts to block access to "public" resources, Latinos quietly and diligently continued their quest for the elusive American Dream.

On May 3, 1954, the US Supreme Court announced a decision in the case of *Hernandez v. Texas*. It ruled all racial and ethnic groups—including Latinos—were protected under the Fourteenth Amendment of the Constitution and were indeed "a class apart" that did not fit into a legal structure that heretofore recognized only black and white US citizens. Up to that point, Latinos had been considered "legally" white, yet suffered the same overt types of discrimination as blacks at the hands of a white, Eurocentric society. Similar to the treatment visited on African Americans; Latinos too, were relegated to segregated churches, public water fountains, restrooms, schools and swimming pools, cemeteries and housing; denied access to restaurants, stores, movie theaters; and employment at private businesses and public institutions.

EXERCISING UPWARD MOBILITY

By the late twentieth century, Latinos had increased their population numbers in California, Colorado, Florida, Illinois, New Mexico, New York, and Texas. Many were transitioning into traditional non-Hispanic jobs and new housing subdivisions and urban neighborhoods located in these states. This trend was prompted by the same rationale as those used for "white flight" (upper- and middle-class whites moving to the suburbs from center city neighborhoods): better schools, housing, public safety, and related quality of life issues.

Latinos also followed employment opportunities into areas of the US that were seen as "new settlement" states for them. By the end of the twentieth century, the number of these states grew by 130 percent; they included: Arizona, Georgia, Massachusetts, Nevada, North Carolina, Oregon, Virginia, and Washington. This was an awakening experience for many white Americans who had never interacted with Latinos or been exposed to them.

Latinos have learned homeownership is one of the major investments for building family wealth. The fact that their family values are closely associated with homeownership has not been lost on them. Rather than remain cloistered in traditional *barrios*, US-born and immigrant Latinos began relocating to neighborhoods where they were a small percentage of the residents. In 2004, the Pew Hispanic Center reported some twenty million Hispanics—57 percent of the total US Hispanic population—lived in communities populated mostly by non-Hispanics. The remaining 43 percent lived in large, growing, and densely populated neighborhoods in areas with a long-standing Latino presence.

A greater number of less acculturated, foreign-born Latinos (48 percent) lived in *barrios* where they were the majority, compared to their more assimilated, US-born brethren (39 percent). But, over half of the people in both immigrant and native-born categories lived in neighborhoods where Hispanics were the numerical minority. Language was a factor: over 75 percent of Hispanics who were "English-dominant" lived in neighborhoods where whites were in the majority; "Spanish-dominant" speakers were evenly divided between Latino and non-Latino majority neighborhoods.

Due to the exclusionary practices and obstacles placed in the paths of past generations, Latinos have had to play economic and educational "catch-up" with their white peers and neighbors—many of whom benefited from legal and social practices and legislation barring Latinos from accessing many of the benefits for which their taxes had paid. But, as non-Hispanic whites continue to age, they will also become a decreasing percentage of the nation's population. Although they accounted for nearly 75 percent of the total population in the latter half of the twentieth century, they represented only 35 percent of the nation's growth between 1990 and 2000. This declining rate of growth is expected to dip to 23 percent between 2000 and 2010 and drop to 14 percent from 2010 to 2030. After 2030, their effect on US population growth is projected to be negligible.

Meanwhile, Latinos have increased their social, political, and economic influence, and their current population numbers are attracting attention from private and public sectors that recognize their value as consumers, employees, taxpayers and voters. Both sectors continue to be challenged in establishing better relationships through more effective and culturally relevant communication efforts. Improved relationships among all US Americans must include mutual respect for each other's culture, heritage and language. US statesman, politician and presidential candidate William Jennings Bryan wrote, "Anglo-Saxon civilization has taught the individual to protect his own rights; American civilization will teach him to respect the rights of others" (Jennings Bryan, *Heart to Heart Appeals*).

Although the path to self-determination for Latinos may remain littered with educational, political, and social obstacles, their economic and political influence is expected to continue growing. Their increasing power will bolster pride in their abilities and allow them to determine how, and to what extent, they wish to interact with members of an increasingly diverse US society. Although pride may not be a virtue, it is the foundation upon which a strong and positive self-image can be established.

Duty, Honor, and Patriotism

Las palabras son enanas y los ejemplos son gigantes.
Translation: Words are dwarfs, examples are giants.
Transcreation: Actions speak louder than words.

Despite their untold economic, social, and political contributions to the United States of America, Latinos are still viewed by many of their fellow citizens as foreigners, immigrants and threats to the country's culture and society. The main reasons for these false perceptions are:

A. The absence of Latino contributions in our nation's recorded history.

B. The negative stereotypes in movies and literature.

C. The lack of positive news media coverage.

It is apparent to an increasing number of academicians, historians, and too few of the general public that Latinos have been systematically excluded from much of US history. To learn that Latinos have participated in every major military conflict—from the US Revolution (in which volunteers from Cuba, Mexico and Puerto Rico fought the British in 1779 under the command of Spanish General *José Bernardo de Galvéz Gallardo*), to the present-day conflicts in Iraq and Afghanistan—one must cull through the catacombs of public and college libraries, ethnic studies curricula, or other equally out-of-the-way repositories of Spanish-language and modern Latino literature.

In such archives you will find Latinos have been ready to prove their support of the principles expressed by the founding fathers of the United States of America in our nation's Declaration of Independence.

> "We hold these truths to be self-evident, that all men are created equal, that they are endowed by their Creator with certain inalienable rights, that among these are life, liberty and the pursuit of happiness. That to secure these rights, governments are instituted among men, deriving their just powers from the consent of the governed."

Among the earliest contributions to US military conflicts were those made by Spain. Judge Edward F. Butler, of the National Society-Sons of the American Revolution's (NSSAR) Ambassador to Mexico (2001-2002) and founder and Charter President of Mexico's NSSAR affiliate has corroborated the fact that from 1776 to 1779, Spain provided financial support to the thirteen colonies in the amount of eight million *reales* for arms, medical supplies and food for their fledgling military forces.

The infusion of capital was necessary because the colonists' printed currency lacked the backing of silver or gold. *Reales* were the currency of Spain's colonies in the Americas and equal to the Spanish *reales de plata* (also known as "pieces of eight") or popularly referred to as the "Spanish dollar." The silver-backed coins circulated in the British and Spanish colonies and beyond as the international monetary standard of its day and was the model for our own US dollar.

Throughout the course of the War of Independence, Spain also delivered military support, arms, munitions, and food to the colonists. According to Butler, in the last three months of 1776, Spain was reported to have sent the colonists nine thousand pounds of gunpowder (via the Mississippi River) and another one thousand pounds by cargo ship to Philadelphia.

In 1779, Spanish, Mexican, *mestizo* and *Tejano* ranchers and *vaqueros* began the first recorded *rodeo* (round-up) of some fifteen thousand head of cattle and hundreds of horses and mules along the *Río Guadalupe*—from *San Antonio de Bexar* to *La Bahia* (modern day Goliad)—for delivery to Spain's General *Galvéz Gallardo* in New Orleans. The cattle were used to feed Spanish troops along the Gulf Coast and some historians believe some of the beef may have reached General George Washington's Continental Army troops at Valley Forge.

A year later, Spain's King Carlos III issued a royal decree requiring a one-time "voluntary" donation from all residents in each of New Spain's settlements in the Americas, ranging from two *pesos* from each Spaniard and one *peso* from each indigenous native. (There is no information about how much *mestizos* were asked to contribute, but based on caste it probably depended on where they fell in the caste system.) Very early in the Revolutionary War, Latinos helped the original thirteen British colonies defray the cost of their war of independence from the English crown.

On the battlefield, General *Galvéz Gallardo* and his troops also captured strategic ports (Mobile, AL and Pensacola, FL) from the British in 1780-1781, aiding the colonists and their military objectives. He received numerous letters of gratitude from prominent colonists, including Thomas Jefferson, yet little historical recognition is given to his early contributions to our emerging nation. The Texas city of Galveston was named in his honor.

ONE NATION, INDIVISIBLE...

As in the Battle of the Alamo and the Mexican-American War, Latinos again took up arms to fight in 1861 for both sides in the Civil War; some 2,500 *Tejanos* pledged their allegiance to the

Confederate States of America (CSA), while nearly one thousand more volunteered for military service in support of Union forces.

By 1863, the North had recruited four companies of *Californianos* (known for their extraordinary horsemanship) in efforts to bolster their side's cavalry units. Nearly 500 served under Major *Salvador Vallejo* and were used to defeat a Confederate invasion of New Mexico. By the end of this bloody civil struggle in 1865, almost ten thousand Spanish-surnamed Americans had served valiantly in regular and volunteer army units on both sides of the skirmish lines.

Significant numbers served in such Confederate units as the 10th Texas Cavalry, the 55th Alabama Infantry, and 6th Missouri Infantry. Colonel *Santos Benavides* of Laredo, TX, ultimately became the highest-ranking Latino in the Confederate Army. As Commander of the 33rd Cavalry, he and his men drove back Union forces from Brownsville, TX, in March 1864.

Of the more than forty thousand books and pamphlets written about the US Civil War, only one book, *Vaqueros in Blue and Gray* by Jerry Don Thompson (with foreword by University of Texas-San Antonio history professor *Félix Almaráz*), focused on the contributions made by *Tejanos* to the US Civil War and Texas. Many of these same accounts have been handed-down for generations by "word of mouth" by the families and friends of these veterans, but neglected by most US historians and public school curricula and textbooks.

In 1866, *David G. Farragut* was the first US naval officer ever promoted to the ranks of Rear Admiral, Vice Admiral, and Admiral. He became the most senior naval officer during the Civil War when he assumed the rank of Full Admiral, a position created by Congress specifically for him. As the Civil War's best-known US naval officer he is remembered for his bravery in battle, which has been immortalized by his battle cry: "Damn the torpedoes, full speed ahead!" Yet, very few Americans—and especially Latino children—have been made aware of his Hispanic ancestry (Schmal, *Hispanic Contributions*).

A FEW GOOD MEN

It was during the Civil War that President Abraham Lincoln created the Congressional Medal of Honorm (MOH)—the nation's highest military award in times of war. It was awarded to members of the military service who distinguished themselves "conspicuously by gallantry and intrepidity at the risk of his/her life above and beyond the call of duty" (Department of the Army: *"Section 578.4, Medal of Honor"*).

Despite minimal publicity or historical documentation, Latinos are among the largest number of non-European white US military personnel to have earned our nation's most prestigious military award. As of 2011, 45 had been awarded the MOH—26 posthumously.

Among the first to be awarded the MOH for bravery during the Civil War were:

> Joseph H. de Castro, a Spaniard serving with the 19th Massachusetts Infantry for bravery displayed at the battle of Gettysburg, July 3, 1863; Philip Bazaar, a Chilean serving in the US Navy, for bravery displayed during the assault on Fort Fisher, North Carolina on January 15, 1865; and John Ortega, a Spaniard serving in the US Navy, for bravery displayed aboard the USS Saratoga, December 1865.

In World War I, David B. Barkley of Laredo, TX, the son of Antonia Cantú Barkley, served in Company A, 89th Division, 356th Infantry. He lost his life on a reconnaissance mission after swimming across the icy Meuse River in France to draw maps of German artillery positions. In addition to the MOH, he also was posthumously awarded France's *Croix de Guerre* and Italy's *Croce Merito de Guerra*.

During World War II, 500,000 Spanish-surnamed soldiers and sailors served in the military services and were recognized for their courageous service, with twelve receiving Congressional Medals of Honor, six of them posthumously*. They included:

> Army Staff Sgt. Lucian Adams (October 26, 1922-March 31, 2003) of Port Arthur, TX; Army Staff Sgt. Rudolph B. Davila (April 27, 1916-January 26, 2002) of Los Angeles, CA; Army Staff Sgt. Marcario Garcia (January 20, 1920-December 24, 1972) was born in *Villa de Castaño, Coahuila* in Mexico, worked as a migrant worker in South Texas and became the first Mexican immigrant to be awarded the MOH; Marine Corps PFC Harold Gonsalves* (January 28, 1926-April 15, 1945) of Alameda, CA; Army PFC David M. Gonzales* (June 9, 1923-April 25, 1945) of Pacoima, CA; Army PFC Silvestre S. Herrera (July 17, 1917-November 26, 2007) was born in *Camargo, Chihuahua* and raised in El Paso, TX; Army Sgt. José Mendoza Lopéz (July 10, 1910-May 16, 2005) was born in *Santiago Ihuitlán, Oaxaca* and raised in Brownsville, TX; Army Pvt. Joe P. Martinez* (July 27, 1920-May 26, 1943) was born in Taos, NM and raised in Ault, CO; Army PFC Manuel Perez, Jr.* (March 3, 1923-February 13, 1945) of Oklahoma City, OK; Army Pvt. Cleto L. Rodriguez (April 26, 1923-December 7, 1990) was born in San Marcos, TX and raised in San Antonio, TX; Army Sgt. Alejandro R. Ruiz (June 26, 1923-November 20, 2009) of Loving, NM; Army PFC José F. Valdéz (January 3, 1925-February 17, 1945) of Gobernador, NM; Army Staff Sgt. Ysmael R. Villegas* (March 21, 1924-March 20, 1945) of Casa Blanca (Riverside), CA.

The Korean War saw eight more Hispanics earn our nation's highest military honor, six of them posthumously.* They included:

Marine PFC Fernando Luís García* (October 14, 1929-September 5, 1952) of Utuado, PR; Marine PFC Edward Goméz* (August 10, 1932-September 14, 1951) of Omaha, NE; Marine Staff Sgt. Ambrosio Guillen* (December 7, 1929-July 25, 1953) born in La Junta, CO and raised in El Paso, TX; Army Cpl. Rodolfo Perez "Rudy" Hernandez (April 14, 1931) born in Colton, CA and raised in Fowler, CA; Marine First Lt. Baldomero Lopéz* (August 23, 1925-September 15, 1950) was born in Tampa, FL and raised in Ybor City, FL; Army Cpl. Benito Martinez* (April 21, 1932-September 6, 1952) of Fort Hancock, TX; Marine PFC Eugene Arnold Obregon* (November 12, 1930-September 26, 1950) of Los Angeles, CA; and Army Colonel Joseph C. Rodriguez (November 14, 1928-November 1, 2005) of San Bernardino, CA.

In the Vietnam conflict, seventeen more Hispanics distinguished themselves for service "above and beyond the call of duty," twelve of them having made the ultimate sacrifice for their country*. They included:

John Philip Baca, born January 10, 1949 in Providence, RI and raised in San Diego, CA; Army Staff Sergeant and Green Beret Raúl (Roy) Peréz Benavidéz (August 5, 1935-November 29, 1998) of Lindenau, TX; Marine Lance Cpl. Emilio Albert De La Garza, Jr.* (June 23, 1949-April 11, 1970) of East Chicago, IN; Marine PFC Ralph Ellis Días* (July 15, 1950-November 11, 1969) born in Indiana County, PA and raised in Shelocta, PA; Army Specialist 4 Daniel D. Fernández* (June 30, 1944-February 18, 1966) of Albuquerque, NM; Alfredo "Freddy" Cantu González* (May 23, 1946–February 4, 1968) of Edinburg, TX; José Francisco Jiménez* (March 20, 1946-August 28, 1969) born in *Mexico City, Mexico* and raised in Eloy, AZ; Marine Lance Cpl. Miguel Keith* (June 2, 1951-May 8, 1970) born in San Antonio, TX and raised in Omaha, NE; Army PFC Carlos James

Lozada* (September 6, 1946-November 20, 1967) born in Caguas, PR and raised in The Bronx, NY; Army Medic/ Spec. 4 Alfred Velásquez Rascón (September 10, 1945) born in *Chihuahua, Mexico* and raised in Oxnard, CA and retired from the Army as a Lt. Colonel; Army Chief Warrant Officer Louis Richard Rocco (November 19, 1938-October 31, 2002) born in Albuquerque, NM and raised in Wilmington, CA; Army Capt. Eurípides Rubio* (March 1, 1938-November 8, 1966) of Ponce, PR; Army Specialist 4 Héctor Santiago-Colón* (December 20, 1942-June 28, 1968) born in Salinas, PR and raised in New York, NY; Army Sgt. First Class Elmelindo Rodrigues Smith* (July 27, 1935-February 16, 1967) of Wahiawa, HI; Marine Major Jay R. Vargas (July 29, 1938) born in Winslow, AZ and retired from the USMC as a Colonel; Army Ranger Capt. Humberto Roque "Rocky" Versace* (July 2, 1937-September 26, 1965) born in Honolulu, HI and raised in Alexandria, VA; and Army Sgt. First Class Maximo Yabes (January 29, 1932-February 26, 1967) born in Lodi, CA and raised in Oakridge, OR.

The latest to be added to this esteemed list of Latino war heroes is Army Sgt. First Class Leroy Arthur Petry of Santa Fe, NM. He was nominated for his actions in Afghanistan, where he served as a Staff Sgt. in the 2nd Ranger Battalion. Petry was formally presented with the MOH by President Barack Obama on July 12, 2011, in a ceremony at the White House and attended by his parents, Larry Petry and Lorella Tapia Petry.

This listing of Latino recipients of the Medal of Honor is not intended to diminish the bravery and service to our nation by others who have earned this recognition. The intent is to underscore the patriotism and courage of Latinos whose service to their country goes virtually unnoticed in the everyday coverage of US heroes and their contributions to our nation.

HONORABLE MENTIONS

Regarding Latinos and military honors, if actions speak louder than words than their heroic exploits should still be resonating throughout our nation, along with those of their fellow recipients of our nation's highest military commendations. There are many examples of US-born, naturalized, and undocumented immigrant Latinos who have taken up arms and fought to defend our democracy. Six of the aforementioned MOH recipients were born outside the US, one each in Chile and Spain and four in Mexico. Others were heroes during times of war, but received little to no recognition for their valor.

One such hero was Marcelino Serna, born April 26, 1896, in *Chihuahua, Chihuahua*. At age twenty, he came to the USA in search of employment and worked in Kansas on maintenance crews for the Atcheson, Topeka & Santa Fe and Union Pacific railroads. He also worked as an agricultural worker in southern Colorado's sugar beet fields.

Serna volunteered for the US Army in 1916 and was assigned to Company B, 355th Infantry of the 89th Division. Most of his fellow soldiers were from Arizona, Colorado, Kansas, New Mexico, South Dakota, and Utah. They participated in some of the most rigorous campaigns of the European theater, including action in the *Lucey* Sector, *Puvenelle* Sector, *Meuse-Argonne*, *St. Mihiel*, and *Ennezin*.

In *St. Mihiel*, Serna's unit was advancing, sloshing in heavy rain through thick brush, when a German machine gunner opened fire on his unit, killing twelve of his fellow soldiers. Serna charged the gun emplacement and tossed four grenades into the machine gun position. Six Germans died, eight others came out with their hands up, which Serna held until reinforcements arrived.

On a subsequent mission, Serna single-handedly captured twenty-four enemy soldiers and killed twenty-six others with only a rifle, a handgun, and hand grenades. General John J.

Pershing, Commander-in-Chief of the American Expeditionary Forces, awarded Serna the Distinguished Service Cross (DSC)—the second highest US combat award.

A few days later, Field Marshal Foch, Supreme Commander of the Allied troops, awarded Serna the French *Croix de Guerre* for bravery. He was awarded two *Croix de Guerre* medals (with Palms), the Italian *Croce al Merito di Guerra*, the French *Medaille Militaire*, the French Commemorative Medal, WW I Victory Medal with five stars, the Victory Medal with three campaign bars, the French *St. Mihiel Medaille*, the French *Verdun Medaille* and two US Purple Hearts. He returned from the war and became a naturalized US citizen. To this day, he remains one of the most highly decorated soldiers in the annals of Texas military heroes.

Serna died in 1991 at the age of 95; yet very few Americans know his name or ever learned of his wartime exploits and heroism. Congressman Ronald D. Coleman (D-El Paso) introduced legislation shortly after Serna's death, requesting Serna be awarded the MOH, posthumously. Representative Coleman stated that although allied countries had awarded him their nations' highest honors, we in his adopted country still had not.

In World War II, Mexico's *Fuerza Aérea Expedicionaria Mexicana* (Mexican Expeditionary Air Force) provided military support to the Allies. Known as the "Aztec Eagles," three hundred members of the 201st Mexican Fighter Squadron were commissioned for active service in February 1945 as a part of the Fifth Air Corps, US Army Air Force and flew fifty-nine combat missions from the Philippine Islands until the war's end in 1945. Five P-47 Thunderbolt Mexican pilots lost their lives in defense of democracy and freedom alongside US forces. Their aircraft were the only combat planes to prominently display the "*tri-colores*" (Red, White, and Green) of Mexico, along with the (Red, White, and Blue) colors of the USA on their airplanes' fuselages.

In the second Iraq War, Marine Lance Corporal *José Gutiérrez* of *Guatemala* was among the first of many undocumented immigrants to make the ultimate sacrifice for his "adopted" country. He was "killed in action" (KIA) March 21, 2003, near the Iraqi port city of *Umm Qasr*. Cpl. *Gutiérrez* was not yet a US citizen, but was granted citizenship under a 2002 Executive Order, allowing relatives of those killed in combat to apply for "posthumous citizenship"—a purely symbolic gesture that provides no benefits for the families of immigrants killed while safeguarding our nation and its principles.

In 2006, the Department of Defense reported thirty-five thousand non-citizen immigrants were actively protecting our nation against the threat of 'terrorism' in the Middle East, yet less than half (fifteen thousand) were eligible for expedited naturalization. Immigrants represent a substantial number of our nation's active military personnel, especially when one considers that in 2010 slightly over 1 percent of the USA's total population was voluntarily putting their lives "at risk" to protect us, our families, and the nation's commercial and political interests around the world.

NO GOOD DEED GOES UNPUNISHED

Greek philosopher Aristotle is credited with saying, "Dignity does not consist in possessing honors, but in deserving them." (Harder, *A Dictionary of American Proverbs*)

Yet, after so many examples of valiant service to the US, Latinos still were not deemed deserving of the recognition or respect they earned on the battlefields. Latinos have had their military service to our nation, ignored, forgotten, and even disrespected.

The 1960 war movie "Hell to Eternity" was based on the WWII exploits of one of four Latinos whose MOH recommendations remain pending: USMC PFC Guy "Gabby" Galbadón. In 1944, Galbadón distinguished himself by "single-handedly" capturing 1,500 Japanese prisoners on the islands of Saipan, Tinian, and the Marianas in the South Pacific. In addition to his bravery, he possessed another secret weapon: a third language. In addition to English and Spanish, he also spoke Japanese. He learned it from his Japanese foster parents and Japanese-American friends in his neighborhood before they were relocated to internment camps following Japan's attack on Pearl Harbor.

Galbadón was awarded the Silver Star (later upgraded to the Navy Cross) for his daring feats. His citation read in part:

> "Working alone in front of the lines, he daringly entered enemy caves, pillboxes, buildings, and jungle brush, frequently in the face of hostile fire, and succeeded in not only obtaining vital military information, but in capturing well over one thousand enemy civilians and troops" (Coates, *Silver Starlight*).

Known as "The Pied Piper of Saipan" for luring so many of the enemy to surrender without firing a shot, Gabaldón has the distinction of capturing more enemy personnel than anyone else in the history of US military history. The producers of the movie documenting his heroic acts felt compelled to attribute his prowess to someone other than a Latino by using white actor Jeffrey Hunter to portray Galbadón as an Italian-American Marine, purposely omitting the fact that he was from East Los Angeles and a California-born US citizen of Mexican heritage.

Gabaldón died August 11, 2006, his consideration for a Congressional Medal of Honor—along with those of Marcelino Serna (WWI), Ramón Rodriguez and Isaac Camacho (Vietnam) and Rafael Peralta (Iraq)—were still pending.

Another example is the story of Felix Z. Longoria, Jr. of Three Rivers, TX, who was drafted into military service November 1944 and assigned to the US Army's 27th Infantry Regiment in the Philippines. Seven months after beginning his tour of duty in the Pacific, Longoria was the victim of a Japanese sniper.

Five years later (in 1950), after his remains were finally returned to Texas, the only funeral home in Three Rivers would not allow his funeral services to be held there because he was a "Mexican" and "the whites would not like it." Adding insult to injury, there was but one burial option for Pvt. Longoria's body: the "Mexican" section of the only cemetery in town—separated by barbed wire from the "whites only" side. In Texas, up until the mid-1900s, Mexican-Americans were socially considered "non-white" and suffered overt "racial" discrimination in public education, housing, and employment similar to that experienced by African Americans in the South (Hanner Lopez, *Racism on Trial-The Chicano Fight for Justice*).

Outraged by the insensitivity of the Three Rivers community, *Tejanos* organized under the auspices of the newly formed, military veterans organization, the American G.I. Forum. With the assistance from then US Senator Lyndon B. Johnson, arrangements were made for Pvt. Longoria's remains to be interred at the Arlington National Cemetery, with full military honors. He became the first Mexican-American veteran to be accorded this honor.

The Commonwealth of Puerto Rico has been a US territory since 1898, when the US invaded the Spanish-ruled Island of Enchantment. Its residents were granted US citizenship in 1917, just in time to be conscripted to fight in World War I. Despite the fact that an estimated 20,000 Puerto Ricans have served in the military and have a proud tradition of service to the USA; as of 2012, they still do not have the right to vote for their Commander in Chief: the President of the United States.

Puerto Ricans face the same lack of recognition as their mainland Latino cohorts who served their country as members of the US armed forces. A prime example of their courageous service was the 65th Infantry Regiment, the *Borinqueneers*, who took part in nine major campaigns in Korea, earning two Presidential Unit Citations, a Meritorious Unit Commendation and two

Republic of Korea Unit citations, four Distinguished Service Crosses (DSC) medals and 124 Silver Stars for heroism.

In Vietnam, US Army Sergeant First Class Jorge Otero Barreto (Vega Baja, PR) continued the Puerto Rican tradition. From 1961 to 1970, he served five tours in Southeast Asia and participated in two hundred combat missions. SFC Barreto is the most decorated US veteran of the Vietnam War. He was awarded a total of thirty-eight military decorations, among them: three Silver Stars, five Bronze Stars with Valor, five Purple Hearts and five Air Medals. Yet, few US residents know of his military exploits.

THE QUIET FORCE

Latinos from all corners of the Americas have distinguished themselves during US military armed conflicts. They continue to enlist and serve gallantly in the US armed forces at rates higher than their percentage of the population. In combat divisions, they remain among the most highly decorated of all US ethnic groups. When one considers the percentage of Latinos who have courageously defended our nation, the fact that their contributions still are not readily cited as examples of patriotism—nor sufficiently shared by US mainstream media and entertainment industries with the general population—is incredulous. It comes as no surprise to learn that within the Latino community many of its military veterans are often referred to as the "Quiet Force."

But thanks to efforts of the VOCES Oral History Project at the University of Texas-Austin's School of Journalism their voices are being heard. The effort is the brainchild of Dr. Maggie Rivas-Rodriguez, who established the project in 1999 to address the void in US history regarding the overlooked involvement of Latinos in WWII. The project's staff—comprised of college students and community volunteers from across the country—

are working diligently to chronicle the contributions made by Latinos/as on the battlefields and home fronts before we lose these aging heroes.

The project was expanded in 2010 to include veterans from the Korean and Vietnam conflicts. Nearly 1,000 stories are now recorded, digitized and available on the project's website (http://www.lib.utexas.edu/voces/). The data is housed at the Nettie Lee Benson Latin American Collection, part of the internationally renowned University of Texas Libraries in Austin, TX.

The results of the project's first ten years include a play "Voices of Valor," three books, a host of educational materials, and a photo exhibit, all of which can be accessed by professors and teachers from around the world. Many of the project's historically relevant photos have been used by the US Air Force, the Japanese American Museum, the National WWII Museum, the Smithsonian Institute's National Museum for American History, and by various news and media organizations across the nation.

Still, an informational vacuum exists, even among the most respected chroniclers of our nation's history. In his highly touted 2008 Public Broadcasting Service (PBS) documentary, "The War," producer Ken Burns overlooked Latino contributions to the war efforts. The 14.5-hour series on WW II failed to include any mention of Latinos, despite the fact that nearly a half million served in that war and were among the most highly decorated.

The reason Burns gave for the omission: "We set out to explore the human experience of war and combat based on a handful of stories told by individuals in only four American towns" (Bauder, *Burns Documentary Angers Latino Veterans*).

The four communities Burns selected to represent the entire nation were Waterbury, CT; Mobile, AL; Sacramento, CA; and Luverne, MN—communities that certainly deserved the focus, but without any substantial number of Latinos. Latino groups from across the country took exception to the exclusion in Burns' documentary; particularly after learning it featured non-white veterans in segments on segregated forces and included Japanese-Americans discussing their internment experiences. It is "limited" perspectives like this by entertainment and media industries that contribute to the marginalization of Latinos and their contributions to our country.

POST-WAR AMERICA

Racial and ethnic biases in the military historically have mirrored those of mainstream society, but serving in the armed forces also forced non-Hispanics and Latinos to interact and learn more about each other and their common interests. The sharing of foxholes, cigarettes, and the pressures of war with a diverse band of brothers provided opportunities for US Americans of all colors and creeds to gain a better understanding of one another.

With the onset of World War II, major shifts in population and employment patterns on the home front occurred and resulted in a rapid diversification of our nation's urban centers and civilian workforce. After the war, and especially during the second half of the twentieth century, Latinos followed employment opportunities and were transformed from a rural to an urban population. US military service and wartime production factories offered a variety of new career and employment opportunities, higher incomes, and increased interaction between white European Americans and Latinos.

WWII, Korea, and Vietnam wars also helped to redefine the Latino identity. No longer was it only people of Mexican, Puerto Rican, and Cuban heritage, but by the latter half of the twentieth century, Colombians, Dominicans, El Salvadorans, and others from Latin America began to change the overall composition of the Latino community.

There were other benefits associated with military service, but perhaps the most important was "The Servicemen's Readjustment

Act of 1944" that was designed to provide a variety of benefits to returning "honorably discharged" war veterans. Known as the "G.I. Bill," it provided federal funds to help veterans readjust to civilian life by defraying expenses related to medical care, home purchases, businesses start-ups, and education. The bill provided for tuition fees, subsistence, books and supplies, equipment, and counseling services for veterans to pursue a higher education. It is still considered by Latino veterans of the armed forces to be the single-most important educational and economic development legislation ever enacted by the federal government.

As for Latinos and their military service, it is safe to say their actions have spoken volumes!

Legends, Myths, and Falsehoods

En la noche todos los gatos son pardos.
Translation: At night all cats appear gray.
Transcreation: Perceptions are the lies we convince ourselves are true.

Stereotypes are generalizations attributable to a defined set of popularly accepted beliefs, or myths. They can be true or false, positive or negative. It is easy to create stereotypes when there is an obvious visible or apparent attribute that can be easily emphasized, such as a physical characteristic, language, accent, or cultural practice. The question is, "Who creates and promotes these simplified and standardized conception or images, and what are their motives?"

Latinos have been misrepresented to our nation's white Eurocentric society by acts of "commission" (stereotypic portrayals of Latinos in media and historical revisions) and acts of "omission" (absence of factual information related their contributions to our communities and country) by the media, entertainment industries, and historical accounts.

Once imbedded, stereotypes are infrequently eradicated. Even in the face of conflicting evidence, most societies cling to stereotypes in order to maintain some sense of superiority over others unlike them. Latinos and other non-whites groups, who have been so easily targeted for stereotyping in a *white Eurocentric* society, have found this practice extremely burdensome as they have attempted to assimilate into the "melting pot" that was supposed to assimilate the entire population of our nation.

Arthur Teitelbaum, a former broadcaster and cultural diversity expert with the Anti-Defamation League, is quoted as saying: "Beware the moments when facts seem to confirm prejudices. Such times are traps, when the well-meaning are misled and the mean-spirited gain confidence" (Pitts Jr., *Separating Fact from Prejudice*). These traps appear to be increasing all around us and have intensified in past years as non-white ethnic and racial groups have grown in numbers and become economically, politically, and socially empowered. Some see these trends as a threat to their way of life and the basis of an "us vs. them" conflict that led to overt discrimination in the past, especially as it related to property ownership, education, and employment opportunities; all critical to financial security in the US.

CREATING ANTAGONISM AND FEAR

Cloaked references to imperialist ideologies and overt racism—as in the case of *manifest destiny*—were already commonplace within many political circles of the 1800s and were frequently espoused by elected and public officials at the highest levels of our nation's government. Early cultural clashes between white European immigrants and non-white inhabitants of the western territories are not well recorded. Eurocentric whites needed to identify (or create) negative racial and cultural differences to justify their understanding of *manifest destiny* and rationalize the "liberation" of the western territories and its resources from its previous tenants.

Academicians and historians point to an early propagator of racial stereotypes: the *dime novel*, an influential medium of the early nineteenth century. These mass-produced books glamorized the West and promoted the concept of good guys versus bad guys. In them *Messicans* and *Injuns* were routinely portrayed as the antagonists: dangerous, inferior, villainous people who were generally slain in the final pages of these short novels.

During that period of US history, books were an inexpensive form of entertainment and quite influential in shaping white European attitudes toward non-white inhabitants of the western frontier. By the mid-1800s caricatures of *sombrero* wearing, mustachioed, armed, drunken Mexicans had been indelibly etched into the minds of many white immigrant settlers.

Following the discovery of gold in 1849, California was granted immediate statehood the following year. Almost as quickly, its legislature enacted the "Greaser Act" in 1855, an anti-vagrancy law that defined vagrants as "all persons who were commonly known as 'Greasers' or the issue of Spanish or Indian blood." The law was intended to keep Spaniards, Mexicans and *mestizos* from owning land or mines—providing justification for the expropriation of their real properties (1855 in Law: *1855 Treaties*).

The law was repealed a few years later but not before it had helped to etch yet another indelible image of Mexicans, *mestizos* and Spaniards into the minds of white European immigrants and settlers entering the still heavily non-white populated Southwest. These types of laws have been periodically re-enacted over the years as the pendulum of anti-Latino sentiments swings back and forth; California's Proposition 187 in 1994 and Arizona's Senate Bill 1070 in 2010 are examples of legislation that had negative repercussions on Latinos in those states.

WITS IN JEST ARE FOOLS IN EARNEST

With the advent of television as the mass media of choice in the US, other creative approaches were soon born. One of those so-called "harmless stereotype" used to lampoon the Latino community was the *Frito Bandito* [*sic*], a cartoon character who ambushed unsuspecting victims at gunpoint to rob them of their corn chips. This national advertising campaign (1967-1971) featured a fat, moustached, unkempt, revolutionary-looking bandit cartoon character that robbed white people to the tune of *"Cielito Lindo."* At one fell swoop, the campaign poked fun at the buffoonish antics of a Mexican revolutionary and/or criminal by denigrating a people, their language, and their culture.

The *bandido* commercials initially appeared during children's TV shows. But Frito-Lay felt the commercials were so *amusing* to youngsters, they opted to use the "Mexican bandit"—created by Foote, Cone & Belding, one of the nation's top ad agencies—in adult prime-time television, print, promotional materials, and other related marketing efforts. Despite protests from Latino advocacy and community groups, which prompted revisions to the character—broken teeth were "capped" and disheveled hair was "coiffed"—the *Frito Bandito* remained an advertising staple and sold a lot of corn chips during its four-year run.

Finally in 1971, under increasing community scrutiny—by members of Congress, local TV station management, and other forces who joined the opposition to the stereotypic ads—Frito-Lay *reluctantly* dropped its "cute" and "innocent" *Frito Bandito* character. For many Latinos across the US, the cancellation of the campaign was a case of "too little, too late." The damage had been done; the majority of white schoolchildren had added another negative stereotype to their arsenal of insults to use against their Latino peers.

While most other corporations ceased questionable campaigns upon receipt of complaints, Frito-Lay remained adamant that its campaign was never intended to be stereotypic or injurious to Latinos. They were not convinced that they had done anything wrong and in many instances projected a cavalier, "I don't give a damn!" attitude.

The *Frito Bandito* stereotype became a prime example of cultural and racial prejudice in advertising; still other national advertisers jumped on the *bandido*-themed bandwagon. Some of the most respected companies spawned some of the most objectionable examples of electronic media commercials, such as:

- **Granny Goose Potato Chips**: Featured fat unkempt Mexican toting guns and bandoliers.

  Inference: Latinos are sloppy, obese, armed, and criminal.

- **Liggett & Myers Cigarettes**: *Paco* never 'feenishes' anything, not even a revolution.

  Inference: Latinos are inarticulate, lazy and lack ambition.

- **R. J. Reynolds Cigarettes**: Mexican bandits.

  Inference: Latinos are sloppy, obese, armed and criminal.

- **Camel Cigarettes:** Typical Latino village, everybody sleeping or idle.

  Inference: Latinos are lazy, shiftless and lack ambition.

- **General Motors Company**: A white man holding three Latinos at gunpoint.

  Inference: Latinos are dangerous, criminal, and are controlled only by force.

- **Philco-Ford Televisions**: Latino sleeping next to a TV set.

  Inference: Latinos are lazy and lack the intelligence to appreciate modern products/services.

- **Arrid Deodorant:** *Bandido* using Arrid's campaign theme: If it works for him, it'll work for you.

  Inference: Latinos epitomize poor personal hygiene and are offensive to the senses.

These "tongue-in-cheek" images and descriptions used by such highly respected companies served to validate negative attitudes and opinions about Latinos by a majority of the white Eurocentric mainstream. They also formed the perceptions and attitudes of our nation's youth—the future practitioners of the advertising, mass media, and entertainment industries who would perpetuate the practices of previous generations. Like wealth and privilege in white America, bias and prejudice also seemed to be handed down to from one generation to the next.

Standard responses to complaints by those perpetuating the stereotypes related to racial and ethnic slurs followed a common theme: "You're too sensitive and are overreacting" or "They're only parodies and aren't meant to be taken seriously!" These were the most frequent responses used when getting caught with one's bigotry showing. Based on what the majority of US Americans considered to be humorous parodies or "poking fun," the advertising and entertainment industries continued to marginalize Latinos by portraying them in "cute," "humorous" and demeaning roles, much like previous portrayals of other minority groups.

There is no question the media and entertainment industries have projected a less than positive image of Latinos as well as that of other non-white, non-male, and racial and ethnic groups. In contrast, the image of white US Americans has been presented almost exclusively in a positive manner, from the rugged cowboy to war hero and from crime fighter to superhero. There was no doubt in the minds of moviegoers and entertainment and media executives as to who were to be projected as the "good guys" and the "bad guys."

IDENTITY THEFT

One of the most popular images used by entertainment and media moguls to represent the nation's "white, rugged individualism" happens to be of Spanish origin: the *vaquero*, or cowboy. Due to the omission of Spanish and Mexican contributions and history related to the Southwest, most US Americans remain unaware that this icon of the West originated in Europe's Iberian

Peninsula and was imported to the New World by Spain. In Spain large herds of cattle required vast amounts of land in order to obtain sufficient forage to sustain them. The need to cover great distances and areas resulted in the evolution of a cow herder on horseback, or *vaquero* (from the Spanish word for cow: *vaca*). Early in the 1500s Spaniards brought horses and cattle—and their cattle herding practices—to the Americas.

Spanish practices were refined in Mexico, where skilled equestrians became known as *charros* (a term used originally by the Spaniards to identify equestrians from *Salamanca* in Spain). Throughout Mexico and the much of the modern Southwest, *charros* remain associated with *charrería* (equestrian culture), *charreadas* (equestrian festivals and competitions) and *rodeos* (round-ups), which are still considered competitive sporting events in Latin America.

Yet, mention the word "cowboy" to most people and they conjure up images of: Bronco Billy Anderson, Gene Autry, Sam Bass, Johnny Mack Brown, Hopalong Cassidy, Buffalo Bill Cody (and his Wild West Show partner Annie Oakley), Gary Cooper, Wyatt Earp, Wild Bill Hickok, Jesse James, Billy the Kidd, Bat Masterson, Roy Rogers and his wife Dale Evans, John Wayne, and others. There were exceptions to the overwhelming list of white western protagonists: O. Henry's "Cisco Kid"—the "Robin Hood of the Old West"—and his trusted sidekick *Pancho*; *Zorro*, the mild-mannered Spaniard *Don Diego de la Vega* who defended the poor and weak in colonial California; and there was *Tonto*, the Lone Ranger's faithful companion, whose name most Spanish-speaking children recognized as meaning "fool," "dumb," or "stupid."

Around the world, cowboys came to personify the rugged individualism of the USA. They are still heroic and mythical characters created and perpetuated by folklore, the dime novel, movies, commercial advertisements, and other entertainment media. The promotion of that image is so pervasive that most citizens of the US are unaware that *vaqueros* in the West were originally Spanish, indigenous people, *mestizos*, and freed African slaves, whose skills were the basic resources used for the taming of the "Wild West."

LOST IN TRANSLATION

It was the Spanish-speaking *vaqueros*, "buckaroos" to English speakers of the time, who named many things associated with modern cowboy practices: bronco (from *bronco*, rough); chaps (leg protection from the *chaparral*); *lasso* (from *lazo*, rope); hoosegow (from *juzgar*, jail or court); lariat (from *la riata*, rope); mustang (from *mesteño*, wild); and *sombrero* (from *sombra*, shade).

Yup, even the "ten gallon hat" is of Spanish-language origin. A *galón* was a braided insignia or hatband *vaqueros* wore on their *sombreros* to denote experience and skills, thus many accomplished *vaqueros* could have worn a ten *galón* hat!

Understandably Hollywood, Madison Avenue, media, and literature continue to perpetuate the myth of white US Americans tamed the West, despite readily available historical sources chronicling the fact that *vaqueros* taught their skills to a great number of white European immigrants and settlers. The influence of these early *vaqueros* is evident today in almost every aspect of cattle ranching and Western sub-culture; but try telling that to pick-up truck driving "city slickers" who don their Sunday-best western duds in an effort to emulate their version of a cowboy.

US lyricist Johnny Mercer must have realized the influence of *vaqueros* (or the passing of the real cowboys) when he wrote the words for his 1930s musical hit, "I'm an Old Cowhand (From the Rio Grande):"

> Step aside, you ornery tenderfeet, Let a big bad buckeroo past.

I'm the toughest hombre you'll ever meet, though I may
be the last.
Yes, sir-ee, we're a vanishing race, No, sir-ee, can't last long.
Step aside, you ornery tenderfeet, while I sing my song:
I'm an old cowhand from the Rio Grande,
But my legs ain't bowed and my cheeks ain't tan.
I'm a cowboy who never saw a cow,
Never roped a steer, cause I don't know how.
Sure ain't a fixin' to start in now.
Yippee-I-Oh-Ki-Ay!

Apparently, constant repetition carries conviction. Repeated
untruths, over a long period of time, erode the facts to the point
where people believe them to be the truth. But like cats in the
dark that appear to be gray, things are not always as they seem—
nor what we would wish them to be.

Quiet as It's Kept

La verdad se corrompe tanto con la mentira como con el silencio.
Translation: The truth is corrupted as much by a lie as by
silence.
Transcreation: The cruelest lies are often told in silence.

M ass media refers to all information and news dissemination technologies, including blogs, the Internet, magazines, newspapers, television and radio. Increasingly, the visual
arts (cinema, radio and TV) have played a key role in influencing
our nation's politics and mainstream society. Since the middle of
the twentieth century, as mass media became the main source of
information for most US citizens, it was already recognized as
effective tools for manipulating and influencing large segments
of society.

Mainstream media continues to play a significant role in
shaping public opinion on a number of economic, political, and
social fronts by virtue of the information they opt to distribute
and the "spin" with which they deliver that information. Through
its delivery, media has further influenced the cultural and social
values of society by promoting a distinctive set of beliefs, values,
and attitudes focused mainly on a white, Eurocentric "one size
fits all" perspective. That perspective is no longer acceptable due
to the rapid diversification of our country's population.

The late television newscaster Walter Cronkite said, "In seeking truth you have to get both sides of a story" (St. Peter, *The
Greatest Quotations*). But as our society becomes more racially
and ethnically diverse, it is also becoming increasingly polarized
along social, class, and political lines; making it more difficult for
non-ethnic members of the media to understand how to access

both sides of any story in which perspectives are not aligned with those of "mainstream" society.

The lack of cultural relevance also is at the root of the change in attitudes some Latinos have developed toward mainstream media. In 2004, the University of California, Los Angeles (UCLA) researchers found that only 4 percent of prime-time's regular characters were Latino, even though they accounted for over 15 percent of the US population. The 2010 census showed Latinos continue to be the nation's fastest growing ethnic population and are now over fifty million strong; still they remain underrepresented in most facets of mass media, especially in local and network primetime television programming.

The National Association of Hispanic Journalists (NAHJ) issued a "Network Brownout Report" on the portrayal of Latinos and coverage of Latino issues on network television news in 2004. NAHJ's retrospective look to 1995 focused on what many already knew about US English-language programming; the nation's news media has been, and continues to be, woefully unaware of Latinos and their concerns.

NAHJ found Latinos remain underrepresented and were still routinely portrayed in less than positive terms by the major networks' news operations. In essence, positive Latino contributions remained nearly invisible on network news programming halfway into the first decade of the new millennium. NAHJ's study found:

- Of an estimated 16,000 stories that aired on ABC, CBS, CNN, and NBC in 2004, only 115, or .72 percent, were exclusively about Latinos. By comparison, the networks aired 131 Latino-related stories (.82 percent) in 2003.

- Out of a total of 548 hours of network news in 2004, only three hours and twenty-five minutes were devoted to Latino stories—a decline from 2003, when four hours and two minutes were allocated solely to Latino news stories.

- One of every three Hispanic stories (34.7 percent) was about immigration in 2004.

- More than one hour of coverage was devoted to the topic, making up almost a third (31.6 percent) of the total time (three hours twenty-five minutes) devoted to Latino stories.

- Half of all Hispanic stories (58 out of 115 stories) did not include an interview with a Latino; coverage lacked depth, with one third (33 percent) of all stories lasting thirty seconds or less.

- Latinos did not often appear in non-Latino related stories. Of an estimated 16,000 news stories in 2004, Latinos appeared as "sources" in only 265 non-Latino related stories (1.7 percent).

- Of the 115 Hispanic stories, forty-seven (41 percent) featured visual images of groups of unidentified Latinos. Of these stories, thirty-one (66 percent) featured immigrants, including images of undocumented border crossings. Only six stories featured Latino reporters; four of which were *Telemundo* network journalists reporting for NBC, the Spanish-language television network's parent.

- A significant proportion of stories about Latinos lacked diversity of opinion. Of 115 stories, more than one third (41 stories) did not cite a single source. Of the stories using sources, 40 percent (46 stories) presented mostly one perspective (or side).

- On a positive note, crime stories centered on Latinos sharply decreased, dropping from twenty-seven stories in 2003 to nine stories in 2004.

NAHJ's ten-year retrospective analysis found from 1995 to 2004, the networks aired approximately 140,000 stories—of those only 1,201 stories (0.85 percent) were about Latinos. Crime and immigration were the focus of most stories about Latinos, accounting for 36 percent of total coverage. During this period, NAHJ also discovered media coverage of Latinos and their issues had not advanced appreciably since 1995, with networks still exploring the same clichéd themes: undocumented immigration and the growing influence of the Latino vote.

Since NAHJ issued its first "Network Brownout Report" in 1996, the US has undergone a historic demographic shift, yet network media has failed to explain this change and its regional and national effects on US society to its audiences. Viewers exposed to network news have learned very little about their fellow Latino citizens and neighbors. Rarely do they see or hear stories about the positive contributions Latinos have made to our nation, our communities, or society in general. Instead, what they have seen is the portrayal of Latinos as "illegal" workers that take away jobs from US workers, use up public services; essentially people taking advantage of a white Eurocentric taxpaying society.

WHERE IS THE LATINO INTELLIGENTSIA?

Professional journalists and news programming producers tend to see themselves as "objective" parties in preparing their reports on any given issue or controversy. Very few claim to be entirely neutral or impartial, but the overwhelming majority makes an effort to sever their personal biases from their reports. Yet with a growing number of Latino organizations, leaders, and experts readily available to them, the majority of non-Hispanic news reporters and producers have not added knowledgeable Latino contacts to their lists of reliable "go to" sources, leaving viewers to surmise there are no such experts.

Could this oversight be a function of the racial/ethnic disparities in our nation's journalist/reporter pool as it relates to issues of importance to our nation's non-white citizens? Media monitoring organizations—like the NAHJ, the national media watch group Fairness and Accuracy in Reporting (FAIR) (http://www.

fair.org/) and the Fourth Estate Project (http://www.4thestate. net/), who analyze media behavior, outlets and news corporations—attribute the oversight to a lack of cultural diversity on the part of media staff.

In its visual analysis of "Newsroom Diversity," the 4th Estate Project found non-Hispanic white journalists wrote the greatest number of feature articles for most of the major metropolitan newspapers in the US and claimed the bylines for the majority of front-page stories on each of the following 2012 presidential election topics:

- Economy-86.6 percent (compared to Asian/Pacific Islander at 7.5, African American at 4.0, and Hispanic/Latino at 1.9)

- Social Issues-88 percent (compared to Asian/Pacific Islander at 8.5, African American at 3.0, and Hispanic/Latino at 0.5)

- Foreign Policy-93.4 percent (compared to Asian/Pacific Islander at 2.0, African American at 2.6, and Hispanic/Latino at 2.0)

- Immigration-94.8 percent (compared to Asian/Pacific Islander at 0.7, African American at 0.7, and Hispanic/Latino at 3.8) (The 4th Estate: *Newsroom Diversity*).

Our nation's undocumented immigration debate, which has dominated the news for decades and especially into the first twelve years of the new millennium, provides an example of how ingrained news media practices have become. General market media and its preponderance of non-Hispanic reporters have provided credibility for—and by default popularized the names of many anti-immigration advocates and their organizations— making many of them *de facto* experts on the US anti-immigration movement. The list of such spokesmen include: Mark Krikorian (Center for Immigration Studies); Jim Gilchrist and

Chris Simcox (Minuteman Project); Dan Stein (Federation for American Immigration Reform); and Roy Beck (NumbersUSA).

Despite a responsibility to provide balanced and objective reporting, the general market media has yet to provide equal opportunities for Latino journalists, content experts, and organizations that provide perspectives from pro-immigrant or comprehensive immigration reform camps. In too many instances the media's coverage of immigration issues and their effects on Latinos has resulted in continuing "acts of omission" as it relates to perspectives from Latino experts and spokespersons.

Adding to the problems associated with a lack of Latinos in the media is the fact that "politicized" perspectives aimed at conservative audiences have become a veritable "gold mine" for cable and talk show media. Among them is the most-listened-to US talk show host Rush Limbaugh, with a weekly audience of fifteen million and a reported contract of $400 million from 2008 through 2016, which makes him one of the highest paid media celebrities (Lewis, *Rush Limbaugh*). The repeal of the Federal Communications Commission's "Fairness Doctrine" in 1987—which required radio and television stations to provide free air time for responses to controversial opinions previously broadcast—meant stations could broadcast editorial commentary without having to present opposing views.

A *Wall Street Journal* editorial opined: "Ronald Reagan tore down this wall (the Fairness Doctrine) in 1987 ... and Rush Limbaugh was the first man to proclaim himself liberated from the East Germany of liberal media domination" (Henninger, *Rush to Victory*). He was not only a pioneer in electronic media's "op-ed" content, but became a role-model for others to follow in promoting political and social controversies, especially those related to anti-Latino immigration and the overall "browning" of America.

Conservative broadcast and cable network programming are not alone in the omission of Latinos and their perspectives. Even socially and politically liberal programs like *The Daily Show with Jon Stewart*, a satirical news program regarding current affairs on cable's Comedy Central, which only recently (May 2011) added Latino comedian Al Madrigal to its cast. HBO's *Real Time with Bill Maher* that features nationally renowned panelists and expert guests seldom includes Latinos, though the political, social, and economic issues the show addresses affect nearly all of our nation's population.

In the face of these aforementioned aspects of media it is easy to understand why attitudes among non-Hispanics towards Latinos may be less than positive.

REVENUE VS. RESPONSIBILITY

Use of opinion and editorial commentary to influence public opinion is not a new or novel concept. The first modern "Op-Ed" page first appeared in 1921 and was the brainchild of Herbert B. Swope, publisher of *The New York Evening World*. Swope realized the page opposite its editorials was filled with too much of what he considered to be "uninteresting book reviews, society items, and obituaries." Concerned with increasing circulation (code for advertising revenues), he wrote:

> "It occurred to me that nothing is more interesting than opinion when opinion is interesting, so I devised a method of cleaning off the page opposite the editorials, which became the most important in America ... and thereon I decided to print opinions, ignoring facts" (Meyer, *Pundits, Poets, and Wits*).

Some 90 years later a modern version of "interesting opinion" is now readily available through the nation's most accessible information dissemination media: cable television and talk radio. A 2008 report compiled by the Media Matters Action Network

(MMAN), documented negative and threatening opinions of Latinos heard almost daily on cable news and syndicated radio shows. MMAN identified CNN's Lou Dobbs and Glenn Beck, along with FOX's Bill O'Reilly, as having contributed to the creation of anti-immigrant hysteria by offering "a steady diet of fear, anger, and resentment" on the topic of undocumented immigration (Media Matters Action Network, *Fear & Loathing*).

The link between immigration and crime rates has garnered considerable attention from researchers, but a growing number of studies find Latino immigrants proportionately commit fewer crimes than their US-born peers. The media's lack of alternative perspectives in its coverage results in the continual portrayal of Latino immigrants as criminals and threats to the white Eurocentric way of life. Although the weight of evidence suggests immigration is not linked to crime, the public consistently views immigrants, especially undocumented immigrants, as criminals and thus a threat to social order (Wang, *Undocumented Immigrants as Perceived Criminal Threats*).

The aforementioned MMAN report found the connection between crime and undocumented immigrants was discussed on ninety-four broadcasts of *Lou Dobbs Tonight*, sixty-six episodes of *The O'Reilly Factor* on Fox News, and twenty-nine of the *Glenn Beck Show* on CNN Headline News. The study found seventy-one of Dobbs', thirteen of Glenn Beck's and eight of O'Reilly's episodes asserted undocumented immigrants were a burden on government services, even though they were legally prevented from receiving public services funded by the federal government (with the exception of emergency medical care). The three also alleged undocumented immigrants did not pay taxes.

Yet the Institute for Taxation and Economic Policy (ITEP) produced a report in 2011, about state and local taxes paid by undocumented immigrants. It estimated $11.2 billion in sales, property, and income taxes were added to the US economy in 2010 by undocumented immigrant taxpayers, workers, consumers, and entrepreneurs. Nationally, about half of the estimated ten to twelve million undocumented immigrants (which includes children) filed tax returns and paid $1.2 billion in personal income taxes, $1.6 billion in property taxes and $8.4 billion in sales taxes (Immigration Policy Center: *Unauthorized Immigrants Pay Taxes, Too*). This information was not shared with their audiences.

Beck, Dobbs, and O'Reilly perpetuated other untruths that further agitated their listeners. Among them were the planned construction of a "NAFTA (North American Free Trade Agreement) Superhighway" from Mexico to Canada; an alleged plan to unite Mexico, Canada and the USA into a "North American Union;" and the threat of a reconquest by Mexico of the Southwest.

The MMAN study found Dobbs also shared with his audiences the threat of a leprosy outbreak resulting from undocumented immigration and reported instances of major voter fraud by immigrants. The latter may have been the impetus for Voter ID laws that were passed in 11 Republican-controlled state legislatures between 2011-2012 (The Brennan Center, *Analysis*). Based on the continuous harangue by these "fear merchants" on immigration, barricading the US Mexico border, residential overcrowding, displacement of US workers, use of tax supported public services, etc., it is not surprising many of their listeners supported a variety of legislative bills aimed at curtailing immigration and Latino-oriented programs across the nation.

Modern versions of editorial opinion masquerading as news are alive and well. There are suspicions that this focus on sensationalism, distortion of facts and misleading information is produced for the sole purpose of inciting public passions that increase audience share and ratings, resulting in greater advertising revenues. Unfortunately, this type of misrepresentation of the facts that hides behind the First Amendment's right to freedom of speech is preferred by many over the more ethical and objective mainstream media's approach to news reporting. Editorial opinion types of news and public affairs programs are designed to appeal to the most susceptible segments of society: the economically disadvantaged, least educated, underemployed, and those who profit from the fear and hate generated by inflammatory media rhetoric.

AIDING AND ABETTING

A July 31, 2008 editorial published by the traditionally conservative newspaper *San Diego Union-Tribune* addressed the aforementioned "groupthink" trend in media:

> "It's common for human beings to fear the foreign or the different, and for fear to be supplanted by hatred. But what is not natural, and should never be shrugged off, is for people to resort to violence to show their displeasure with those who have a different skin color or practice a different religion or speak a different language. It is no coincidence that this kind of ugliness coincides with an immigration debate that makes scapegoats out of those who come into the country illegally."

The editorial referenced the July 2008 incident in Shenandoah, PA, where a 25 year-old, undocumented Mexican immigrant, *Luis Eduardo Ramirez Zavala*, was beaten by at least six teenagers who used racial slurs as they pounded and kicked him into unconsciousness. The youths stomped the father of two so violently that an imprint of the religious medallion he wore around his neck was imbedded on his chest. The victim died a few days later, leaving behind his children and fiancée. According to town officials it appeared to be a "hate" crime, especially because the teens made a point of telling the victim to "go back to Mexico," calling him a "dirty Mexican," and warning other Mexican residents to do likewise or end up like *Ramirez Zavala*.

Derrick Donchak and Brandon Piekarsky faced a maximum penalty of life in prison on the hate crime charge, but the judge who presided over the trial, sentenced Piekarsky to a term of from six months and seven days to twenty-three months, while Donchak was sentenced to a term from seven to twenty-three months in prison for simple assault and alcohol-related crimes for their respective roles in the beating death. Shortly thereafter federal authorities convened a grand jury, which indicted the pair on hate crime charges. In October 2010, an all-white jury of six men and six women found the two youths guilty on all counts. Donchak and Piekarsy each face up to life in prison and a $250,000 fine for violating their victim's civil rights.

The Pennsylvania attack was not an isolated incident. Suffolk County prosecutors charged seven teenagers in Patchogue, NY, in the deadly November 2008 assault on *Marcelo Lucero*, an Ecuadorian immigrant. The teenagers were reportedly engaged in a regular and violent pastime that they described as "beaner-hopping" or "Mexican-hopping"—hunting Latinos for physical attacks. Prosecutors believed other young men were involved in as many as eight such attacks. One of the attackers, Jeffrey Conroy, was found guilty of killing *Lucero* in the hate crime attack and was sentenced to twenty-five years in prison.

In 2006, two "skinheads" viciously attacked a 16 year-old named David Ritcheson in Houston, TX. According to news reports, the two broke Ritcheson's jaw, knocking him unconscious, while screaming "white power!" and calling him a "spic" and a "wetback." The two burned the teen with cigarettes, kicked him with steel-toed boots, poured bleach on him, and tried to carve a *swastika* on his chest. They also sodomized him with a patio umbrella pole. David Tuck, nineteen, was sentenced to life in prison for his part in the attack, while Keith Turner, eighteen, received a ninety-year sentence.

It took thirty surgeries before Ritcheson, who was confined to a wheelchair and wore a colostomy bag, was able to return to school. A year after the attack, the high school student had still not been identified in news accounts by name, but he decided to go public by speaking before a U.S. House of Representative's Judiciary Committee. In his testimony, he recalled the horrific experience for lawmakers who were deliberating over strengthening federal hate crime laws. Three months later, Ritcheson committed suicide by jumping off a cruise ship into the Gulf of Mexico. Why he took his own life remains unknown (Mock, *Hate Crimes*).

There is a substantial number of impressionable people who are easily swayed by the sentiments being expressed by anti-immigrant supporters and the media hosts that provide them the soapboxes from which to proselytize?

"The media is doing a disservice with coverage that is misleading the public about Latinos who live in the U.S.," said National Hispanic Media Coalition (NHMC) President and CEO Alex Nogales of Los Angeles, CA. As a result of television and radio talk show programs posing as news, an impressionable segment of US Americans perceive Latinos—US native-born and immigrants alike—as threats to white US Eurocentric values.

In a recent NHMC poll conducted by Latino Decisions, 50 percent of non-Latinos think the term "welfare recipient" describes Latinos "very" or "somewhat well" (51 percent), as well as "less educated" (50 percent) and "refuse to learn English" (44 percent). Surprisingly, the same poll found respondents also held positive views of Latinos: over 75 percent of those polled thought Latinos were family-oriented (90 percent), hard-working (81 percent), religious (81 percent), and honest (76 percent) (Lilley, *Poll*).

If the unfounded threats attributed to Latinos by the ranting of anti-immigrant media hosts and guests have not sufficiently underscored the losses suffered as a result of senseless hate crimes in our society, perhaps the wasting away of impressionable white youth in our nation's prisons should!

HABIT RULES THE UNREFLECTING HERD

In the past general market media executives opposed the addition of non-white and ethnic content, except for the occasional *Cinco de Mayo* celebrations in news and public affairs programming—an observance actually created by Latinos in California to commemorate a Mexican victory over the French in 1862 that influenced the outcome of the US Civil War (Hayes-Bautista, *El Cinco de Mayo*). Media and programming decision-makers frequently expressed doubts over the fit between Latino and white, Eurocentric American audiences. Some candidly shared a common opinion: "Inclusion of Latinos and their perspectives in our news and/or local programming could result in 'tuning-out' by our general market audience." The concern over alienating white audiences (and the advertising revenues associated with them) resulted in the absence of Latino perspectives and content in local news, allowing for misconceptions about their political loyalties to be formed and perpetuated.

Today many English-language media executives feel Spanish language television, radio, and print media adequately address Latino community needs and interests, allowing them to focus on the news and entertainment programming needs of non-Hispanic white (NHW), English-speaking audiences. A few see the handwriting on the wall and are expanding their programming to fit the needs of changing demographics in their local markets, especially in markets where the minority is becoming the majority.

Non-whites, mainly Hispanics and Asians, made up 92 percent of US population growth in the first decade of the new millennium; many of them are moving into large cities or their suburbs. Non-whites now make-up more than 50 percent of the population in twenty-two of our nation's largest cities—up from fourteen metropolitan areas in 2000, and just five in

1990. According to Census figures, the majority of every major racial and/or ethnic group in these large cities now lives in the suburbs.

Even though Latinos are more frequently included in general market news and programming at local levels they are still not yet "prime-time players" at local or network levels, especially when it comes to producing, writing, and on-camera roles. There have been a few exceptions but the fact we can easily identify them speaks to the limited number of examples. A case in point: of the nearly sixty prime-time series on the major TV networks in 2006, only five (.08 percent) had non-white performers in leading roles, and only two (.03 percent)—*Ugly Betty* and *The George Lopez Show*—were scripted solely around Latinos.

As of 2007, Latinos remained the most underrepresented segment of the US population on non-news, network television. Even with the advent of *Ugly Betty* (cancelled in April 2010) and the *George Lopez Show* (cancelled in May 2007), Latinos accounted for less than two percent of all characters on English-language "prime time." When they were included it was generally in secondary or "traditionally negative" roles: unskilled workers, illiterates, undocumented immigrants, gang members, drug dealers, and other scofflaws.

George Lopez may have vindicated himself with his November 2009 entry into late night television programming with *Lopez Tonight* on cable television channel TBS (Turner Broadcasting System). In its first week it outdrew the competition by averaging more than 1.6 million viewers and beating its competition in the highly coveted young adults audience categories. The show averaged 1.6 million viewers, over 1.1 million households, 597,000 "Adults 18 to 34," over one million "Adults 18 to 49," and hit a high with one episode, scoring 2 million viewers and 1.2 million "Adults 18 to 49."

Among "Adults 18 to 34" and "Adults 18 to 49," *Lopez Tonight* outperformed the season-to-date averages for *The Daily Show*

·

with Jon Stewart, The Late, Late Show with Craig Ferguson, Late Night with Jimmy Fallon, Jimmy Kimmel Live, and *Last Call with Carson Daly.* It also beat out the season-to-date average for *The Late Show with David Letterman* and the series premiere of *The Wanda Sykes Show* among "Adults 18 to 34." The show was a big hit on the multicultural front; Latinos accounted for one third of the audience, while African-American viewers accounted for one fourth. In addition, the series enjoyed a higher concentration of Latino viewers (33 percent), Hispanic "Adults 18 to 34" (40 percent) and Hispanic "Adults 18 to 49" (34 percent) than any late-night talk show on the major networks (Gorman, *Lopez Tonight Scores Big First Week Ratings*).

In November 2010, the show was bumped to a later time slot to accommodate Conan O'Brian's late night entry into the TBS line-up. Despite A-list guests, an informal party atmosphere, and Lopez's irreverent Latino-flavored comic *persona*, the network felt the show did not produce anticipated audience levels. In August 2011, citing drops in viewership TBS again asked Lopez to move his late-night program—this time off their network.

Yet, Latinos are becoming more visible. ABC's *Dancing with the Stars* and FOX's *American Idol* remain among the most popular with US viewers and also reflect our nation's changing demographics. The shows' casting of Latino participants, and winners, have made them popular with Latino audiences.

ABC's highly successful *Modern Family* introduced a multicultural extended family to viewers featuring Sofía Vergara (Colombian) as the voluptuous Gloria Delgado-Pritchett, whose stereotypic Spanish accent and mispronunciation of English words and phrases (ala *Charo* and *Lupe Velez*) are an integral part of the show's humor. Rico Rodriguez (USA) plays Vergara's on-screen son Manny Delgado, an urbane and scholarly pre-teen, which is a good thing! Latino actors are being prominently displayed in a number of television network shows and may soon provide viewers with a variety of roles that more accurately reflect our nation's racial/ethnic population and "real life" situations.

Yet, the images most US Americans are exposed to in many programs continue to be inarticulate, uneducated, poor, unskilled, criminal and undocumented immigrants in secondary and "extra" roles. These perceptions contribute to the negative impressions people have, as do the continuing news coverage and biased broadcasts of negative and controversial issues frequently associated with Latinos: drugs, gangs, and immigration.

A 2009 report by the Pew Research Center's Project for Excellence in Journalism in Washington, DC found most of what the public learns about Latinos "comes from event-driven news stories in which they are one of many elements discussed." From February through August 2009, only a fraction of the news stories—57 of 34,451 (or .00165 percent) they reviewed—focused directly on Latino life experiences in the US. During the six months examined, Pew found "only 2.9 percent of the news content studied contained substantial references" to US Hispanics/Latinos, which was more attention than any other ethnic or religious group analyzed, except for Muslims (Project for Excellence in Journalism, *Hispanics*).

Despite the lack of positive or proportional media coverage, Latinos are entering the ranks of film, music and sports careers, corporate executives, elected officials, and successful business owners at unprecedented rates. These success stories are creating positive perceptions among Latinos, but go relatively unnoticed by traditional English-language media.

IT'S ALL ABOUT THE JEFFERSONS

In the case of the news media, conformity with traditional exclusion of Latinos is no longer advisable, or profitable. It is in the best interests of our nation's media and their owners to provide accurate and positive news coverage of Latinos in order to shed light on their growing contributions to society as consumers, employees, students, taxpayers, and voters. In 2010 the majority of the population of four states, and a growing number of our nation's largest urban cities, had become "majority" non-European white.

Underscoring this growth is the school-aged population that will produce our future workforce, consumers and taxpayers. In 2009, one-fourth of the nation's kindergartners were Latino, an accelerating trend that will see non-white children become the majority by 2023. These enrollment levels are most evident in the Southwestern US, where non-white students at the K-12 grade levels were already 37 percent of student enrollments; their state proportions were: 54 percent in New Mexico, 47 percent in California, 44 percent in Texas, and 40 percent in Arizona. They are expected to become the majority of students in several neighboring states in the near future (Yen, *Hispanics*).

An increasingly diverse population and its influence on our society dictates we put an end to the mythical threats of impending doom to the US American "way of life." The rate of violent crime in recent years is at its lowest point since 1968, even in the midst of a major recession. Although 84 percent of all white murder victims are killed by whites, the *Drudge Report* and *Fox News* provides extensive coverage of any incident in which a non-white person harms a white person. In the short term, fear, controversy, and conflict may increase media ad revenues and profits (and influence political agendas), but at what costs to a woefully uninformed segment of our society?

Once a year the US observes the histories, cultures and contributions of its citizens of Spanish, Mexican, Caribbean and Latin American heritage. That it is condensed into a 30-day period is appreciated, but many Latinos feel it effectively isolates nearly one fifth of the nation's population (and its contributions) into a "separate but equal" window that is opened but once each year.

It may require more than a week or a month to recognize Latino accomplishments and their contributions to the US, as in the case of Hispanic Heritage Month. It started as a weeklong celebration in 1968 under Executive Order of President Lyndon Johnson; it was extended to its current 30-day period—September 15 to October 15—in 1988 by Ronald Reagan.

Granted the barriers to seeking the truth may be difficult to overcome but when something as important as the demographic shift we are currently experiencing in the US is occurring, the truth is corrupted as much by omissions and silence as by lies.

Shining Examples

Hasta las estrellas más pequeñas brillan en la oscuridad.
Translation: Even the tiniest stars shine in the dark.
Transcreation: The best examples in one's life are those
worthy of emulation.

Most Latinos can recount personal experiences with stereo-types and slurs used by teachers, peers, co-workers, and neighbors. The lack of accurate representation of Latinos in the entertainment and news media has contributed to the misconceptions and stereotypes non-Hispanics have formed of Latinos. The movie industry in the United States has become the most prolific source of entertainment in the world and perhaps the most influential in creating long-lasting images of the people portrayed in them. The popularity of motion pictures provides yet another avenue by which stereotypes can be communicated and perpetuated.

Professor Charles Ramírez Berg of the Radio-Television-Film department at the University of Texas-Austin, claims the *bandido* series of early silent films in the US contributed greatly to the stereotyping of Mexicans by continuing to portray them as greasers, rapists, thieves, drunks, and murderers (Ramirez Berg, *Latino Images in Film*).

The movie industry produced a raft of overtly racist films during its silent era, among them: *The Greaser's Gauntlet* (1908), *Ah Sing and the Greasers* (1910), *Tony the Greaser* (1911), *The Greaser and the Weakling* (1912), *The Girl and the Greaser* (1913), *The Greaser's Revenge* (1914), *Bronco Billy and the Greaser* (1914), and *The Greaser* (1915).

"The *bandido* stereotype not only oversimplified Latinos, the very definition of stereotype, but also 'reinforces the cleanliness, sobriety, sanity, overall decency, and moral rectitude of the White Anglo-Saxon Protestant (WASP) in the white hat.' Consciously or not, movie studios used the *bandido* to reaffirm US America's values and morality," explained Ramírez Berg.

THE WINDS OF CHANGE

Starting with the silent era, movie stars were generally white European-Americans who established themselves as swashbucklers, cowboys, and other types of heroes. Over the years they became the Silver Screen's examples of All-American men and women—a practice that has been perpetuated by generations of industry executives and producers. In early films Latinos were generally cast in stereotypic roles: duplicitous, sneaky, and looking for sexual conquests of white women. Except for the early silent film era, Latinos were seldom cast in starring roles; they were mainly *second bananas* to white protagonists, who in the end almost always got the town's gratitude, the adoration of the leading lady, and often as not rode-off alone into the sunset on their trusted steeds.

While on the subject of leading ladies, there was the exceptional career of Myrtle Gonzalez of Los Angeles, CA, who starred in nearly eighty silent era motion pictures from 1913 to 1917. She is regarded as Hollywood's first Latina movie star. However, for the most part Latinas were cast mainly in one of two roles in the Golden Age of Hollywood: the alluring *señorita* (usually of high social standing based on wealth, class or family status); or the irascible, hot-blooded *vixen* (sultry, unsophisticated, excitable, and feisty). Among the early stars of these Hollywood films were the *classy Dolores del Río* and the *sassy Lupé Veléz*.

Other notable actresses who followed in their footsteps were *Raquel Torres, Maria Montez, Elena Verdugo* and *Katy Jurado*. *Jurado* has the distinction of being the first Latina nominated for an Academy Award as Best Supporting Actress in the 1954 movie *Broken Lance*. Only two others have been nominated since; *Salma Hayek* for Best Actress in *Frida* (2002) and *Adriana Barraza* for Best Supporting Actress for *Babel* (2006). None of the three were born in the US.

As the silent era of motion pictures continued the need to compare "good guys" to more contemporary foils resulted in the introduction of yet a different stereotype: the licentious "Latin Lover." Actors like *Antonio Moreno, Ramón Novarro* and *Rudolph Valentino* became overnight sensations. The distinctive and swarthy looks of these *"don Juans"* caused an unanticipated reaction: they swept female moviegoers off their feet.

Their replacements in "talkies" were more urbane, exotic types like *José Ferrer*—the first Latino to win an Academy Award for Best Actor in "Cyrano de Bergerac" (1950)—*Ricardo Montalbán, Gilbert Roland, César Romero,* Anthony Quinn and *Fernando Lamas*. They too had a lasting impression on movie fans. A 2006 on-line survey of five hundred people found over 36 percent of the respondents described "Latin Lovers" as "someone who really knows how to romance you." Another 17 percent replied, "A beautiful person with dark skin and hair."

Another Hollywood notable was *Thomas Goméz* (1905-1971), the first US-born Latino nominated for an Academy Award for his role in *Ride the Pink Horse*. In the 1947 movie, he portrays *Pancho*, "a wise fool, the peasant with a heart of gold who speaks broken English through a missing front tooth, runs around barefoot, unshaven, wearing a tattered *sombrero*." (Sound familiar?) As the publicity department at Universal so adroitly expressed it: "Thomas Gomez is a big, greasy, *tequila*-swilling slob, who has one brief glow of nobility" (Hewitt, *Hispanics and the Oscar*).

Mexican actor *Alfonso "Indio" Bedoya* (1904-1957) may have immortalized the stereotypic *bandido* role in the 1948 movie, *The Treasure of the Sierra Madre*. In an exchange with Fred C. Dobbs (the role played by Humphrey Bogart), a Mexican bandit "Gold

Hat" (portrayed by *Bedoya*) tries to convince Dobbs he and his colleagues are friendly *Federales*. Dobbs asks, "If you're the police where are your badges?"

Gold Hat replies with his now famous outburst: "Badges? We ain't got no badges. We don't need no badges! I don't have to show you any stinkin' badges!"

THE PRICE OF FAME

The aforementioned silver screen pioneers opened the door for others who longed for the klieg lights of tinsel town and stardom in other fields of entertainment. By the late twentieth century, Latinas and Latinos had made their presence felt in movies, music, and sports. But, in order to gain that fame, most were required to shed their Spanish surnames and "Latinoness." The fear of offending white people was still at the forefront of the movie industry's efforts to promote and sell their wares.

This list of those who were crossing over to the "light side" included several of what would become the brightest stars in their respective fields: *Esteban Ernesto Echevarría Samsón* (Steven Bauer), *Florencia Biscenta de Casillas Martinez Cardona* (Vicky Carr), *Marta Victoria Moya Burges* (Linda Cristal), *Enrique Tomás Delgado* (Henry Darrow), *Baldemar Huerta* (Freddie Fender), *Margarita Carmen Dolores Cansino* (Rita Hayworth), *Antonio Rúdolfo Oaxaca Quinn* (Anthony Quinn), *Luis Antonio Damaso de Alonso* (Gilbert Roland), *Ramón Gerardo Antonio Estévez* (Martin Sheen), *Richard Steven Valenzuela* (Richie Valens), and *Jo Raquel Téjada* (Raquel Welch).

By trading-in their Spanish surnames for those more closely associated with white Europeans, they assumed they would become acceptable to mainstream movie fans and have a better chance for success. However, the cost was great for them and the Latino community; the jettisoning of their surnames and cultures also kept them from becoming recognizable and positive role models for an emerging Latino population.

By the beginning of the twenty-first century a growing number of music entertainers and motion picture/television actors were taking pride in their Latino identities and heritage. In fact, many had become box-office attractions in starring roles—without having to change their names. The list includes: Jessica Alba, Trini Alvarado, Antonio Banderas, Penelope Cruz, Raymond Cruz, Rosario Dawson, Alana de la Garza, Kathe Del Castillo, Cameron Díaz, America Ferrera, Andy García, Salma Hayek, Eva Longoría, John Leguízamo, George López, Jennifer López, Mario López, Demi Lovato, Vanessa Marcil, Eva Mendez, Esai Morales, Ana Ortiz, Rosie Perez, Tony Plana, Sara Ramirez, Adam Rodriguez, Mercedes Ruehl, Zoë Saldana, and Rachel Ticotín, to name a few.

Yet the dearth of Latino (and other non-white actors) recognized for their acting talents is not surprising. A months-long investigation by *The Los Angeles Times* resulted in a February 25, 2012, editorial about the membership of the Academy of Motion Picture Arts and Sciences (AMPAS) that revealed the organization, like much of the media and entertainment industries, is overwhelmingly non-Hispanic white (NHW) and male. The *Times* investigation found that of the Academy's 5,112 members, the voting members were almost 94 percent (4,805) NHW and 77 percent (3,936) male. According to AMPAS officials, of the 178 people accepted for membership in 2011, 30 percent (53) were women and 10 percent (18) were non-white.

Why is the make-up of the Academy relevant? In 2010, Nielsen reported 43 million Latinos bought 351 million movie tickets, an increase from the 37 million that bought 300 million tickets in 2009, making them a critical share of the movie-going audience in the US. The movie industry continues to develop more marketing initiatives and ways to make their films more attractive to Latinos, but inexplicably fails to understand the need for more diversity within their own ranks.

It's interesting to note Mexican filmmaker and actor *Emilio "El Indio" Fernández* (March 26, 1904-August 6, 1986) posed for the initial design of the AMPAS Oscar statuette, which has been given to all the winners since 1929. While working in Hollywood, *Fernández* befriended Mexican actress *Dolores del Rio*—wife of MGM's art director and AMPAS member Cedric Gibbons. *Del Río* introduced *El Indio* to Gibbons, who was then in charge of supervising the award's design. Reluctant at first, *Fernández* was finally convinced to pose nude to create what today is known officially as the "Academy Award of Merit"—or affectionately among the nominees: "Oscar."

AND THE BEAT GOES ON

Music is another art form that has provided positive exposure for Latinos. From the incomparable talents of the late *Desi Arnaz, Ray Barreto, Celia Cruz, Xavier Cúgat, Beny Moré* and *Tito Puente* to international superstars like *Julio Iglesias, Plácido Domingo* and Mexican composer *Armando Manzanero,* who wrote and recorded the classic *"Somos Novios,"* also known in English as "It's Impossible."

Other Latinos have made many notable contributions to the music world. *"Bésame Mucho"* (Kiss Me a Lot)—written in 1941 by 14-year old Mexican *Consuelo Velázquez*—became the international anthem of lovers during World War II. The song is reported to have had more than two million performances on radio and television and was recorded by renowned artists, among them: Josephine Baker, Dave Brubeck, Vikki Carr, *José Carreras, Charo,* the Coasters, Nat King Cole, *Xavier Cúgat, Plácido Domingo,* Bill Evans, the Flamingos, Connie Francis, Dexter Gordon, Chris Isaak, Harry James, Spike Jones, Diana

Krall, Frankie Laine, Steve Lawrence & Eydie Gorme, Julie London, *Trini Lopéz*, Dean Martin, Carmen McRae, Les Paul, Art Pepper, the Platters, *Tito Puente*, and Artie Shaw, to name a few. It was also a frequent—yet never recorded—live concert offering by the Beatles.

Speaking of the Beatles, the first Latino band to record a national hit was Cannibal & The Headhunters of East Los Angeles, CA. In 1965, their song "Land of 1,000 Dances" climbed to #30 on the *Billboard Hot 100* charts—a feat that earned them the opening act on The Beatles' second US tour. The following year, Question Mark (Rudy Martinez) & The Mysterians of Bay City, MI, topped the *Billboard Hot 100* chart with "96 Tears." They are ranked #213 on the Rolling Stone magazine's list of the "500 Greatest Songs of All Time."

Music icons *Leandro "Gato" Barbieri*, Vikki Carr, *José Carreras, Plácido Domingo, Gloria Estefan, Jose Feliciano, Julio Iglesias,* Linda Ronstadt, *Carlos Santana*, and *Lalo Schifrin* continued the crossover trend. They were followed by a number of more recent stars, including *Christina Aguilera, Marc Anthony, Selena Gomez, Enrique Iglesias, Los Lobos, Los Lonely Boys, Lucero, Demi Lovato, Luís Miguel, Ozomatli,* Pit Bull, *RBD, Ricky Martin, Shakira, Thalía,* and Daddy Yankee. Additionally, these modern perform- ers have become as popular with non-Hispanic music fans as they are among their Latino *aficionados*.

TAKE ME OUT TO A BALLGAME

Latinos are also making their presence felt in other areas of the entertainment industry; they are emerging as stars in a variety of professional and amateur sports.

According to a 2012 study of major league contracts by *The Associated Press*, Latinos are among the highest paid players in Major League Baseball (MLB). At $30 million per year, the

Yankees' Alex (A-Rod) Rodrigez is the richest of the rich, baseball's highest-paid player for the twelfth straight season.

Baseball has benefited from an impressive list of former, current and future Latino stars—from Ted Williams to Sammy Sosa and from A-Rod to the members of the 2009 Little League World Champions, the Park View All-Stars from Chula Vista, CA.

In 2005, in recognition of past and current contributions, MLB named twelve active and former players to its first Latino "All-Star" baseball team. The team included catcher Ivan (Pudge) Rodriguez (Puerto Rico), 1st baseman Albert Pujols (Dominican Republic), 2nd baseman Rod Carew (Panama), shortstop Alex Rodriguez (Dominican Republic), 3rd baseman Edgar Martinez (Puerto Rico), outfielders Roberto Clemente (Puerto Rico), Manny Ramirez (Dominican Republic), Vladimir Guerrero (Dominican Republic), starting pitchers Pedro Martinez (Dominican Republic), Juan Marichal (Dominican Republic), Fernando Valenzuela (Mexico), and relief pitcher Mariano Rivera (Panama).

In announcing the line-up, MLB Commissioner Bud Selig said Latinos possess a "deep passion for the game of baseball, and have made immense contributions to the national pastime." And not only on the field! Modern day MLB teams include the names of Latino owners such as Art Moreno (Los Angeles Angels of Anaheim), Linda Alvarado (Colorado Rockies), and the late José Canchola (Arizona Diamondbacks).

The National Football League (NFL) has featured Latino quarterbacks such as Joe Kapp (Vikings-Patriots), Tom Flores (Raiders-Bills-Chiefs), Jim Plunkett (Patriots-49ers-Raiders) and J.P. Losman (Bills). The 2006 National Conference playoffs pitted QBs Jeff García (Eagles) and Tony Romo (Cowboys) against each other.

Perhaps the most prominent Latino quarterback today is Mark Sanchez, a first round pick in the 2009 NFL draft by the New

York Jets. He was the second QB taken and fifth overall selection. He played college football at the University of Southern California (USC) and became only the fourth rookie QB in NFL history to win his first playoff game, and one of only two to win two play-off games in a single season. With Sanchez, the Jets made another play-off appearance, losing to the Pittsburgh Steelers in the January 23, 2011 AFC Championship game.

In 1998 offensive lineman Anthony Muñoz of the Cincinnati Bengals was the first Latino inducted into the Pro Football Hall of Fame in his first year of eligibility. During their playing days, he and Max Montoya (1979-1989) anchored the Bengals offensive line. They have since been joined by many other giants of the gridiron, including: Chicago Bears guard Roberto Garza (2005-present), Pittsburgh Steelers guard Willie Colon (2006-present), Detroit Lions guard Manny Ramirez (2007-present), and two member of members of the San Diego Chargers: defensive end Luis Castillo (2005-2012) and guard Louis Vasquez (2009-present). The 2011 NFL season playoffs and Super Bowl included two gifted rookies: New England Patriots tight end Aaron Hernandez and New York Giants wide receiver Victor Cruz. Both returned for the 2012 season and still celebrate their touchdowns with *salsa* dance moves.

With the advent of soccer-style field goal kickers Latinos have been a part of the NFL game for years, among the most notable "sidewinders" were Mexican Raúl Alegre (1983-1991), Argentinian Martín Gramática (1999-2008), Mexican Efren Herrera (1974-1982), and US-born Danny Villanueva (1960-1967).

Soccer, or *futból*, is now the second most popular sport in the US among the key age group of 12-24. (The NFL tops the list and baseball has slipped to fourth behind basketball.) Much of the games attractiveness is its star-studded teams and players from Spain and Latin America, which includes: captain of the Argentina national team *Lionel Andrés Messi* who plays professionally for Spain's *FC Barcelona*; Mexican national team member *Javier Hernández*, popularly known as *Chicharito* (little pea), who plays professionally for England's Manchester United; and captain of Portugal's national team *Cristiano Ronaldo dos Santos Aveiro*, aka: *Cristiano Ronaldo*, who plays professionally for Spain's *Real Madrid*.

Even the National Basketball Association (NBA) has developed a Latino flavor with players like: *José Juan* "J.J." *Barea Mora* (Puerto Rico), who helped the Dallas Mavericks win the 2011-12 championship, and is now a teammate of *Ricky Rubio* (Spain) with the Minnesota Timberwolves; Charlotte Bobcat *Eduardo Nájera* (Mexico); Chicago Bull *Andres Nocioni* (Argentina); New York Knick *Carmelo Anthony* (USA); Los Angeles Laker *Pau Gasol* (Spain); Milwaukee Buck Charlie Villanueva (USA); San Antonio Spur *Manu Ginobili* (Argentina); and Toronto Raptor *Carlos Delfino* (Argentina).

The NBA launched *Noche Latina* (Latino Night) events designed to recognize its Latino fans and players from across the US and Latin America. *Noche Latina* took place in four of the top ten Hispanic markets during the 2007-08 season and was expanded in 2009 to include Los Angeles, Miami, Phoenix, San Antonio, Dallas, Chicago, Houston, and New York. The NBA has one of the largest and fastest-growing Latino fan bases in US professional sports, and it plans to continue building fan interest in the game through community outreach and events.

Since the latter half of the twentieth century, Latinos have also emerged as stars in several non-traditional sports—from golf's *Chi Chi Rodríguez* (Puerto Rico), Lee Treviño (USA), Nancy Lopéz (USA) and *Lorena Ochoa* (Mexico), to racecar drivers *Milka Duno* (Venezuela), *Jorge Goeters* (Mexico), *Juán Pablo Montoya* (Colombia), and top fuel dragster driver Erica Ortiz (USA).

STICKS AND STONES

Why are positive role models important to the young and growing Latino populace? Simply, negative labeling has a lasting detrimental impact on people who experience it. Studies have found individuals perform poorly in situations where they feel they are being stereotyped and the results of stereotyping and its related discrimination have lingering adverse impacts (Nauert, *Long-term Effect*).

In this study, researchers had a group of women participate in a math test. They were told the test would determine whether or not they were capable and smart in math, subtly injecting stereotypes about women and math skills. A second group took the same test, except it received support and coping strategies to deal with the stress they would encounter.

Following the test, the two groups performed a series of tasks designed to gauge their aggression levels, their ability to focus, and their exercise of self-control. Regardless of the groups, those who felt they were discriminated against—based on gender, age, race or religion—all experienced significant lingering effects, leaving them at a disadvantage. Even after generations removed from prejudicial situations, people can still carry the "psychological baggage" that negatively affect them and their families.

The abovementioned research underscores the detrimental effects of past negative labeling and why positive role models are critical to success, especially for our nation's fastest growing segment of school-aged children. For those who have received support and coping strategies all of their lives, such influences may be taken for granted; but for young Latinos, they can definitely provide the psychological boost needed to nurture their self-esteem.

US American novelist, essayist, playwright, poet, and social critic James Baldwin may have captured the importance of psychological development and positive role models when he wrote:

"It is a great shock at the age of five or six to find that in a world of Gary Coopers you are the Indian."

It should be easy to appreciate why today's Latinos are less interested in giving up their culture to assimilate into a society where they, their language, and their contributions are still not fully recognized or valued. The number of stars that are beginning to shine may still appear faint to many, but collectively they are becoming beacons for generations of Latinos looking for a brighter future.

Accentuating the Positive

Las palabras amables enfrían mejor que agua.
Translation: Kind words refresh better than water.
Transcreation: Kindness can be heard by the deaf and seen by the blind.

Much like the US History taught in schools, most of the media messages Latinos see, hear, and read are the stories of a people from a different America. When Latino issues and events have been included they are generally relegated to footnotes or separate sections of textbooks, rather than part of the mainstream narrative of where and how they live.

This reality has essentially marginalized many Latinos, denying them a place in the identity of our nation's social mainstream, despite the many indelible marks they and their ancestors have made as the USA has expanded its borders and territorial holdings. The absence of positive representation in English-language media—along with being the fastest growing segment of the US population—created the perfect conditions for the introduction of alternative choices for Latinos to general market media.

By the end of the twentieth century, Spanish-language media had taken hold in the US and was rivaling many of its English language competitors in major urban markets, even among US-born, English-dominant Latinos hungry for positive reflections and images of themselves in news and entertainment programs. Turning to media in which they were depicted in a positive light was a desirable alternative to available media options for many Latinos, regardless of their citizenship, acculturation levels, or immigration status.

South Africa's president Nelson Mandela, an expert on the effects of racial and ethnic segregation, may have been referring to the need for such an emotional and psychological reinforcement when he said, "If you talk to a man in a language he understands, that goes to his head. If you talk to him in his language, that goes to his heart" (Mandela, *Mandela in His Own Words*).

LEADER OF THE PACK

In May 2008, Univision Communications announced its flagship television station, KMEX-34 in Los Angeles, had become the highest rated local television station in the entire country—in any language. According to the Nielsen Station Index (NSI), KMEX-34 had captured the largest number of "Adults 18-49" viewers during that month. In recent years KMEX has attracted more of this prized consumer demographic than most other English and Spanish language stations in the USA.

According to industry pundits, the reasons for the milestone were: *telenovelas* (soap operas) reaching key points in their stories, and a week of random reality shows and re-runs broadcast by the English-language broadcast networks. Univision claimed Latino viewers connect with its type of programming because of its cultural relevance. "Viewers at the end of the day want to watch high-quality programming that they connect with, regardless of language," said Univision Network president Cesar Conde (Dunham, *History is Made*).

In September of 2010 Univision reached another milestone by becoming the nation's most watched network among television viewers aged 18 to 49, the first time a Spanish-language television network had outperformed traditional general market networks in this key demographic category. In television, the 18

to 49 year-old demographic is considered so important to advertisers that ABC, NBC, and Fox pay more attention to these
demographic ratings than they do to viewership as a whole.

Compared to the English-language broadcasters, Univision's
audience is markedly younger. During September 2010, 2.1 million of Univision's prime-time average of 3.8 million viewers
were members of this critical demographic. By contrast, only 1.8
million of CBS' 5.7 million viewers were in that category. This
may also be a function of white, middle-aged and elderly US
Americans' migrating towards "conservative leaning" cable and
radio outlets.

In recent years, the Univision network and its local affiliates'
newscasts have been among the highest-rated in an increasing number of the nation's largest metropolitan areas: Chicago,
Dallas, Houston, Miami, New York, Rio Grande Valley, and the
San Jose/San Francisco Bay Area. As a national broadcast network, Univision ended its 2005-2006 season as the fourth largest in "prime-time" (generally 8:00-11:00 p.m. in Eastern and
Pacific time zones and 7:00-10:00 p.m. in Central and Mountain
time zones) among "Adults 18 to 34," beating-out NBC, UPN,
and WB. By 2007, it consistently ranked among the top-rated
networks, outperforming ABC, CBS, NBC, and Fox.

From September 22, 2008, to June 21, 2009, Univision dominated Friday night for the 33rd time, outperforming ABC, CBS,
NBC, FOX, and CW among Adults 18-34, according to Nielsen.
The Nielsen Station Index (NSI) reported KMEX Univision 34
in Los Angeles and WXTV Univision 41 in New York led all
other stations during the first quarter of 2009 by securing the
#1 and #2 early evening newscasts among "Adults 18 to 49" and
not just among Latinos. This occurred in the two largest media
markets in the entire country.

Its airing of the 12th annual *Latin Grammy Awards* show
also made Univision the top rated network on Thursday night,
November 10, 2011, among "Adults 18 to 34." An estimated

11.1 million viewers tuned-in to all, or part, of the three-hour live broadcast. The awards program attracted more viewers in the three top demographic groups—Total Viewers 2+, Adults 18-49, and Adults 18-34—than the combined audiences of the most recent English-language broadcasts of the *Academy Awards, Golden Globe Awards* and *Primetime Emmy Awards*.

Univision rival, *Telemundo* has also been thriving and became the fastest-growing, Spanish language, broadcast network in prime time among total viewers—"Persons 2+" and "Adults 18-49"—from October 2010 to October 2011. Compared to October 2010, *Telemundo's* Monday through Sunday prime time delivery grew among total viewers ("Persons 2+") from 823,000 to 1,132, 000 (+38 percent) and among "Adults 18-49" from 447,000 to 583,000 (+30 percent). It appears we are in the midst of a "tipping point" relative to television viewing in the US.

IF A TREE FALLS IN THE FOREST...

Spanish-language radio is also experiencing unprecedented growth in the US. Its formats are outpacing its competitors in terms of audience share. By 2007, Spanish-language radio ranked second among all radio formats and was gaining fast on the nation's English language leader: Country.

Nationally syndicated and Los Angeles-based, Spanish-language deejays *Eduardo Sotelo* (*Piolín*, Spanish for Tweety Bird) and *Renán Almendárez Coello* (*El Cucuy*, The Boogeyman) were being heard by millions of listeners daily. At the start of the new millennium, *El Cucuy* routinely attracted more listeners in Los Angeles than English-speaking personalities Rick Dees and Howard Stern. *Piolín por la Mañana* became the most listened to radio show host in the entire US, in both English and Spanish language, with 4.3 million listeners per day at the start of 2011.

The two major US radio networks, Univision Radio Network and Spanish Broadcasting System (SBS) continue to build listeners with a variety of musical formats. Univision's network includes seventy owned/operated (O&O) stations in seventeen markets, including all ten top markets and reach 16 million listeners a week. SBS owns and/or operates stations in seven of the top 10 US Hispanic media markets. It comes as no surprise Spanish-language media performed best in the larger Hispanic-populated metropolitan areas, but successes are also being reported in many smaller markets.

There are people in the forest anxious to hear the sound of "falling trees." Corporate America is also hearing the trees fall. Their national and local advertising buys have made Spanish-language media a growth industry. Apparently, Latino-oriented radio programming was making welcomed sounds in what had been thought of as a remote, unpopulated forest.

BEYOND THE HEADLINES

The US Hispanic population has expressed a thirst for culturally relevant information and the growth of Spanish-language print publications was another indication of that appetite. According to the National Association of Hispanic Publications (NAHP), by 2007, its members' publications were reaching over forty-one markets in thirty-nine states, the District of Columbia and Puerto Rico for a combined circulation of over 14 million. Along with expanding news coverage of local, national, and international issues important to readers in the US and Latin America, Spanish-language and bilingual print media was also providing more coverage of events and activities in their local communities.

Among these print publication companies is impreMedia, the country's leading Hispanic news and information company with seven different platforms: web, mobile, video, audio, social media, newspapers and magazines. The impreMedia network publishes Spanish-language newspapers in the following markets:

- New York (Founded in 1913, *El Diario La Prensa,* is the USA's oldest and largest daily in New York)
- San Francisco/San Jose (*El Mensajero* is the Bay Area's top-rated publication)
- Los Angeles (Founded in 1926, *La Opinión* is the nation's largest circulated daily)
- Chicago (*La Raza* is Chicago's leading publication)
- Orlando (*La Prensa* is Central Florida's leading newspaper)
- Houston, San Antonio & Rio Grande Valley (*RUMBO,* serves these fifth, ninth and tenth largest markets, respectively)

A partnership with the McClatchey Company added three more publications in Florida, while California's Central Valley and the Dallas/Fort Worth Metroplex provides an additional nine print publications and eleven online properties. With mobile media, they have a combined monthly reach of 7.7 million adults. Their markets are home to nearly 29 million readers, which represent 59 percent of the Hispanic population and $580.9 billion in consumer buying power.

Despite the continuing sophistication, reach, and frequency of Spanish-language and bilingual print publications, most media planners and buyers still rely on traditional media buying criteria used for English-language newspapers and magazines. First they consider paid subscription and audited circulation, secondly their demographic or targeted readership. This has been a time-tested methodology for established English-language publications, which are now experiencing declines in readership as they compete with radio, television, Internet-based news, social media outlets, and Hispanic media.

This traditional number-crunching formula fails to recognize the overwhelming majority of Hispanic publications are variations on the "small-business" model where entrepreneurs provide information and news they deem important to their readers and local areas. In this model, many of the publications are generally distributed free of charge (to promote higher circulation and reach) and the costs of production generally covered by retail advertising and paid legal notice revenues.

SOME NEWS IS GOOD NEWS

In a highly competitive and information-rich environment, an increasing number of corporations, nonprofits, and public sector organizations are recognizing the importance of media exposure as part of their overall marketing efforts, not to mention its value in building credibility and trust among targeted segments of an increasingly diverse marketplace. Therefore, "earned media" has become a new avenue to consider. It is cost-free publicity gained mainly by editorial influence and refers specifically to publicity gained in newspaper, television, radio, and Internet. It can take a variety of forms: news releases, letters to the editor, Op-Eds, editorials, and even features and articles.

Traditionally a common response by publishers of community newspapers to timely and important news releases and/ or promotional information from companies or organizations that do not advertise in their publications has been to toss such information into the "circular file." Those communicators who understand the "small business" mindsets of these entrepreneurs have periodically placed "image" or "institutional" (non-sales or promotional) ads in such publications to create a more receptive attitude towards an advertiser's "earned media" messages.

With a paid image or institutional ad an advertiser still gains public recognition and brand awareness with that publication's readers; not to mention the appreciation from a small business owner who will be more receptive to publishing news release and other information from that "supporter." The overwhelming majority of the consumer public does not differentiate among the many goals and objectives of internal departments; however, they do recall if the messages they see are "relevant" to them. The cost of an image building ad is a small price to pay to establish positive relationships with those who influence your targeted consumers, businesses, students, taxpayers, voters, and workers.

MEDIA AS THE MESSAGE

In his books, *Understanding Media, The Extensions of Man* and *The Medium is the Message*, Marshall McLuhan introduced the notion that the form of a message (be it print, visual, musical, etc.) has a great deal to do with how such information is perceived and processed. His premise was based on the fact that modern electronic communications (radio, television, film, computers and the Internet) would have far-reaching sociological, aesthetic, and philosophical consequences that would alter the ways media consumers experience their environments.

McLuhan advised readers to look beyond the obvious and seek the non-obvious changes or effects that are enabled, enhanced, accelerated or extended by changes in media. He was of the opinion the message communicated by any medium is not determined by its actual content, but in the resulting changes in social behaviors and values the medium brings about. He wrote: "Control over change would seem to consist in moving not with it, but ahead of it. Anticipation gives the power to deflect and control force."

Inasmuch as considerable population growth and attendant social advances by Latinos were of little interest to general market media, it hastened the desire by Latinos to modify their media consumer behaviors, affecting the media balance across the United States. A reluctance on the part of general market media to ignore a growing segment of the population prompted Latinos to look for alternatives to those traditional general market outlets. Based on limited and negative coverage of their presence and growing influence, many turned to emerging Spanish-language media outlets for that coverage. The ability to provide socially and culturally relevant news coverage and entertainment programming not only addressed a major void, but also created a new paradigm in US media. Spanish-language media was a controlling factor in the demographic change; not by moving with it, but ahead of it.

Spanish-language media captured the attention of both Spanish- and English-dominant Latinos and a growing number of marketers, advertisers, and communicators wishing to reach the country's largest ethnic consumer market. National, regional, and local advertisers continue to increase their efforts to communicate to, and attract, members of the US Hispanic Consumer Market (HCM) and increasingly rely on national and local Spanish-language media.

The following list of advertisers includes some of the most recognized brands and services in the country, and perhaps contains a surprise or two. Ad Age's 2008 Hispanic Fact Pack provides a representative snapshot of media expenditures in 2007 and percentage of increase from the previous year (2006):

Name:	Media Expenditure:	Change:
1. Lexicon Marketing Corp.	$218,108.2	24.4
2. Procter & Gamble Co.	163,078.1	-4.3
3. AT&T	119,320.6	-10.0
4. General Motors Corp.	100,848.6	-2.7
5. BMP (Univision)	91,273.3	-14.8

6. McDonald's Corp.	89,676.7	6.6
7. Toyota Motor Corp.	80,687.6	16.9
8. Sears Holdings Corp.	79,568.9	-4.5
9. Verizon Communications	79,277.8	-12.8
10. Johnson & Johnson	76,791.4	-3.6
11. Ford Motor Co.	73,406.0	-0.3
12. The Walt Disney Co.	67,025.2	3.8
13. Cerberus (Chrysler)	66,109.7	1.9
14. Nissan Motor Co.	61,314.9	82.7
15. Wal-Mart Stores	59,890.3	-10.3
16. TVAtlas.com	55,071.6	14.8
17. Hyundai Corp.	53,945.2	-12.8
18. America Directo	52,466.3	14.2
19. Sprint Nextel Corp.	51,752.2	98.3
20. Deutsche Telekom	50,085.0	15.4

ASSIMILATION OR ISOLATION?

Of these aforementioned "national" advertisers on US Spanish-language television networks, the number one spender in 2006 and 2007 was Lexicon Marketing Group, a Los Angeles, CA-based business that caters to Spanish-speaking consumers. Its product? *Inglés sin Barreras* (English without Barriers), the world's top selling, English learning, video program.

In spite of this readily available information, general market media has provided "soapbox" for those alleging Latinos have an aversion to learning English and otherwise refusing to acculturate into US mainstream society, like the many immigrant groups who have done so in the past. In an October 8, 2007, segment of "Good Morning, America," co-anchor Diane Sawyer interviewed conservative media commentator Rush Limbaugh. The anti-immigration advocate claimed Latinos in the US did not want to learn English.

> "Yes, they work hard to put roofs above their heads and food on their tables and for this we respect them. But they have little interest in learning English themselves, and instead demand that we make it possible for them to function here in Spanish" (*Hola or Hello?* Good Morning, America).

His comments went unchallenged by Sawyer, a celebrated TV journalist, leading viewers to accept her report and Limbaugh's allegations as fact. When journalists do not challenge unfounded sweeping assertions by public figures, it allows audiences to assume such reports are true. After all the interview had been conducted by a professional journalist and broadcast over one of the nation's most popular television network's morning news programs.

It has become obvious to dedicated journalists and informed media consumers alike, US media operations must be better informed of the changing demographics of our nation. As Latinos carve out a larger "share of market" as media consumers, English-language media must also implement its own corporate social responsibility practices. As in the case of the private and public sectors, media must also diversify its employee and management staffs if it is to become culturally relevant and competent in providing accurate, objective, and balanced coverage of the nation's racial and ethnic communities. That is, if they wish to broaden their appeal and attract the growing number of eyes and ears that their advertisers expect.

INGLÉS OR SPANISH?

"English only!" is a mantra being chanted by American jingoists and nativists opposed to the encroachment of the Spanish speakers. Many in these camps, like Limbaugh, incorrectly refer to Latinos as "rejecters of English" and "resisters of assimilation." If proponents of "English-only" and anti-Latino immigration are to be believed, Spanish-speaking, US-born citizens and recent Latino immigrants resist learning English, unlike white Europeans and other non-English speaking immigrant groups who voluntarily chose to dive headlong into the homogenizing "melting pot."

Latinos are exercising their options related to assimilation and their choices seem to counter those who accuse them of being "rejecters of English." A 2007 survey conducted by the New Generation Latino Consortium and New American Dimensions found contemporary young Latinos embraced US culture and its idioms at higher rates than members of previous generations who had faced a variety of overt social, economic, and political barriers to assimilation. The poll was based on a national survey of 766 respondents between the ages of 14 and 34 (of which 80 percent were US-born) and was fielded with a 25 "online" questionnaire, which found:

- There was a clear preference for English in print and electronic media. All the top magazine and newspaper titles identified by respondents were in English. For electronic media, 70 percent preferred the Internet in English and nearly 80 percent preferred video game content in English.

- In terms of TV media consumption, English-language TV and cable readily beat out Spanish-language TV more than two to one as most often watched. About 40 percent watched broadcast networks and 34 percent watched cable networks most often, while only 15 percent said they watched Spanish-language TV most often.

- Young Latinos are either fully bilingual or prefer English. Some 37 percent indicated they mostly spoke English overall, while 55 percent say they spoke both English and Spanish equally. Only seven percent identified Spanish as the language they speak most.

- The most popular English-language programs cited by young Latinos included: "The Simpsons," "That 70's Show," "Grey's Anatomy," "CSI," "Family Guy," "Lost," and "Friends." (The "George Lopez Show" was the top Latino TV program.)

- Among networks focusing on Latino youth, "*Mun2*" was the most popular, followed by "*MTV en Español*" and "*Sí TV.*" "*Mun2*" led Latino-focused networks as the most watched at 29 percent, trailed by "*MTV en Español*" and "*Sí TV.*"

- US celebrities and movies occupied the top positions in the minds of young Latinos. The top three actors were Johnny Depp, Denzel Washington and Al Pacino; the top movies were "Pirates of the Caribbean 2," "Superman Returns," and "X-Men 3" (Chitel, *Young Latinos*).

Rather than resisting US culture and its language, the majority of second- and third-generation Latinos appeared to be embracing both. Farmworker, labor leader, and civil rights activist César Chavéz, said, "The preservation of one's own culture does not require contempt or disrespect for other cultures" (Chavez, *Education of the Heart-Culture Quotes*). Young Latinos continue to exhibit unique cultural values, experiences, attitudes, and behaviors; challenging the popular myth that most of their media consumption habits are based on a preference for "Spanish-language" content.

It is true that US-born Latinos are becoming increasingly comfortable in receiving information in Spanish. The main reason for that lies in their intrinsic bilingual abilities; the second, and equally important, factor is that Spanish-language media is more relevant to them when it comes to cultural, economic, political, and social matters. It also speaks to their hearts and values in much the same way English-language media has historically spoken to white Eurocentric Americans.

Latinos do not reject the English language as much as they choose to function in both languages. Why? Because, they can.

IT'S BEEN A LONG TIME COMING

Commercially, the Hispanic Consumer Market (HCM) is now openly coveted by businesses wishing to increase sales and build brand loyalty, but socially Latinos may still have a ways to go to rectify the effects of their "class apart" existence of the past. For generations they existed with economic, political, and social boundaries defined for them by a white majority. By the end of the twentieth century, US citizens of Hispanic, Latino, and *mestizo* descent were beginning to exercise economic, political, and social influence outside of their traditional geographic haunts— Mexican Americans in the Southwest, Cuban Americans in the Southeast, and Puerto Ricans in the Northeast—in their quest for better employment, education, and housing opportunities. At long last, the "Sleeping Giant" appears to be stirring from its slumber.

Still, US-born and naturalized Latinos, along with undocumented immigrants, are routinely lumped into a single monolithic group and seen by many of their fellow citizens as threats to the US American way of life. Prejudices and stereotypes promoted by overt nativists and hate mongers have fanned the flames of suspicion about Latinos. Anti-Latino attitudes and actions by a small, vocal segment are adding to negative reactions of epidemic proportions on the part of a shrinking white Eurocentric population.

There is a bit of irony in the popular phrase used by those who urge their fellow US Americans to "Take back our country!" The obvious question is "From who?" The paradoxical nature of the provocation is not lost on the indigenous people of the Western Hemisphere and the initial wave of European Spaniards, who together with indigenous people, began populating the continent with *mestizo* offspring long before English colonists arrived in the New World.

There is a substantial information gap in the US when it comes to Latinos and their history. The availability—and sharing—of bias-free, non-subjective information about them and their contributions to our nation will lead to a better understanding of their growing influence.

To effectively interact with Latinos, general market media, its audiences and the general public must become better informed of their history and contributions to this nation. Spanish-language media has recognized the void in news about this rapidly growing segment of the population and is filling that need—from which other media can learn and profit. In a world of increasingly diverse information sources and content, bilingual and Spanish-language media are demonstrating cultural relevance works and that their messages are proving to be those even the deaf can hear and the blind can see.

To Be or Not
to Be?

No te comprometas, eres todo lo que tienes.
Translation: Don't compromise yourself; you are all that
you have.
Transcreation: Open your arms to change, but don't let go
of your values.

In his seminal book regarding the origin and struggle for life
among the planet's species, written in 1859, Charles Darwin
introduced the theory that populations evolve over the course
of generations through a process of natural selection. He shared
several key observations, among them:

> "Individuals less suited to the environment are less likely to
> survive and less likely to reproduce; individuals more suited
> to the environment are more likely to survive and more
> likely to reproduce" (Darwin, *On the Origin of the Species*).

His theories were (and remain) controversial because they contra-
dicted traditional religious beliefs upon which popular thoughts
on evolution were based. Even though the topic of evolution
remains contentious, "natural selection" remains the most widely
accepted scientific model of how species on our planet evolved.
Darwin explained,

> "Individuals who survive are most likely to leave their inher-
> itable traits to their offspring. This slow process results in
> a new population that gradually adapts to the environment

and ultimately creates new variations—and eventually a new, stronger, more adaptable species emerges."

To a number of sociologists, demographers and marketing researchers, such theories of evolution apply not only to biology, but can also be applied to culture. Hispanics, Latinos, and *mestizos* throughout the Americas may be proving that point. They have withstood efforts to dominate and absorb them by two of the major world powers of their times. They adapted to external, social, language and religious practices and evolved from an indigenous society into one that today retains customs and values from both their Spanish conquerors and native environs.

Since the mid-nineteenth century to the new millennium, Latinos have been dealing with a common challenge in their cultural evolution: adaptation to foreign societies. Their current challenge is from the most formidable, yet inveigling world power: the United States of America. Through colonialism, Spain forced its influence on the indigenous people of the Western Hemisphere and subsequent *mestizo* offspring for over five centuries. The adaptation process in the US also began under "forceful" invasions but over the years has become mostly a voluntary—albeit unrequited—effort on the part of most Mexicans, Puerto Ricans, Cubans and other Latin American immigrants. These unreciprocated efforts on the part of a white Eurocentric society have puzzled generations of Latinos who believed the United States of America to be the land of equality and justice for all.

INTO THE CRUCIBLE

It's easy to see why the confusion exists. The Latin motto *E pluribus unum* (from many, one) was taken from the Roman poem *Moretum*, attributed to Virgil and considered by historians to be the source of the motto used for the Great Seal of the United States of America.

In the poem Virgil describes an early morning in the life of a poor old farmer (*Simylus*) and his servant, an African woman (*Scybale*) who rise before dawn to make bread and prepare a *moretum* (herb cheese) that consisted of garlic, parsley, coriander, *rue* (an intensely bitter herb whose use in cooking has declined considerably, but widely used in Europe's Mediterranean region and especially during the days of the Roman Empire), salt, and cheese, which were mashed together and formed into a ball and drizzled with oil and vinegar. Virgil describes the mashing of the ingredients and their blending into one: "*It manus in gyrum: paulatim singula vires deperdunt proprias; color est e pluribus unus.*" (His hand moves in circles until the separate ingredients lose their individual colors, and out of many colors, comes one.) (Dryden, *The Works of Vergil*).

In addition to its use on the Great Seal of the United States of America, *E pluribus unum* has also been used to refer to the original thirteen colonies that became "one" nation. The motto was recommended in 1776 by a Congressional committee appointed to design the national seal. Interestingly, one of the early concepts was the sketch of a shield that would be part of an emblem. It had six symbols representing the countries from which the "united states" were initially populated: the rose (England), thistle (Scotland), harp (Ireland), fleur-de-lis (France), lion (Holland), and an imperial two-headed eagle (Germany). The shield concept was not adopted, but it provided a clue as to the committee's perspective of which immigrants were establishing a racially singular society (MacArthur, *E Pluribus Unum*).

The reference to a crucible that would homogenize all immigrants coming to the new country first appeared in Israel Zangwill's 1908 play entitled "The Melting Pot," in which the protagonist declared:

> "Understand that America is God's Crucible, the great Melting-Pot where all the races of Europe are melting and reforming! A fig for your feuds and vendettas! Germans and Frenchmen, Irishmen and Englishmen, Jews and

Russians—into the Crucible with you all! God is making the American" (Gerstle, *American Crucible*).

In keeping with the principles of the Doctrine of Discovery and Manifest Destiny, admission into the "crucible" was limited to the white races of Europe. The play was basically an updated version of William Shakespeare's *Romeo and Juliet*, but these lovers were of Russian Jewish and Russian Christian heritage. Among the play's ironies were that America was a new country with no room for old hatreds, and keeping biases and prejudices was pointless, evil, and probably impossible. Implicit in the crucible theory was God's will to coalesce "Americans" into a single, unadulterated, national race of white European immigrants seeking to be part of this new society; they had only to surrender their nationalities, ethnic cultures, and external trappings to become assimilated with those already in the pot.

As easy as it sounded, the concept was not applicable, nor acceptable, to all white European immigrants. Many did not identify, nor wish to be tagged, with the all-encompassing label associated with "English" or "Anglo" Americans for a variety of reasons. Among them are cultural, political, and religious differences. Some non-English Europeans—the Dutch, German, Greek, Irish, Italian, Polish, Middle Eastern, Scottish, and Scandinavian immigrants—found the term "Anglo" to be inappropriate when used to identify them.

The melting pot remained a popular metaphor used to describe the assimilation of white Europeans into a national white society. But, once immigration patterns shifted away from Europe and towards Asia, Africa, and Latin America, the melting pot concept was no longer an accessible option for non-Europeans wishing to assimilate into the "American" mainstream.

SUSTAINING A NATIONAL IDENTITY

Not having much of a choice in selecting the values and culture of a new society, white European immigrants opted to identify with

Anglo Americans. It was a logical and easy alternative, given their common external and physical appearances. By merely remaining silent many avoided telltale foreign accents and easily passed the "color" test routinely applied to more obvious "non-whites," who were socially and legally barred from the benefits and prerequisites afforded whites in the US.

In the latter half of the twentieth century, during the height of the US civil rights movement, our nation and its institutions began to address the challenges of equality for all citizens—regardless of race, color, and creed. The idea of a melting pot was unacceptable to non-European whites and was substituted with a more inclusionary alternative: the "salad bowl." Unlike Virgil's *Moretum*, where the distinctive ingredients were "blended" into a singular homogeneous broth; the salad bowl allowed for non-white immigrant groups to keep their distinctive colors and tastes (i.e., their ethnic customs and cultures) while coexisting with others in a diverse and "multicultural" society.

Call it what you will, melting pot or salad bowl, the two concepts had their proponents and opponents. The white majority supported the "from many, one" approach to maintain a uniform national and racial identity; while non-whites, who faced social, legal and political barriers to assimilation opted for retention of their "distinctive" racial and ethnic cultural values and languages.

FROM MINORITY TO MAJORITY

In May of 2012, *The New York Times* reported non-Hispanic white (NHW) births were no longer the majority. According to the story, Census Bureau data found NHWs accounted for only 49.6 percent of all births in the twelve month period ending July 2011, while non-European whites—Latinos, Blacks, Asians and mixed race individuals—reached 50.4 percent, a majority of US births for the first time in US history. (Indigenous people will argue this is actually the second time, inasmuch as their ancestors were the majority of the population in North America prior to—and for several years following—the USA's Declaration of Independence in 1776.) *The Times'* article concluded:

> "Such a turn has been long expected, but no one was certain when the moment would arrive, signaling a milestone for a nation whose government was founded by white Europeans and has wrestled mightily with issues of race, from the days of slavery, through a civil war, bitter civil rights battles and, most recently, highly charged debates over efforts to restrict immigration."

At the beginning of the new millennium, the US was already moving in the direction of "ethnic pluralities" in its two most populated states: California and Texas. Latinos were already the overwhelming majority of the population in a growing number of cities across the country, among them: East Los Angeles, CA (97 percent), Laredo, TX (94 percent), Brownsville, TX (91 percent), Hialeah, FL (90 percent), McAllen, TX (80 percent), El Paso, TX (77 percent), Santa Ana, CA (76 percent), and Oxnard, CA and Miami, FL (66 percent each).

In 2000 California's non-white population constituted a majority in nearly half of the ninety cities with populations of 50,000 or more. With 4.7 million, Los Angeles had the largest Hispanic population among US counties and was expected to exceed 50 percent by 2008. California officials reported non-whites accounted for more than half of the population growth since 1998 and constituted 55.5 percent of its growth in 2005. Latinos, the fastest growing segment, accounted for 46 percent of the total non-white growth.

The state of Texas projected that between 2000 and 2040, the non-Hispanic white (NHW) population would increase by four to 12 percent, while the African American population would increase by 40 to 70 percent, and Hispanics would grow by an incredible 180 to 350 percent. By 2040, the percentages of the Texas population for the following groups were estimated to become: 8 to 10 percent African American, 25 to 32 percent non-Hispanic white, and 50 to 60 percent Hispanic.

By 2002, Hispanics officially accounted for 36 percent of the total population in the nation's five largest counties, or 9.1 million of the 25.4 million people who lived in the counties of Los Angeles (CA), Cook (IL), Harris (TX), Maricopa (AZ), and Orange (CA).

Between July 1, 2005 and July 1, 2006, Hispanics accounted for nearly half (1.4 million) of the nation's population growth of 2.9 million. By May 2008, they had reached 45.5 million, becoming the largest ethnic group in the country, with single race and multiracial blacks trailing behind at 40.7 million. Hispanics exceeded 500,000 in sixteen states and became the largest ethnic population in twenty others. By 2009, non-whites under 15 years of age had become almost half of the population in the US.

By 2010, Hispanics had become the largest ethnic population in the states of Arizona, California, Colorado, Connecticut, Florida, Idaho, Iowa, Kansas, Massachusetts, Nebraska, Nevada, New Hampshire, New Jersey, New Mexico, Oregon, Rhode Island, Texas, Utah, Vermont, Washington, and Wyoming. The US population had topped 300 million; but within that total number, not so subtle changes were taking place. California had a non-white population of 20.7 million, or 21 percent of the nation's total. Texas had 12.2 million and 12 percent of the US total. The US was undergoing profound and accelerated changes, spurred by increased rates among non-whites, particularly among Latinos.

In spite of unprecedented population growth, the path to assimilation and acculturation for Latinos in parts of the US was still a challenge due to a history of physical, legal, and social barriers. For more than five hundred years, *mestizos* in the Americas have demonstrated that evolution is not a force, but a process. Due to their geographic concentration and rapid rate of growth in the US, they are creating alternative paths to traditional patterns of assimilation and acculturation not available to previous indigenous and immigrants groups seeking access into a white Eurocentric society.

"To be, or not to be acculturated and assimilated, and to what extent?" is the question facing many of today's Hispanics, Latinos, and *mestizos*. Collectively, they have reached a level of critical mass that no longer relies on mainstream society defining who they are, or should be; they are now defining themselves and increasingly assuming the roles they choose to play as US citizens, taxpayers, students, voters, and workers. They continue to keep their minds open to acculturation and assimilation, but are realizing they don't have to abandon their cultural values in the process of becoming bona fide citizens of a country that for many of them is part of their ancestral homelands.

Redefining the Work Ethic

El trabajo duro purifica el espíritu.
Translation: Hard work purifies the spirit.
Transcreation: Never stand begging for what you have the
power to earn.

Due to a national economic recession and attendant unemployment rates reaching into the double-digit range, an alarming and flourishing urban practice has blossomed: the least educated, least employed and least vested segments of society are "dropping-out" of the workforce, home ownership, and mainstream society. Their numbers are increasingly evident as many plied a new trade: public begging.

The practice of panhandling has become a common sight on many streets, parking lots and other high-trafficked thoroughfares across our country. Obvious by their absence among the growing number of street beggars are Latinos. If and when you see them on street corners, roadsides, and highway medians they aren't asking for handouts; on the contrary, they're trying to sell you their labor, fresh vegetables, fruit or flowers, lawn care services, or whatever else will earn them money.

Throughout our nation's history the work ethic has been a personal asset most Americans have come to recognize and admire; most believe hard work, combined with perseverance, has helped to make our country the world's economic power it is today. It is a personal characteristic that has been rewarded in almost every aspect of our society: in the classroom, on the sports field, in the home and in the workplace. It has been a major factor in an individual's ability to prosper and succeed —one that is obviously understood and exemplified by Latino workers.

Since the latter part of the last millennium, US businesses had begun outsourcing a substantial number of jobs to offshore vendors—downsizing workforces while reporting record profits. US heads of households were spending more hours at work than ever before and special interest business groups appeared to be unduly influencing the nation's legislative processes. Supposedly rooted in consumerism and shareholder stock value, financial transactions accounted for two-thirds of all economic activity across our nation.

Meanwhile residents were being bombarded daily by myriad advertisements urging consumers to buy, buy, buy. As a society, US residents have been conditioned to associate success with the acquisition of material possessions, rather than the practical and essential necessities considered important to past generations. Consumers are encouraged to seek immediate gratification and amass as much material wealth as possible.

Conservative estimates indicate the average US resident uses thirty times the goods as the average third-world resident. Advertising campaigns and their emphasis on the "good life" have led US consumers to believe the attainment of wealth (marketable assets, such as real estate, stocks, and bonds) is the ultimate goal in life.

Yet, despite our nation's global leadership in consumerism, Sociology Professor G. William Domhoff of the University of California-Santa Cruz found not all of our citizens are sharing in the prosperity. He found the top one percent of US households owned 34.6 percent of the nation's wealth; the next 19 percent, the middle class, held 50.5 percent. That meant 20 percent of the US population owned 85 percent of the nation's wealth, leaving only 15 percent to 80 percent of the population: the working class, the underemployed, and the unemployed (Domhoff, *Who Rules America?*).

REJUVENATING THE WORK ETHIC

At nearly 23 million, Hispanics represented 15 percent of the U.S. labor force in 2011. By 2020, they are expected to comprise closer to 20 percent. Findings by the "State of Hispanic America" series of studies on employment by the National Council of La Raza (NCLR) in Washington, DC underscored the growing importance of Latinos to the nation's workforce and economy. Its study, *Moving Up the Economic Ladder: Latino Workers and the Nation's Future Prosperity*, offered a comprehensive view of Latino workers and linked their actual and potential income strength to the country's future economic health as the nation began the twenty-first century. It is not only their increasing population numbers that will affect our economy but their propensity to enter the workforce at an early age (Cattan, *Moving Up*).

From 2000 to 2010, Latinos in the US had the highest work force participation rate of any group 16 years of age and older. Based on 68.6 percent in 2000 to 69.0 percent in 2010, they were expected to continue leading the nation in this category well into the foreseeable future.

Employment numbers among Hispanics increased by almost 1 million from 2005 to 2006, with foreign-born Latinos who arrived after 2000 accounting for about 24 percent of the total US employment increase. In 2006, Hispanics made up 13.6 percent of the US workforce; yet accounted for 36.7 percent of employment growth in 2006, which actually increased the number of US employees.

Undocumented immigrants accounted for about two-thirds of the increase among recently hired workers. The Pew Hispanic Center estimated that more than half (7 of the 10-12 million undocumented immigrants in the US) were employed and represented nearly 5 percent of the nation's civilian workforce and two thirds of new construction jobs. Pew cited their numbers as high in specific job categories: roofers (29 percent), agricultural work-ers (24 percent) and construction laborers (25 percent).

These numbers are expected to decline in the second decade of the century as the anti-immigration debates heats-up again and undocumented immigrants (along with our nation's econ-omy) head South. While perceptions of Latinos historically have been less than positive, this has not prevented them from seeking work, getting hired, or making social and economic progress.

Despite relative low levels of education and job skills among immigrants and increased competition for jobs, Latinos continue to be employed at levels higher than any other segment of the US population. Their employment projections were even rosier due to the growth rate of Hispanic-owned businesses between 1997 and 2002, which grew by 31 percent, compared to a national average of only 10 percent for all US businesses. Revenue generated by Hispanic-owned businesses in 2002 was $222 billion, up 19 per-cent from 1997, which provided a needed boost to the economy.

According to the Selig Center at the University of Georgia, buying power among Latinos increased appreciably and grew at a faster rate than that of the overall US population. From 1990 to 2014, the nation's Hispanic buying power will grow dynami-cally; in sheer dollars their economic clout will rise from $212 billion in 1990, to $489 billion in 2000, to $978 billion in 2009, and projected to reach $1.3 trillion in 2014. The 2009 amount will exceed the 2000 value by 100 percent—a percentage gain far greater than either the 45 percent increase in non-Hispanic buying power or close to half (49 percent) of the total increase in buying power for all US consumers. Hispanic buying power will grow faster than that of African-Americans at 54 percent, Native Americans at 65 percent, and Asians/Pacific Islanders at 89 per-cent (Humphreys, *The Multicultural Economy*).

Even though a Federal Reserve's survey of household finances showed white, black, and Asian/Pacific Islander populations all gained ground, wealth for the *median* Latino household did not keep pace. Household income for Latinos in 2005 was $35,967, statistically similar to the previous year. However, Latino total wealth rose, which is reflected in data showing increased average Hispanic household income levels compared to other segments of the US population.

The data indicated a growing income gap within Latino communities; but even as the total number of lower income households grew, many middle- to high-income families accumulated sufficient incremental wealth to raise the overall bar. No matter the cause of declining median income, the implications went mainly unnoticed amid the general rejoicing over the overall rise in Latino household income, which was attributed to an increasing number of family members in the same household joining the workforce.

YOU'VE COME A LONG WAY...

Another notable economic bright spot has been the increase in wages earned, especially among college educated Latinos. NCLR found advanced education has become an effective long-term strategy for increasing family income and wealth. By 2006, nearly 60 percent of Hispanics over the age of 25 had completed high school and another 12 percent had completed a four-year college degree. The number of Latinos eighteen years and older with a bachelor's degree had grown to 3.1 million, more than doubling the 1.4 million in 1996—a major accomplishment, inasmuch as Latino education attainment levels had historically been among the nation's lowest.

And by the 1990s, Latinas were making major inroads into blue-collar and professional careers. Those who entered the workforce were more likely to be better-educated, work fulltime, and hold jobs with major employee benefits, allowing them to contribute to their personal economic well-being, as well as that of their immediate family's. Also, Latina college graduates were earning more than their white and black female counterparts.

These aforementioned examples of economic progress are significant in light of the following 2007 findings by the Pew Hispanic Center:

A. Latinas were less educated than non-Hispanic women; one third had less than a high school education, compared with 10 percent of non-Hispanic women. •

B. Nearly half (49 percent) of Latina immigrants have less than a high school education, while (46 percent) of the US-born have some college education.

C. The labor force participation rate for all Latinas (59 percent) is similar to the participation rate for non-Hispanic women (61 percent); however, US-born Latinas had the highest participation rate (64 percent).

Given their younger age, population growth rate, and employment earning trends, the future health of our nation's economy is closely linked to the Latino workforce. Despite having the highest workforce participation rate in the US, between 2000 and 2010 their median wage level did not keep pace with that of non-Hispanic workers, regardless of the economic upswing attributable to additional family incomes generated by Latina wage earners.

The Latino work ethic and attendant earning power translate into taxable and disposable incomes. More spending on consumer goods, services, and housing by this growing population will increase corporate revenues, stock value and contribute tax revenues to public coffers—essential to a healthy economy and a higher quality of life.

OWNING A PIECE OF THE ROCK

Government, public, academic, and private studies also found homeownership, a standard indicator of financial growth, has also increased substantially among Latinos. Homeownership is yet an indicator of economic stability and a major factor in building wealth and Latinos were increasingly taking steps to acquire their "piece of the rock." An estimated 44 percent of all Latino households in the fifty states and District of Columbia were buying (or owned) homes in 2005, while 48 percent of second generation and 57 percent of third generation Latinos were homeowners, compared to 34 percent of first generation immigrants.

These advances in homeownership were certainly affected by the burst of the housing bubble and its attendant recession that began at the end of 2007. The ensuing shock to financial markets—and the more than $7 trillion in lost housing wealth—prolonged and deepened the downturn and has had a braking effect on the nation's economic recovery. After reaching a record-high—49.8 percent in 2006—homeownership among Latinos slipped to 47.9 percent in 2011. Although the housing market is showing signs of stabilization, the healing process is not progressing as fast for Latinos in many parts of the country.

By 2020, Hispanics are expected to be half of all new home-buyers. Low mortgage rates, affordable housing prices and consistent Hispanic population growth are seen as the reasons for the expansion. Ironically, another major factor is the availability of government-backed Federal Housing Administration loans (from which Latinos were initially excluded when the program was enacted in 1935), used by over one-half million Hispanic families to purchase or refinance homes since 2008.

Judging from the economic situation our country found itself at the end of the millennium's first decade, the economic contributions made by Latinos have helped to ensure the US economy remained viable. The beneficiaries of their financial contributions were, and will continue to be, taxpayer-supported public agencies that are expected to provide services to an aging non-Hispanic white population that will soon rely on Social Security and Medicare to help them through their golden years.

Latinos and their collective energy and youthfulness are poised to rejuvenate our country's economy. They already have demonstrated they will not stand begging while they have the power to earn a living. Their taxpaying potential can contribute mightily to financial stability of our nation. The question we must answer is: "Will an aging, non-Hispanic white, US population become sufficiently motivated to provide the necessary short-term support for public education, vocational training and higher education that will prepare Latino students and employees to meet our future economic and workforce needs?"

Life, Liberty, and Pursuit

Todo es posible para el que sabe trabajar y persistir.
Translation: All is possible for one who knows how to work and persevere.
Transcreation: The A-B-Cs of success: Ability, Breaks and Constancy of purpose.

Attention to the growing Hispanic population by private, public, and nonprofit sectors cannot be limited to demographics and consumerism. Recognition of and respect for Latino culture and values must be factored into advertising, marketing, and public relations plans if they are to effectively reach, communicate, and engage this growing segment of the nation's population. Most research related to Latinos has found that the two most important issues confronting them remain inextricably linked education and economic development.

Many Latino educators and parents believe the adage, "Everybody is a genius. But if you judge a fish by its ability to climb a tree, it will live its whole life believing that it is stupid." Although unsubstantiated, this quote is often attributed to Albert Einstein, but its premise remains indisputable. Academically, one can argue Latinos are like "fish out of water" when it comes to traditional white Eurocentric social, cultural, and historical subjects taught in school textbooks and curricula.

Yes, there are exceptional Latino students who have exercised their innate intelligence and higher than average academic skills to learn the ABCs of "tree climbing" without having to abandon their cultural heritage, but they remain the exceptions to the rule.

A good number of them have been the "first" in their families to successfully compete and excel in a variety of white Eurocentric cultural, educational, and social environments.

At the start of the new millennium The Heritage Foundation reported that although Latinos endured numerous barriers to education (e.g., low levels of individual income and limited proficiency in English), the US public education system continually short-changes them in learning basic skills. It also found Latino students performed markedly better, on average, in private and parochial schools than in public schools and were prone to continue their formal education beyond high school. In Catholic schools the Latino dropout rate decreases to about 9.3 percent, compared to the 47 percent in US public schools (The Heritage Foundation: *Why Catholic Schools Spell Success*).

Experts believe the emphasis on religion, specifically Catholicism, has provided Latino students some of the "cultural relevance" they miss in typical public school curricula and textbooks. A University of Chicago Economics Department's study found that 27 percent of non-Hispanic black (NHB) and Latino Catholic school graduates who started college went on to graduate, compared to only 11 percent of non-Hispanic white (NHW) urban public school graduates.

The Heritage Foundation concluded the probability of inner-city students graduating from high school increased from 62 percent to nearly 90 percent when they attended a secondary Catholic school. Furthermore, compared with their public school counterparts, non-white students in urban Catholic schools can expect to earn approximately 8 percent more in future wages.

Exposing students to supportive (and culturally relevant) educational environments produces positive results. Such environments can raise student (and parent) expectations and can even be accomplished in public schools located in non-white communities. The success of the late, renowned math teacher Jaime

Escalante of the Los Angeles Unified School District's James A. Garfield High School (and the focus of the movie "Stand and Deliver") demonstrated that Latino students excel if challenged by their teachers to meet higher standards.

By demanding that his students enroll in college-level Advanced Placement (AP) programs in 1987, Escalante had more calculus exam takers than all but four high schools in the entire US. His protégé Angelo Villavicencio, a teacher at Ayala High in Chino Hills, CA, was able to pass 80 percent of his low-income, non-white, calculus students in 1995 using the same approach: raising students' and parents' expectations. The two demonstrated that bridging the cultural gap is easier when you engage "culturally competent" teachers who recognize and appreciate the approaches required to address the educational needs of Latino students and families. They were teaching "fish" to climb trees!

The public school systems should have been quick to replicate these successes; yet AP classes remain limited to a select few, supposedly the best and the brightest. The fact is that over the last half century public schools have limited competition for AP classes and diminished the quality of public education, which has prompted a trend towards enrollment in private academies and college preparatory schools among those able to afford them.

However, for most Latino families, public schools remain the only affordable option for educating their children. Despite being the majority of incoming students in a growing number of school districts across the nation, they remain exclusively focused on white, Eurocentric culture and US History. Public education has been a challenge for most Latino students and families whose culture and heritage remains more closely tied to the Western Hemisphere.

IF YOU CAN'T JOIN 'EM, BEAT 'EM!

The founder of the American Civil Liberties Union (ACLU), Roger Nash Baldwin said, "Silence never won rights. They are not readily handed down, but are forced upward by pressures from those oppressed below" (Zach: *Silence Never Won Rights*).

Accounts of legal efforts to provide for equal access to public education in the United States is not typically associated with Latinos, or included as part of their civic contributions to the United States. Even among many of the best educated legal minds in the country, desegregation of public schools is commonly thought to have begun with the 1954 US Supreme Court case: *Brown v. Board of Education* (Topeka, Kansas). The Court ruled separate public schools denied black children equal educational opportunities. The case was touted as a landmark decision by the nation's highest court and overturned earlier rulings such as *Plessy v. Ferguson* (1896) by declaring state laws that established segregated public schools for black and white children violated the Thirteenth and Fourteenth Amendments of the US Constitution.

Actually, the earliest US court cases challenging "separate but equal" schools occurred in Southern California almost a quarter century earlier. The 1931 case *Roberto Alvarez v. Owen* (aka: *Alvarez v. Board of Trustees, Lemon Grove School District*) was the first successful school desegregation court decision in the US, which is overlooked in many history textbooks, legal studies, and media accounts (Walsh, *50 Years*).

In 1930, Lemon Grove, CA, was described as a bucolic community located a few miles east of San Diego. Non-Mexican members of the community grew alarmed at what they perceived as a disturbing trend in the number of Mexicans attending school with their children. They expressed their concerns to the Lemon Grove School Board and recommended a separate school be built for Mexican children. They cited overcrowded classroom conditions, illiteracy in Mexican homes, wide spread use of Spanish as the language of choice at home, and insinuations that Mexicans were "filthy" people as the rationale for their demands for the separate school.

Alvarez v. Board of Trustees, Lemon Grove School District is notable because it was Mexican parents who initiated legal action to eliminate segregation of schools and won. This ruling established the rights of Latino children to equal education in spite of sentiments on the part of a white-Eurocentric community that favored separation of students and actual deportation of their US-born and legal immigrant parents. The case against the Lemon Grove School District is a testament to the determination of Latino parents and their efforts to ensure equality in education for their children (Alvarez, *The Lemon Grove Incident*).

Despite this early court victory, segregation in California continued. Less than a hundred miles north of Lemon Grove, schools in Orange County maintained a segregated education system from 1911-1947; separate schools for whites and Mexican-Americans, regardless of the students' citizenship or immigration status. At the end of WWII, California was the largest state in the nation to maintain separate schools for non-white children. Public schools would routinely enroll "fair-skinned" Latino students into "whites-only" schools, but rejected siblings from the same families with darker skin. Public funded institutions were employing a caste system to distinguish white European children from indigenous and *mestizo* populations.

In March 1945, five families—Méndez, Estrada, Guzmán, Palomino and Rámirez—challenged the practice of segregation by Orange County schools in the US District Court in Los Angeles in the case of *Mendez, et al v. Westminster School District, et al.* The plaintiffs claimed their children, along with five thousand other children of Mexican heritage were victims of discrimination based solely on the color of their skin and thereby forced to attend separate schools in the Westminster, Garden Grove, Santa Ana, and El Modena school districts.

These parents led a community challenge against discrimination that changed school segregation in California and established yet another legal precedent for ending segregation in public schools in the USA. In commemoration of the lawsuit, the US Postal Service issued a first class stamp on September 14, 2007, memorializing the importance of the case and recognizing the Latino parents who understood that if their community was to take its rightful place in mainstream society, their children required the same quality of education provided to white children.

The *Mendez v. Westminster* case lasted two years and was decided in San Francisco in 1947. It "legally" ended segregation in Orange County and throughout California, eight years before the *Brown v. Board of Education* landmark decision. The National Association for the Advancement of Colored People (NAACP), the American Civil Liberties Union (ACLU), the American Jewish Congress (AJC), and the Japanese American Citizens League (JACL) supported and contributed *amicus* briefs to the lawsuit. Two of the key participants in the case were attorneys Thurgood Marshall of the NAACP and California Governor Earl Warren (1943-53). Marshall became the first African American Supreme Court Justice and Warren was named Chief Justice of the Supreme Court of the United States in 1953, and is credited with several other major decisions regarding racial segregation, civil rights, and police arrest procedures in the US.

TAKING CARE OF BUSINESS

Education within the Latino community receives a tremendous amount of attention and rightfully so. It is often paired with economic development because of the symbiotic relationship that exists between these two critical needs. Latinos understand that a good education is directly related to financial security, and vice versa. Gainful employment or profits from private business ownership provide financial freedom to live in neighborhoods of one's choice, send one's children to better schools, and contribute to the development of one's community through a variety of public taxes and personal philanthropy.

Contrary to popular stereotypes of being "lazy" or "feckless," Latinos (as a group) have proven to possess a strong work ethic and entrepreneurial spirit that allow them to pursue the American Dream. Instead of asking for "hand-outs" on street corners, they recognize that steady income is the best way to provide for their families. This desire to improve their quality of life may explain why in recent years (2000-2010) Latinos consistently led the nation's racial/ethnic groups with nearly a 70 percent workforce participation rate for workers 16 years of age and older. Due to the economic recession and a higher unemployment rate, in 2011 that number dropped to under 60 percent (US Department of Labor: *The Latino Labor Force*).

Prior to the economic recession in the US that took place during the second half of the new millennium's first decade, Latinos were credited with launching small businesses at record rates. The states with the fastest growth of Hispanic-owned businesses between 1997-2002 were: New York (57 percent); Rhode Island & Georgia (56 percent each); and Nevada & South Carolina (48 percent each).

Counties with the highest number of Hispanic-owned businesses were: Los Angeles, CA (188,472); Miami-Dade, FL (163,188); Harris, TX (61,934) and The Bronx, NY (38,325). According to the Census Bureau, during this five-year period the number of Hispanic-owned businesses grew by almost 44 percent to 2.3 million—a growth rate that far exceeded all businesses in the US.

By the year 2000, Hispanics represented the highest percentage of US business start-ups, with Latinas leading that growth.

Of all the new Hispanic-owned businesses launched during the last decade of the twentieth century, nearly 40 percent of them were registered to women. Between 1997 and 2002, the number of Latina-owned firms (those with 51 percent or more ownership) increased from 337,800 to 553,600—a 64 percent increase—with nearly $30 billion in sales and 200,000 employees.

BULLISH ON AMERICA

A 2006 study by Intuit (producers of Quicken, TurboTax and QuickBooks software) and the Institute for the Future uncovered predictable but unexpected trends in US entrepreneurship. It suggested a new wave of business owners was emerging and projected substantial changes in the structure and composition of small businesses by 2017. The study cited three demographic trends that were certain to affect small businesses in the new millennium: the first was an increase in workforce diversity; the second was a rise in personal business start-ups; and the third was an expansion of entrepreneurial education (News Release: *Intuit Study*).

It also found that by 2017 the majority of entrepreneurs would no longer fall into the "middle-aged, white-male" category; instead they will come from a variety of age, ethnicity, gender, and traditionally underrepresented groups, which includes an increasing number of immigrants.

As our nation continues its recurring and increasingly heated debate over the influence and role of immigrants there is evidence backing the argument that the overwhelming majority doesn't come to take jobs away from Americans. On the contrary, immigrants have been "job creators" and have contributed to our nation's economy for more than 130 years. While the entrepreneurial spirit of immigrants in the US is not well documented, they have been more likely to be self-employed than native-born citizens in every census since 1880.

While largely disconnected from local economic development planning, immigrant-owned businesses have become the engines for economic stimulus in many communities throughout the US. Research showed that more businesses are being started by the foreign-born than by native-born entrepreneurs, driving growth in business sectors from food manufacturing to health care. The following examples shed more light on the subject:

- In 2005, first-generation immigrants founded twenty-two of Los Angeles's 100 fastest growing companies, among them nationally renowned firms: *El Pollo Loco*, Panda Express, LuLu's Desserts, and Forever 21.

- The Little Village area of Chicago—a Latino enclave since the 1960s when Latinos revived the community after descendants of white European immigrants fled to the suburbs—has become one of the city's biggest sources of sales tax, rivaling the up scale stores on Michigan Avenue known as the Magnificent Mile.

- In New York, majority-immigrant neighborhoods such as Flushing, Queens, Sunset Park and Brooklyn have experienced job growth at a much higher rate than the city as a whole. And although immigrants' efforts may not be as glamorous as the much ballyhooed sports stadium, ethnic business districts like Flushing's Main Street have helped to recapture tax revenues from suburban shoppers.

- In 2000, foreign-born individuals comprised 36 percent of New York City's population, yet accounted for nearly half (49 percent) of all self-employed workers in the Big Apple.

In an increasingly global economy of outsourcing and corporate mergers/acquisitions, the previously referenced Intuit study suggests that small businesses will become more important to local economies. And with Latinos expected to drive much of the population growth, the demand for businesses that serve domestic and immigrant Latino communities is also expected to continue its upward growth trend.

It should come as no surprise that so many people from other countries are emulating our nation's immigrant ancestors by coming to America, despite the risks of discrimination, jail terms, separation from loved ones, and threats to their personal safety. More than any other period in the history of this country, immigrants continue to contribute to our nation's economic growth and progress.

INDEPENDENT SORTS

In 2005, over 25 percent of the nation's nearly 1.7 million Latino businesses were located in California, a state in which 15 percent of all businesses are Hispanic-owned and 11 percent of those businesses are located in the greater Los Angeles metropolitan area. This makes sense when one considers that approximately 25 percent of the total US Hispanic population is located in Southern California.

Self-employment provides an opportunity for personal independence and job satisfaction. For many it's an alternative to underemployment or the lack of employment opportunities. Latino business owners believe they possess relevant insights into the marketplace and that their cultural values will serve them well in a changing marketplace. In addition to strong ties to their crafts and professions, Latino business owners tend to hire a higher number of Latino workers, resulting in community economic development.

To trace the economic vitality of any community it is a common practice to count the number of times a dollar circulates within its boundaries before leaving to enter the mainstream economy. According to the Harvest Institute of Washington, DC, a dollar circulates in Jewish communities twelve times or more, in Chinese communities over nine times, and in Latino communities over six times before merging into the general economy, where it circulates indefinitely (Jackson, *Help One Another*).

The fact that Latinos are willing to tackle jobs and provide services many US citizens won't even consider, demonstrates these *wannabe* US workers and taxpayers not only understand the price of prosperity in our society, but are anxious to "invest" in their own success.

It is universally accepted that products and services at competitive prices drive most consumers' decisions; but with all things being equal, corporate responsibility, cultural relevance, and related factors also result in trial and brand loyalty. To gain an advantage over their competition, promoters of products and services must find ways to create interest among current and potential customers. In light of current demographic trends, private companies, government agencies, and nonprofit organizations are developing new (or repackaging old) products and services to reach members of an increasingly diverse marketplace.

A substantial portion of the US Hispanic population may not yet be formally educated or possess a college degree, but through their innate talents and high workforce participation rates they are ensuring their children will be. They understand that in spite of their limited access to education and limited economic opportunities, nothing is impossible for those who understand the ABCs and *Ñ* of success.

Can You Hear
Me Now?

Mi voto es mi voz.
Translation: My vote is my voice.
Transcreation: The voice of the people is louder than the
boom of any cannon.

Thanks to an estimated 75 percent of the estimated 10 million Hispanic votes cast for President Barack Obama in the 2012 presidential election, Latinos have finally become a factor in national politics. Still many Americans view them as mainly unassimilated, disinterested, and as undocumented immigrants not legally eligible to vote. As the major political parties and their minions debated the effects of diversity and immigration on the US, Latinos have been quietly afoot establishing their financial and political clout.

As a voting bloc, Latinos were credited with being a major factor in the election of President Obama in 2008. The William C. Velasquez Institute (WCVI) reported the Latino electorate grew to more than 12 million registered voters. According to a Pew Hispanic Center analysis of national exit poll data from Edison Media Research, a record 10 million Hispanic voters helped carry President Obama to victory by a two to one (68.6 to 28.7 percent) margin over Republican Senator John McCain in the 2008 Presidential election. This 79.85 percent turnout figure for Latino voters represented 7.43 percent of all votes cast in the US.

The Census Bureau reported that 5.6 million Hispanics voted in the 2006 general election for an increase of 18 percent over

2002, a year in which a federal election was conducted with no presidential race on the ballot. They were reported to have influenced the ousting of Republicans from power in Congress in 2006 and were also credited with reelecting Republican President George W. Bush to a second term in 2004.

These voting trends were previews of what can be expected in future elections, especially when compared to only a 7 and 5 percent increase among white and black voters, respectively. Decidedly strong opposition by Republican candidates across the nation to immigration reform, education funding, inclusion of Latino contributions and accomplishments in history textbooks and curricula, and other issues of concern to Latinos is expected to continue driving them to the polls.

Latinos are definitely expected to continue gaining influence in the political arena. Geographically, by 2025 they are projected to be major political players throughout the country. For example, 40 percent of all US residents will live in California, Texas, Florida, New York, and Illinois, states that will elect approximately 40 percent of all members of Congress and control 68 percent (184) of the electoral votes required to elect the President of the US. Latinos are on their way to becoming the majority in California and Texas and the largest, single ethnic group in the other three states.

Why are these trends relevant? Across the country, non-Hispanic white (NHW) voter turnout decreased by nearly a million votes from 1992 to 1996, while black turnout grew by fifteen thousand and Latino voters increased by 690 thousand. The National Association of Latino Elected & Appointed Officials (NALEO) reported that only 59 percent of adult Hispanics were eligible to vote in 2004, compared to 97 and 94 percent of non-Hispanic whites and blacks, respectively. It found Latinos represented approximately 10 percent of the national vote in 2008, a considerable increase over the 8.5 percent in 2004. Latino voting has increased nearly 50 percent in the past decade, and voter registration has grown by 33 percent since 1996. Percentages are considerably greater in heavily Hispanic populated states and urban areas.

Historically, Latinos have had low voter turnout but their political influence is now beginning to reflect a critical mass, which is reflective of their rapidly growing population numbers. The Pew Hispanic Center attributes their low turnout numbers to two factors: 1) the youth of the Latino population (over 33 percent are under the voting age of 18 years of age; and 2) the high proportion (22 percent) of adults who are not yet US citizens. In 2010, Hispanics were over 16 percent of the nation's population, but slightly over 10 percent were eligible to vote.

Since 1995 the average annual number of immigrant naturalizations has surpassed 650,000, compared to 150,000 in 1970. In 2006, Pew reported the number of naturalized citizens in the US grew to nearly 13 million from 1995 to 2005—a historic increase that also revealed the nation's changing ethnic composition; not to mention the growing potential of Latinos to affect public policy through the ballot box. Over half of the nation's legal immigrants had become naturalized citizens—the highest level in a quarter century and a 15 percent increase since 1990, when the proportion of naturalized immigrants dropped to historic lows.

CHANGE IS IN THE WIND

As in most developed countries, non-voters in the US tend to be concentrated among the young and the poor. Taking into account the young age of native-born and naturalized Latino citizens—and the ineligibility of most immigrants to vote—a number of community-based organizations (CBOs) have undertaken numerous citizenship and voter registration initiatives focused on "get out the vote" efforts. One of them, the Southwest Voter Registration Education Project (SVREP), a non-partisan, political advocacy organization, has managed to register over 2.2 million voters throughout the Southwest and Florida since 1974.

The Wall Street Journal (WSJ), in a 2007 article reported on a national campaign by Spanish-language media and community advocacy and grassroots groups to spur millions of eligible Hispanics to become naturalized citizens in order to influence the outcome of future elections. *WSJ* reported: "More than eight million green-card holders—that is, legal permanent residents—are eligible to become US citizens, and the majority of them are immigrants of Latin American origin, according to US government data."

Univision (the nation's top-rated Spanish television network) provided its considerable clout to convert a disenfranchised, Spanish-speaking community into a viable voting bloc. The television network and its community partners realized that a citizenship drive and subsequent voter registration efforts could transform Latinos into political players in key cities and states.

Given past voting patterns, political experts feel the Latino growth rate and naturalizations, and subsequent voter registration and voting, will benefit Democrats at least twice as much as it will Republicans. Historically Latino voters have tended to register and vote as Democrats and in the 2010 mid-term elections, Republican candidates who took a hard line on immigration reform were handily defeated with the help of Latino voters, mainly among those of Mexican heritage, who represent about 66 percent of the nation's total Hispanic population.

And nowhere was this partnership more visible than in Florida, the traditional Hispanic GOP stronghold. A May 2008 *Miami Herald* article reported Democrats had overtaken Republicans among the state's registered Latino voters in what signaled "a trend that, if it continues, could have far-reaching implications for future elections and US foreign policy." (It did! Florida became the "cherry on top" of the 2012 elections for President Obama when its final vote count gave him the majority of nation's popular votes in addition to a substantial advantage in the electoral college tally; albeit too late, as the outcome had already been determined.)

Immigration from Latin America by various nationality groups into Florida and the maturation of younger generations of Cuban Americans are diluting the influence of older Cuban Americans who have traditionally supported conservative GOP planks. Democrats (18 percent) and Undecided voters (14 percent) grew substantially since January 2006, while Republican registrations increased by only 2 percent. Pundits saw this as a major "tipping point" in Florida politics.

According to an April 2011 *Politico.com* story, Cuban-Americans remained committed to conservative principles and continued to vote Republican, but their number of the state's Hispanic population is being overtaken as an influx of Democratic-leaning Puerto Ricans into Central Florida reshapes the state's voting patterns. The growth of Puerto Rican voters has (for the first time in the state's history) helped to register more Latinos as Democrats than Republicans.

The 2010 census data showed a 57 percent increase in Florida's Hispanic population, far outpacing the state's overall total of 18 percent, and accounted for 23 percent of the state's nearly 20 million residents. A 2009 Census report put the number of Puerto Ricans at nearly 730,000—fast approaching the 1.1 million Cuban-Americans in the state. Based on these increases by Puerto Ricans, a political power shift appears to be in the offing.

IDENTITY POLITICS

South Florida has also become a major source of campaign funds for high-visibility Latino candidates from throughout the nation, even a few Democratic candidates received financial support from the mostly Republican Cuban American donors. In spite of apparent and long-established partisan loyalties, there is an inexplicable increase in "inter-party" collaboration. In 2005 Los Angeles Democratic and mayoral candidate Antonio Villaraigosa tapped into Miami's political fundraising machine. Other Democrats who benefited from this unprecedented cross-over anomaly were presidential primary candidate (and former New Mexico Governor) Bill Richardson and New Jersey Congressman Bob Menendez.

The 2004 election of former US Secretary of Housing and Florida Republican US Senator Mel Martinez was another example of "crossover" politics being practiced by Latinos in Florida. He received strong support from Puerto Rican Democrats in his victory. This and other examples of identity politics (support of Latinos by other Latinos) may be blurring former class and partisan voting practices among Latinos.

The obvious sign of Latino voter turnout is visible in the increasing number of elected office holders and presence in legislative chambers across the country. Data collected by Strategy Research Corporation, the California Secretary of State, the US Census and the Newspaper Association of America indicated there were nearly 4,500 elected Latinos across the US in 2000—an increase of over 40 percent since 1985.

Other signs of that growing legislative influence are becoming more visible. In 2003, the California State Assembly elected Fabian Nuñez, a 37 year-old freshman Democrat from Los Angeles, as its Speaker of the House. He assumed his duties in 2004 and termed-out of office in 2008. In March 2010, John Perez, a 40 year-old Los Angeles Democrat, was given the reins to the eighty-member house. Across the nation the number of Latino state legislators increased from 156 in 1996 to 237 in 2006. Arizona, California, Florida, New Mexico, New York, and Texas all had at least 10 percent Latino representation in their legislative chambers.

There are other "firsts" in US politics, beginning in 2004 with the election of two Latinos to the US Senate: Mel Martinez (R-FL), who has since decided not to stand for reelection, and Ken Salazar (D-CO), who has since been appointed by President Obama to serve as his Secretary of the Interior. Former US Representative Bob Menendez (D-NJ) joined them in January 2006 to bring the number of Latinos in the US Senate to three.

In 2010, fellow Republican and former Florida House Speaker Marco Rubio was elected to fill the US Senate vacated by Martinez. Rubio's meteoric rise to prominence continued as he garnered national attention as a potential vice presidential candidate in former Massachusetts Governor Mitt Romney's challenge to President Obama in the 2012 election. Others joining him on the GOP list of Latinos with a bright future were New Mexico's first female Governor Susana Martinez and Nevada's first Hispanic Governor Brian Sandoval.

WHAT DOES THE FUTURE HOLD?

Latinos are experiencing significant population growth and winning elections at an unprecedented rate. Although they constitute nearly 16 percent of the population, Latino legislators made up less than four percent of all US lawmakers, including Puerto Rico. States with historically high percentages of Latino voters include California, Colorado, Connecticut, Florida, Illinois, Nevada, New Mexico, New York, New Jersey, New Mexico, and Texas. High voter turnout in non-traditional, Hispanic-populated states has also begun in Georgia, Kansas, Maryland, Michigan, Nevada, Rhode Island and Washington, all of which have elected Latinos to state offices.

Examples of political success are becoming more frequent at local, state and national levels. Latinos are rapidly becoming a political force and increasingly capable of electing (or preventing the election of) candidates from either of the two major parties. Political pundits predict Latinos could actually influence which of the two current major parties will dominate US politics into the 21st century. Research into party affiliations at the start of the new millennium uncovered the following trends:

A. Registered voters of Mexican ancestry made up 60 percent of the Hispanic electorate; almost half (47 percent) claimed to be Democrats, 18 percent identified as Republicans and 22 percent as Independents.

B. Those of Cuban ancestry made up six percent of Hispanic voters; more than half (52 percent) claimed to be Republicans, 20 percent said Democrats and nine percent Independents.

C. Puerto Ricans accounted for 15 percent of the Hispanic electorate; half (50 percent) said they were Democrats, 17 percent Republicans and 15 percent Independents.

In the 2000 presidential election, Latinos represented approximately 15 percent of California's registered voters, 11 percent of Florida's, 15 percent of Arizona's, and 30 percent of New Mexico's. Two years later, the Pew Hispanic Center reported 14.5 million US Hispanics (over 35 percent of the US Hispanic population) were eligible to vote. That number was projected to be closer to 25 million in 2012—an increase of some 38 percent. The largest increases in voting came in the California and Texas Democratic primaries.

In California, Hispanic share rose to 30 percent in 2008, up from 16 percent in 2004. In Texas, voter share increased from 24 percent in 2004 to 32 percent in 2008. Florida's Democratic primary also showed an increase, from 9 percent in 2004 to 12 percent in 2008. These three states are home to nearly 60 percent of all eligible Hispanic voters. Pundits and researchers say there is no reason to believe that this rate of voter growth will soon subside.

THIS AIN'T YOUR FATHER'S POLITICS

Nationally, Democrats have maintained a two to one advantage over Republicans in party registration among Latinos, which has not changed significantly since the 2000 presidential election. If anything, the Republican Party and its increasingly conservative and anti-Latino positions have driven Latino voters to the Democratic Party in droves. The enactment of Arizona's anti-immigrant legislation in 2010, Senate Bill 1070, is being supported by GOP partisans across the US, resulting in copycat immigration and voter identification legislation in many other states that also contributed to the animosity among Latinos toward the GOP.

A July 2010 CNN/Opinion Research Corporation poll found 57 percent of Hispanics said Democrats agreed on issues that Latinos care about; only 32 percent felt the same about Republicans. In the same poll, 56 percent said the GOP is doing a bad job of reaching out to African-Americans, Latinos, and other non-whites. Latinos are also becoming disenchanted with the inability of Democrats and President Obama to challenge the Tea Party-energized Republicans on several issues, ranging from jobs, the economy, health care, tax reform, and last but not least, comprehensive immigration reform.

A March 2012 edition of *Time* magazine featured its first Spanish headline in its history: "*Yo decido*" (I decide). It was tied to the magazine's feature article: "Why Latinos will pick the next president." The focus of the cover story was the impact Latino voters could have in the presidential election, which would be a test of how seriously both parties are in their efforts to establish meaningful relationships with Latino voters.

Politicians and their "machines" are aware of Latinos and their voting influence; however, they still lag far behind the more successful corporate marketers and communicators in how to effectively reach and engage Latinos. That lack of awareness is resulting in disconnects by political candidates and their targeted voter segments, even at the highest office levels. Policy decision-making and access to the exclusive backrooms where political strategies are developed remain uncharted territory for most politically oriented Latinas/Latinos. Until they are identified, recruited, and involved in comprehensive policy-making decisions and integrated outreach strategies, voter loyalty will remain more of a virtual goal rather than a reality.

Latinos have become a significant voting bloc but are still, for the most part, being taken for granted by Democrats—and excluded by Republicans. However, despite substantial efforts to increase Latino voter support by presidential primary candidates, "high-level" and "high visibility" Latino involvement has been sporadic. The 2008 presidential primary campaigns of Democrats Hillary Clinton and Barack Obama had Latinos involved at the highest levels of their respective campaigns, from national co-chairs to strategic management and consultants; as well as a credible cross-section of local, regional and national endorsers and campaign staff managers.

Senator Clinton named Patty Solis Doyle—her longtime aide and assistant during Bill Clinton's 1992 presidential campaign—as her campaign manager, making her the first Latina to manage a US presidential campaign, but her appointment was short-lived. In February 2008 she was removed from her position for allegedly mismanaging the campaign, a move that didn't go unnoticed among Latino community leaders, influencers, and voters.

Granted, political expertise is essential for most campaign positions, but former President George W. Bush's campaign staff recognized the need for an expert in cultural relevance. They hired Hispanic marketing maven Lionel Sosa of San Antonio, TX, who is credited with helping Bush attract as much as 44 percent of the Hispanic vote in 2004. Sosa, a recognized expert in Hispanic consumer marketing and voter behavior, has worked on eight Republican presidential campaigns since 1980.

Political campaign managers are learning that when it comes to creating awareness and loyalty among Latinos, the candidates and their campaigns are no different from the marketing of any other brand, product or service. Attention to cultural relevance may explain why US Senator Mel Martinez—the first Cuban-born US Senator—was chosen to chair the Republican National Committee (RNC) as it geared up for the 2008 presidential election. His appointment as the first Latino to serve as chairman of a major party signaled an effort to show signs of cultural sensitivity—and inclusion—in the GOP's efforts to woo Latino voters.

Although Latinos supported President Bush in record numbers in 2004, they were significantly less enthusiastic about GOP candidates in the 2006 mid-term elections. Much of the decline in support was attributed to increased anti-immigration and anti-Spanish language "bashing" attributed to conservative and nativist elements of the GOP.

Not to be undone in their efforts to gain ground as a result of the waning popularity of the GOP among Latinos, Democrats in 2006 named US Senators Ken Salazar (who lost his Colorado seat in Congress in 2010) and Robert Menendez (New Jersey) to co-chair its Senate Democratic Hispanic Task Force. Their mission was to build bridges between the Latino community and the Senate Democratic Caucus. But as both the Republicans and Democrats are learning, naming Latinos to titular posts for national initiatives and political campaigns is a good first step, but not the complete answer.

In October 2007 Senator Martinez resigned his RNC position, becoming the latest casualty in the GOP's bitter internal fight over immigration reform and dealing another setback to President Bush's effort to gain Latino support for his administration's programs. Martinez made the announcement after he expressed frustration over the vitriolic tenor of anti-immigration posturing within the GOP. He later announced he would not seek re-election and resigned his US Senate seat August 7, 2009.

HOW TO WIN FRIENDS
AND INFLUENCE PEOPLE

A spate of GOP sponsored state legislation related to anti-immigration enforcement and voter suppression initiatives is also taking its toll. An example of such anti-Latino immigration posturing was GOP stalwart Newt Gingrich, who first expressed his attitude towards Latinos and Spanish-speakers in a speech to the National Federation of Republican Women in March 2007.

He proclaimed, "We should replace bilingual education with immersion in English so people learn the common language of the country and they learn the language of prosperity, not the language of living in a ghetto [*sic*]."

Any politically savvy politician worth his or her salt should know the difference between a ghetto and a *barrio*. But why let cultural competence get in the way? Demonizing the Spanish language is tantamount to demonizing the people who speak it, especially when a recognized political leader is doing it. Gingrich continued his rants against the Spanish language, when he said bilingualism poses "a long-term dangers to the fabric of our nation" and "allowing bilingualism to continue to grow is very dangerous." Comments like these further distanced Latinos from the GOP (Hunt, *Gingrich*).

Like most politicians who count on the public's short memories, Gingrich announced the launch of his *Americanos* group in early 2011—a national initiative to recruit Latino support for the GOP and his candidacy for the presidency in 2012. His media consultant was Lionel Sosa.

Partisan politicians need to overcome several obstacles related to Latino voters. The anti-immigration rhetoric of some GOP candidates frequently overshadowed other issues during the 2010 mid-term elections, such as when Tea Party-backed Republican Senate candidate Sharon Angle of Nevada ran ads portraying undocumented immigrants as thugs and gang members. She lost to Democratic incumbent Harry Reid, who credited Latinos for his victory.

Both major parties promise to address issues important to Latinos and claim they are committed to advancing legislation and policies that will unlock the political, economic and social potential of the nation's fastest-growing consumer and voting bloc. But unlike many of their corporate and public brethren, experts in Hispanic marketing and Latino issues are still not sufficiently involved in strategic policymaking being framed by the "king makers" in either party. One thing is becoming clear; those campaigns that recruit culturally competent Latinos with an ounce of "street smarts" will likely have more credibility.

The election of Latinos to political office is also affecting lobbying and governmental affairs activities. Like most elected and appointed officials, Latinos are susceptible to political largess: campaign donations, dinners, fact-finding junkets and other perks; but due to a traditional community orientation, many are most receptive to those who support programs and services that benefit their constituents. The challenge is knowing which they are.

Latino politics remain locally driven. A substantial number of elected office holders base their political agendas on matters important to advocacy organizations and constituents who played major roles in electing them. These relationships between Latino political and community leaders are not too different from those of non-Hispanic officeholders, except for the fact they are often more profound because of a shared experience of exclusion among Latino elected officials and the communities they represent.

Community relationships on the part of Latino office holders underscore the need for corporations, public agencies, and
nonprofit organizations to establish and maintain their own relationships with community leaders—as well as Latino office holders—as an "indirect" way to influence public policy. CBOs have
access to elected Latinos and their staffs, mainly because many
of them were the springboards used to win elected office for a
substantial number of candidates. They are also trusted resources
and sounding boards related to community and civic concerns for
a growing number of non-Hispanic politicians.

MALICE DRINKS HALF
OF ITS OWN POISON

In 1994, California's Proposition 187—a controversial ballot
measure that sought to limit services to undocumented immigrants—won a resounding victory. While supported by a substantial number of voters, "Prop 187" became a rallying cry for the
state's Latino advocacy and activist groups, who saw the measure
as nothing more than a veiled form of discrimination affecting
all Latinos: US citizens, naturalized, legal, and undocumented.

The proposition was ultimately struck down as unconstitutional by the courts in 1998, but not before it was challenged
by Latino advocacy and immigrant-rights groups who credited
the measure (and its political champion, Republican Governor
Pete Wilson) with invigorating Latino advocacy CBOs and voters, and transforming their communities into a political force in
California and neighboring states.

Reference to Wilson's influence in motivating Latino activists and voters was made in a November 2008, *Los Angeles
Times* opinion piece by Tim Rutten, in which he underscored
the overwhelming support by Latino voters in Senator Barack

Obama's victory over Arizona Republican Senator John McCain. Rutten wrote:

> "The significance of that landslide was amplified by the fact that Latinos are clustered in the Western states that Obama pried from the red column. Seventy-three percent of Colorado's Latinos went for the Democratic candidate, as did 76 percent of Nevada's and 69 percent of New Mexico's. More striking, Latinos helped deliver to Obama two of the three Sunbelt states crucial to Reagan's first realigning victory. In California, 77 percent of Latinos went for the Democrat, as did 57 percent of Florida's. Even the third, Texas, seems to be teetering on the blue precipice. Political history is a funny thing…. Who would have guessed that Pete Wilson would be one of the architects of Barack Obama's victory?" (Rutten, *Opinion*).

Political enfranchisement and the polls have become valuable tools for Latinos in their interaction with traditional US politics. It is apparent to a growing number of *politicos* that the game as they knew it had reached a "tipping point" in influence with an increasingly diverse electorate. Which party will recognize and act on that reality in earnest is still anyone's guess.

Like non-Hispanic whites, Latinos contribute to local economies through the taxes they pay on gas, retail sales, excise, property (through ownership, and indirectly through rents), FICA, and their payroll deductions. Therefore, they expect to have their voices heard on local, state, and national issues, if not through media or public discourse, then through the ballot box. Latinos have already started snatching victory from the jaws of defeat in local and statewide elections. As their voter strength and sophistication grow, they can expect to win more elections and begin shaping the social and economic futures of their communities—and to an increasing extent, the nation.

In politics, the relative age of Latinos is another point to consider. They are younger than the rest of the US population. In 2008, Latinos had a median age of 27.6 years, compared to 36.6 for the nation. White European Americans were the oldest at 40.8. Due to their young age, Latinos potentially have a promising political future: 37 percent of Mexican Americans and 31 percent of Puerto Ricans are under the legal voting age of eighteen. More than 20 percent of historically conservative Cuban Americans are 65 years or older, compared to only 4 percent of Democratic-leaning Mexican Americans, who at almost two-thirds, represent the "lion's share" of the Hispanic population.

Maria Teresa Petersen, executive director of *Voto Latino*, agrees that naturalization and maturation of Latinos will affect future US voting trends. "Each month, approximately 50,000 US Latinos turn eighteen years of age, 87 percent of them eligible to register to vote," she adds. The Hispanic teen population was predicted to grow 62 percent by 2010. By comparison, the growth rate among all US teens for the same period is forecast at only 10 percent.

The William C. Velasquez Institute (WCVI) found there were over 12 million registered Latino voters who cast approximately 9.7 million votes in the November 2008 presidential election. This represented an 80 percent turnout and accounted for over 7 percent of all US voters. WCVI data analysis found dramatic increases in non-white voting were more supportive of Obama in 2008 than for Kerry in 2004. The data found Democratic voting grew significantly compared to 2004, while Republican voting declined slightly.

Surprisingly, very few voters said the election was about race, yet if only non-Hispanic whites had gone to the polls, McCain would have won. Two-thirds of the white vote in the South backed McCain, while the overwhelming majority of blacks backed Obama. President Bush received about one-tenth of the black vote in his reelection campaign, but even that reliable

Republican black vote backed Obama in 2008. But, the decisive ethnic factor was the Latino vote; Obama reportedly won 66 percent, 16 percentage points more than John Kerry in his 2004 bid for the presidency.

THE TIDE IS TURNING

In the 2010 midterm elections, Latino voters turned out for some races in unprecedented numbers and actually affected their outcomes. *The New York Times* reported the results as "history-making" on many fronts. In addition to the aforementioned election of Susana Martinez of New Mexico, the nation's first Hispanic female Governor and Brian Sandoval, the first Hispanic Governor of Nevada; Raul Labrador was the first Latino ever to represent Idaho in the US House of Representatives and Jaime Herrera Beutler became the first Latina congresswoman from the state of Washington (Lacey, *Latinos Reached*).

As a result of Marco Rubio's election to the US Senate from Florida, along with the upset victory by Bill Flores over Representative Chet Edwards (a 10-term incumbent in Texas), eight Hispanic Republicans in the US House and Senate joined 18 Hispanic Democrats—three fewer than before the mid-term elections as a result of losses by Congressmen Ciro D. Rodriguez and Solomon P. Ortiz of Texas and John Salazar of Colorado.

Latinos overall showed a clear preference for Democrats and were credited in Nevada with also saving Harry Reid (the Senate majority leader) in his race against Tea Party-backed Republican Sharron Angle. Hispanics comprised 15 percent of the total electorate and ended up giving Reid 90 percent of their votes. Likewise, according to analysts and exit polls, Senator Barbara Boxer of California and Senator Michael Bennet of Colorado owe their victories to Latinos and their aggressive get-out-the-vote campaigns.

Election eve polling by Latino Decisions, a polling and research organization, showed double-digit increases in Hispanic voter turnout from 2006 to 2010. But the aforementioned races weren't the only ones in which they made a difference. A November 2010 Pew Hispanic Center report, "The Latino Vote in the 2010 Elections," found that while Latinos helped some Democrats win, more also voted Republican, compared to 2006.

National House exit poll results show that among Latino voters, Democrats had an advantage—64 vs. 34 percent—over Republicans in US House races, although those winning high offices, like Governor or Senator, were Hispanic Republicans. The Latino Decisions survey showed these GOP candidates didn't necessarily garner more of the Latino vote. For example, in the governor's race for New Mexico, Susana Martinez received 38 percent of the Latino vote while her Democratic opponent garnered 61 percent. So much for the identity politics argument made earlier about Florida, when compared to other areas of the country!

As technology shrinks the world and diverse Latino communities recognize the benefits of working together to promote common goals and interests, a more comprehensive national political agenda is emerging. Political party leaders may wish to embrace this trend and begin to recruit Latinos for top-level positions in their respective campaigns—a move that would signal their party's cultural relevance, which could also result in political dominance and long-term loyalty.

VOTER ID: SECURITY OR SUPPRESSION?

As mentioned earlier, efforts to thwart turnout among non-white voters were initiated by GOP partisans who imposed requirements that some voters would be unable to meet. In several states, voters will be required to show a photo ID at the polls. Kansas Governor Sam Brownback said his state's bill is necessary to "ensure the sanctity of the vote."

According to an April 26, 2011, editorial by *The New York Times*, "Kansas has had only one prosecution for voter fraud in the past six years." But because of this "threat" to democracy in Kansas, some 620,000 voters lacking government IDs may lose their right as US citizens to vote. The conservative wing of the Republican Party has their fingerprints all over this legislation. It was written by Kansas Secretary of State Kris Kobach, who also drafted Arizona's controversial SB-1070, an anti-immigration law that was challenged in state and federal courts and had several of its key points ruled unconstitutional.

Eight states enacted photo ID laws and more than 30 other states are jumping on the same bandwagon, as Republicans attempt to outdo one another in proposing bills with new voting barriers. The Wisconsin bill refuses to recognize college photo ID cards issued by its state university, thus eliminating many student voters. Texas Governor Rick Perry thought voter ID warranted emergency legislation and made it one of the first bills to be passed by the majority Republican legislature; it too rejected college and university-issued student ID cards. It was challenged and struck down by a federal court that called the voter-identification law the most stringent of its kind in the country (Fernandez, *Court Blocks*).

Obviously, the coalescing of diverse Latino groups into voting blocs is creating a formidable political force—a reality that should not be lost on either of the nation's existing (or potentially new) political parties. What binds Latinos of diverse geographic regions together is their common experiences with prejudice and discrimination at the hands of a non-Hispanic and a culturally-uninformed majority that has served to unite diverse Latino subgroups toward common causes and goals.

Silence is no longer an acceptable alternative for Latinos in addressing their inalienable rights as US citizens, employees, students, taxpayers, and voters. They are demonstrating that their voices are louder than the boom of any cannon and becoming impossible to ignore.

Challenge Your Assumptions

Aunque salga de manos afueranos, el dinero siempre huele a rosas.
Translation: Although it may come from unfamiliar hands, money always smells like roses.
Transcreation: Stop to smell the roses.

In the past, much of the hesitancy in targeting the Hispanic Consumer Market (HCM) or Latino communities by most private and public entities was blamed on a lack of Spanish-language skills, previously failed attempts, and the assumption that Latinos could not afford nor appreciate the benefits of one's products or services—or all of the above.

The health and sustainability of any corporate, public, or nonprofit organization is directly linked to the loyalty and support of its stockholders, stakeholders, taxpayers and employees. Establishing mutually benefiting relationships with Latinos requires positive relationships with Hispanic-owned businesses, community-based organizations and media: in essence, those that influence their attitudes, behaviors and opinions.

Record-setting US economic growth in the latter half of the twentieth century resulted in quantifiable improvements in Latino social and economic status. From 1990 to 2000, total US "minority" buying power nearly doubled over the previous decade, growing at a faster rate than the nation overall. This was also a major indicator of the consumer sophistication occurring among consumers "of color." Latinos made major contributions to this record economic growth in the 1990s, with both their high rates of workforce participation and consumer spending.

The Selig Center, reported Latinos led all other major US ethnic and racial groups in the rate of growth of purchasing power and had become a vital part of the economies in their neighborhoods and surrounding communities. Hispanic purchasing power between 1990 and 2010 grew by 413 percent; followed by Asian/Pacific Islanders at 397 percent, Native Americans at 251 percent, African Americans at 222 percent, and non-Hispanic whites at 165 percent.

The HCM demonstrated an increased understanding and ability to purchase a variety of products and services available to them. In 2005, market research indicated Latinos were well above the average (over-indexed) in purchase and use in almost all categories of "high-tech" electronics, particularly "in-home entertainment" and "smart-phone" categories. This included many of the latter's incremental revenue-generating add-ons that ranged from ring-tones, long-distance calling and total calling minutes per month plans, use of text messaging, data/photo transfers, and purchase of high-speed Internet access.

Factors related to their cultural identity also affected Latino attitudes toward food purchases. A 2000 Census Bureau comparison of household family size had Latinos at 3.62, blacks at 2.74 and whites at 2.43—the national average was 2.59. Larger families mean proportionately higher spending levels for home-cooked and out-of-home meals.

MOVIN' ON UP

Despite lower levels of education (as a group) and social and economic discrimination, Latinos have managed to see some of their financial and social aspirations become realities. Proof of that progress is reflected in the number of them entering the ranks of the middle class. By the end of the twentieth century, the Latino middle-class was entrenched as a viable consumer and economic force.

According to the National Association of Hispanic Real Estate Professionals (NAHREP), Latinos are also beginning to drive growth in housing demand. During the third quarter of 2011, their homeownership rose to a rate of 47.6 percent, growing by 288,000 units, accounting for more than half of the total growth in homeownership (53 percent) in the US during that period—driving it to its highest level with 6.5 million homeowners.

A national study released by the Tomás Rivera Policy Institute (TRPI) at the University of Southern California, revealed the Latino middle-class grew at a whopping 80 percent during the 1980 and 1990 decades—a rate three times higher than that of non-Hispanic whites. The presence of a Latino middle-class began dispelling the belief that all Latinos were poor, underedu-cated, and lacked ambition—unfounded stereotypes carried-over from entertainment and news media depictions (Tomas Rivera Policy Institute, *National Study*).

In Southern California—home to 25 percent of the nation's Hispanic population—Pepperdine University studies revealed the existence of a substantial and steadily growing Latino mid-dle-class in the five-county Southern California region (Los Angeles, Orange, Riverside, San Bernardino and Ventura). It was composed of both US- and foreign-born groups that shared numerous cultural values and behaviors. In other areas of the country with established Latino communities (i.e., Florida, Texas, and the Chicagoland area), parity had also been reached and exceeded.

The NAHREP report, "2011 State of Hispanic Homeownership Report," also found upscale Latino house-holds—those earning more than $100,000 per year—accounted for 21 percent of all households. Between 2000 and 2010, their number more than doubled, going from 1.3 million to 2.9 million.

KEEPING UP WITH THE JONESES

The Latino middle-class is rapidly catching-up to their non-Hispanic white peers. It stands to reason they can afford (and appreciate) many of the products and services readily available to other US consumers. However, bridging the cultural gap that exists between Latinos and the private, public, and nonprofit sectors wishing to reach them must be resolved if there are to be mutually beneficial results.

The most obvious example of their growing economic contributions to our nation is the amount of money Latinos are paying into the Social Security program. It is ironic that their contributions to this federal entitlement program (from which they were initially barred) will ensure retirement funds to an aging non-Hispanic population.

As expressed in previous chapters, education and employment opportunities are the keys that unlock the doors to the American Dream in the US. They allow families to become more discerning consumers and civic-minded citizens. This fact is not lost on a growing number of corporations, public agencies and nonprofit organizations that are opening their doors to an increasingly diverse population and marketplace.

In an era of keen competitive activity, where little distinguishes quality and price of products and services among competitors, Latinos look to other factors that will help them decide what to buy—and from whom. They want to maintain their cultural values, enjoy the fruits of their labors, and have the opportunity to live their lives unfettered by the prejudice and discrimination encountered by themselves and previous generations.

At the start of the new millennium, the Hispanic consumer marketing and community outreach had been allocated resources in the plans and budgets of most large companies and organizations interested in engaging this consumer giant. But, senior management's interest in reaching a larger share of the HCM still may not have been fully understood (or supported) with the same fervor by all employees.

In the past, a popular excuse for not funding ethnic-specific outreach had been that this segment of the market was being adequately reached through English-language campaigns and media, negating the need for additional resources to develop separate "in-language" campaigns. This rationale was generally attributable to the long-held belief in the melting pot concept of assimilation: Latinos would eventually go the way of previous immigrants and assimilate into the English-speaking mainstream, in spite of their non-European white heritage.

A lack of Spanish-language skills, along with varying degrees of cultural enlightenment, also contributed to the belief that Spanish-language or Latino outreach campaigns could not be as easily monitored or evaluated as English-language efforts. The truth of the matter is that efforts to communicate with Latino audiences require perspectives and skill sets not readily available to most non-Hispanic professionals. Inasmuch as every sale has the five basic obstacles to overcome—need, money, urgency, desire and trust—accuracy, cultural relevance and political correctness require professionals who possess language capabilities and cultural competence to ensure campaigns address these barriers—or at the very least, know how and when to access such expertise.

Another consideration has been who would oversee Latino initiatives. Many marketing and communication managers still tend to be skeptical about the benefits of such efforts, especially if funding for general market campaigns for which they were responsible were subject to reduction. Many practitioners have identified this type of "foot-dragging" as part of a more prevalent concern on the part of managers: a concern with organizational power and advancement. In most professional environments the amount of financial resources one controls is generally associated with power and incluence, essentials to climbing the career ladder. As you can imagine, power is not readily relinquished.

MAPPING OUT THE JOURNEY

To minimize the "silo effect"—independent efforts by internal departments with little (or no) coordination with their fellow departments' objectives—senior management must establish policies and procedures for implementing effective community and HCM outreach initiatives. Companies with the best bottom lines and greatest market shares related to Hispanic (and other targeted) consumers generally have practitioners with the professional and cultural expertise to effectively design and direct such outreach, and more often than not allocate the financial resources to ensure success. Generally, increased "share of voice" (paid advertising or earned media coverage) results in a higher "share of market." Most veteran practitioners understand and subscribe to this time-tested "rule of thumb."

Credit must be given to the ingenuity of visionary professionals who foresaw Hispanic population growth and planned for it. Despite the many reasons given for previous failures to integrate "emerging" and "target" markets into general market campaigns, early efforts helped to launch a process of inclusion within companies and organizations that understood the value of racial, ethnic, and gender diversity in their organizations.

The initial inclusion of blacks and women into entry-level and middle-management staff positions allowed for increased sharing of divergent points of view with predominantly white male executives and managers. As a result, substantial strides were made to ensure communication efforts became culturally relevant and politically correct. Still, many of these same executives failed to acknowledge the successful initiatives that had worked in addressing racial and gender differences with blacks and women did not translate into successful outreach efforts with culturally and geographically diverse Latino audiences.

A common language—English—facilitated the inclusion of African American and women into general market initiatives related to marketing: advertising, community outreach, citizen participation, merchandising, and promotions. Historically, creative and policy decision-making had been under the control of white males, but that changed to include previously excluded non-male white groups. Representation in the creative process on the part of historically excluded segments of the population led to a reduction of gaffes related to race, ethnicity, and gender, resulting in more effective and politically correct campaigns. If you have doubts, just look at the industry leaders in ethnic market share and see how they are developing and sustaining consumer trial and loyalty while enjoying increased profits.

DEGREES OF SEPARATION

Approaching the Latino community or Hispanic consumers was, and remains, one of the more difficult challenges facing culturally-challenged, monolingual English-speakers. In the early 1980s, Lionel Sosa and Ernest Bromley of the San Antonio, TX-based Sosa & Associates advertising agency unveiled an "Acculturation Index Group" (AIG) concept, which basically identified acculturation and assimilation levels of Latinos in the US. The AIG was a useful tool for early target marketers and political campaigns in how to be more effective in reaching Latinos from the national (macro) to the local (micro) levels, and even within specific zip codes. At the time, AIG was a new tool for proponents of the "think global, act local" approach to marketing and community outreach initiatives.

On one end of the AIG spectrum was the least acculturated/assimilated group of Latinos, and the most divergent from the nation's white Eurocentric mainstream. This group was primarily foreign-born, Spanish-language dominant, consisting of a high number of adults with minimal amounts of formal education, and mostly unfamiliar with US mores values, and behaviors.

On the other end, was the most acculturated/assimilated, English-dominant group that reflected consumer patterns most similar to their NHW counterparts. Its cohorts were primarily second-generation (and beyond), US-born and educated, and quite familiar with most cultural, economic, political, and civic aspects of white Eurocentric society.

Between the two ends of the spectrum was the bilingual-bicultural group, which formed the largest segment of the HCM, estimated to be between one-half to two-thirds of the entire US Hispanic population. These bilingual/bicultural Latinos were (and still are) the most difficult to classify. They are neither as culturally isolated as the least assimilated, nor as fully acculturated into mainstream society as their white Eurocentric peers. In essence they could effectively navigate in and out of either end of the Latino spectrum.

By 2008, Cesar Melgoza and David Perez, of Latin Force Group in New York, NY, had further refined the HCM into five yet more distinct categories and estimated percentages of the Hispanic population:

- *HA-1: Americanizado* (Americanized) = 15.1 percent
   English dominant (practically no Spanish)
   US-born (generally 3 or more US generations)
   Little-to-no Latino cultural practices

- *HA-2: Nuevo Latino* (New Latino or "retro-acculturated")
  = 26.4 percent
  > English preferred (some Spanish)
  > US-born (generally 2nd generation)
  > Some-to-moderate Latino cultural practices

- *HA-3: Bi-cultural* = 27.4 percent
  > Bilingual (equally/nearly)
  > Immigrant (child/young adult) or 1st generation
  > Moderate-to-considerable Latino cultural practices

- HA-4: Hispano = 17.0 percent
  > Spanish Preferred (some English)
  > Immigrated as an adult, in US 10+ years
  > Predominant Latino cultural practices

- *HA-5: Latinoamericano* (Latin American) = 14.1 percent
  > Spanish Dominant (almost no English)
  > Recent Immigrant as adult (less than 10 years)
  > Primarily Latino cultural practices
  > Identifies with home country more than US

Exact Latino segmentation remains a challenge for practition-ers who develop outreach or communication programs for the diverse Latino audiences and markets. Non-Hispanic research is also being conducted on a number of recent immigrant and established cultural groups. In 2008 the Manhattan Institute released the findings of its 2006 Assimilation study. Using a scale of 0-100, it measured levels of assimilation for the ten largest immigrant groups in the US in three specific areas: economics, culture, and civic involvement.

Four of the ten groups were of Latin American origin: Mexican, Salvadoran, Cuban, and Dominican.

Size:	Nationality/Country:	Economic:	Cultural:	Civic:
1	Mexico	66	51	22
2	Philippines	100	72	65
3	India	96	39	40
4	China	90	40	47
5	Vietnam	99	53	55
6	Korea	100	64	55
7	El Salvador	71	55	29
8	Canada	100	100	43
9	Cuba	100	65	53
10	Dominican Republic	84	71	48

In the economic category, Latin-American immigrant groups (with the exception of Cuba) were not as assimilated as the other six groups; they ranged from a low of sixty-six (Mexican) to a high of one hundred (Cuban).

Regarding culture, the four Latino groups ranged from a low of fifty-one (Mexican) to a high of seventy-one (Dominican), the average being slightly higher than mid-point in the index ratings. Civic involvement ranged from a low of twenty-two (Mexican) to a high of fifty-three (Cuban). The Manhattan Institute concluded that for outreach efforts to effectively engage the greatest number of any immigrant group, practitioners must consider the lowest levels of assimilation by members of each immigrant group that is part of their target audience.

TRANSLATE OR TRANSCREATE?

A popular notion for reaching Spanish-speaking audiences was to simply adapt strategies and tactics similar to those created for blacks or women audiences, with one major difference: translation of English copy into *español*. It wasn't (and still isn't) quite that simple! But as with other consumer segmentation refinements, it is becoming easier to understand why.

There are numerous examples of mistakes committed in attempting to "literally" translate media campaigns into Spanish without giving the necessary attention to cultural, regional, and contextual factors. Most writers agree that a translation can never be equal to the original work. It can approximate, but its effectiveness can only be judged by its accuracy in how close it really gets to communicating the concept in its original language. Translation errors have proven to be costly and, much to the surprise of management, avoidable.

Among the most popular culprits contributing to the least effective translations are the oft-cited "legal requirements," "pride of authorship," and "creative license" used by many English-speaking executives, creative professionals and legal staffs who demand "literal" translations of their ad copy, themes, and text. Over the years, this concern with literal precision in translations has been relaxed as a result of numerous and unintentional, yet costly, mistakes.

In the early stages of ethnic, "in-language" marketing communication, whenever incorrect or inaccurate aspects of any campaign were raised, many creative professionals became defensive and challenged changes in the translation of their creative concepts. This was a logical reaction by individuals who operated in an "English-only" environment where nuance, puns, double entendres, and innuendo help to shape messages to targeted English-speaking audiences.

In English, the reference to someone being "up to one's ears" in work or debt is clearly understood to mean "deeply involved" or "overwhelmed." A phrase in Spanish to describe the same concept is "*Hasta las cejas*" (up to one's eyebrows). If the original English message, visuals, graphics, or context contain references to "ears" the analogy and its cultural relevance is lost. If there is no reference to eyebrows, the message becomes confusing—or worse, nonsensical.

Another common defense for inaccurate translations was, and I paraphrase: "These concepts, treatments, or drafts have been reviewed by another Spanish-speaker who validated the use and accuracy of the language we are using."

In many of such instances the people who reviewed Spanish language materials for creative writers and designers were often assumed to be proficient in both languages. However, these bilingual "experts" were often in jobs unrelated to advertising, marketing, journalism, or public relations. Also, these well-meaning accomplices had limited professional experience in oral or written communications—or ad copywriting. In English language assignments, professional practitioners do not normally rely on a receptionist, cafeteria employee, or delivery man to edit or revise text or campaign concepts simply because they speak English. Yet, some practitioners frequently turned to the nearest or most accessible Spanish-surnamed individual or "self professed" Spanish-speaker to review concepts, messages, and treatments aimed at Latino audiences.

The problem—as well as the solution—leads back to "who" was in a position to determine such skills? Field-testing should be S-O-P (standard operating procedure) and is highly recommended. But, the review of marketing and communication materials targeting Latino audiences by Spanish-speaking professionals is only one of several professional steps that must be taken to ensure effective use of grammar, idioms, and cultural relevancy of communications. Insuring one's message accurately communicates in Spanish that which was conceptualized in English is the ultimate goal—an elusive one for those not familiar with the culture, history, and level of in-language literacy of those at whom the information is aimed.

Spanish-English dictionaries, computerized translation software, and translation "apps" are becoming commonplace in offices of those who occasionally develop or review Spanish-language materials. But these types of resources are limited in that they mostly provide literal translations without the benefit of contextual or cultural reference points. Many of these types of resources compare English words to common substitute words in Spanish, which in many cases may not have the same meaning or nuance as the intended concept, text or theme.

Traditionally, the "literal" approach to translations has been the one used by non-Spanish speakers who had to make judgment calls about "in-language" communications, often without knowledge of the targeted audiences' idioms, cultures, or degrees of assimilation.

LOST IN TRANSLATION

Many Spanish speakers enjoy a "play on words" game called "*No es lo mismo.*" (It's not the same). It's the use of puns or homonyms: "*No es lo mismo: 'Me río en el baño.' o 'Me baño en el río'.*" (It's not the same: "I laugh in the bath tub." as "I bathe in the river.") Already, by translating the phrases literally into English the word game has lost some its original humor and entertainment value.

The noun *río* is Spanish for "river" and the noun *baño* is Spanish for bathtub; whereas the indicative, present form of the verb *río* in Spanish is "I laugh" (from the infinitive verb: *reír*, to laugh) and the indicative, present form of the verb *baño* in Spanish is "I bathe" (from the infinitive verb: *bañar*, to bathe). As demonstrated by this example, context is critical in conveying the intended thoughts from one language to another.

It is the opinion of most bilingual communication experts that the best translators are actually "transcreators"—those who have language skills in composing works similar to those being "translated." A lack of expertise in either language (or subject) seriously limits one's chances of arriving at the most effective communication of the original concept from one language to another.

Language is the most fundamental communication tool of any culture. Those involved in bilingual communications understand that effective transcreations require an ability to move easily among the words and context used in both the initiating and receiving languages, as well as the specific cultures and key reference points of the targeted audiences.

As in English, there also must be a "targeted" level of comprehension. Over the years, an inability to understand the nuances of the Spanish speaker's culture has resulted in countless *mea culpas* (Latin plural for "my fault."). Such mistakes underscore the need for literacy in both language and culture in order to effectively convey the intended meaning of English-language materials to targeted cultural and Spanish-speaking groups.

THE ENVELOPE, PLEASE

Many early attempts at Spanish language campaigns resulted in irreparable damage to corporate reputations and brand images among targeted Latino customers. Many of these now infamous blunders can be attributed to good intentions; nevertheless, they still elicit raised eyebrows (as well as a few chuckles) among enlightened professionals. Here are a few examples:

- The defunct Braniff Airline's ad informing Spanish-speakers they could fly in luxuriant leather (*cuero*) seats. Braniff's invitation to fly '*en cuero*' (in leather) was perceived as '*encuero*' or naked.

- Chicken magnate Frank Perdue's line, 'It takes a tough man to make a tender chicken,' came out literally as: '*Toma a un hombre duro para hacer un pollo tierno'* (It takes a sexually aroused man to make a chicken tender).

- Volkswagen launched a US ad campaign featuring its 2006 GTI model on a black and white billboard that featured two words in big, bold letters: *'Turbo Cojones.'* The word *'cojones'* is Spanish for testicals or in English slang: "balls." Complaints from Spanish-speakers offended by the vulgarity of the ad copy prompted VW to remove the billboards and print ads in key Hispanic markets of: Miami, New York, and Los Angeles.

What these aforementioned examples demonstrated was the need for language to be culturally relevant, accurate, appropriate, and respectful. You should be aware that Spanish has both a formal and informal way of communicating, depending on the relationship you have established with the audience. By using the familiar *"Tu"* for "You" when the formal *"Usted"* is expected, one risks sounding presumptuous or even disrespectful. Not the first impression you want to make.

The use of commonly understood words in Spanish does not ensure comprehension. One must use the appropriate words—and in the proper context—used by Spanish-speakers to describe the concept wishing to be conveyed in English. To effectively "transcreate" an English-speaker's message into Spanish, it is essential that both the sender and receiver of the message understand the concept wishing to be communicated.

A concept that might be receptive to a young, athletic, and trendy audience may not resonate with an older, cosmopolitan, and urbane segment of the marketplace. This is why it is prudent to use experienced, professional communicators who relate to both Spanish and English languages, as well as to the "mind sets" of the intended audiences, not unlike market segmentation processes and related demographic research used for English-language campaigns.

In the end, language is simply a tool with which we attempt to replicate in other peoples' minds the concepts and emotions we wish to convey from one language to another. Marketing and communication campaigns are an interdependent collection of language, culture, and symbols; the comprehension of these campaigns by the targeted audiences will determine one's success.

The "once burned, twice shy" communicator has been hesitant to attempt subsequent Latino outreach efforts due to the fear of yet another failure, or because of their lack of confidence in how to best reach their targeted audiences. A common reaction to questions about continuing outreach to the HCM or Latino audiences has been: "We tried that once and we didn't get the desired or anticipated results."

Welcome to show business! For that is what messaging is— an attempt to capture the attention of targeted audiences in a positive, entertaining, and relevant manner. It's one thing to have a well-designed ad or campaign message miss its mark because of poor aesthetics, wrong use of media, or promoting a product during the wrong time of the year; it's another to offend the audience through inappropriate language or culturally irrelevant themes and concepts.

Still, there is an upside to such failed attempts! Some Latinos have actually been impressed by mangled translations, which often were accepted as good intentions in efforts to recognize their market's existence, language, and culture. But are good intentions enough, or is one expected to strive for the same level of excellence in Spanish that we have come to expect from English language efforts? Your competitors already know the answer to that question.

Can the private and public sectors afford to wait for the "inevitable" assimilation of Latinos into the US melting pot? Many corporations, public agencies, and nonprofit organizations think not; they are looking to their communication experts for ways to best address the increasing challenges of cultural relevance in communications to the Latino community.

A question for many non-Spanish speaking practitioners is simply, "Do you possess the necessary skills to deal with the evolution of the marketplace from a traditional 'one size fits all' environment, to a diverse multicultural bazaar?" If not, then the next question might be: "Is my company, agency, or organization prepared to invest in experts who can provide us with culturally competent perspectives?"

A major difference between today's Hispanics, Latinos, and *mestizos* and past generations is the phenomenon known as globalization. Inexpensive air travel, Internet communications, and the growth of Spanish-language media outlets (that provide culturally relevant content) allow both native-born and immigrants to maintain ties to their extended families, cultural roots, and motherlands.

Latinos are ready, willing, and able to invest their consumer dollars in those companies that want them as customers. By making assumptions that have outlived their their "uselessness" in determining if someone is a potential buyer of your products or services in today's marketplace can cost you market share and profits.

Go ahead, stop and smell the roses! You could profit from the experience.

Cultural Common Sense

Quien desea aprender, pronto llegará a saber.
Translation: Who desires to learn will quickly come to know.
Transcreation: Adapt or perish is nature's inexorable imperative.

"Core competency" is the fundamental knowledge, ability, or expertise in a specific subject area or skill set. It is what gives an organization its competitive advantages in creating and delivering products and/or services to its targeted audiences. In essence, it is the internal values of an individual, organization, or business. The term is relatively new and is believed to have originated in a 1990 *Harvard Business Review* article written by C.K. Prahalad and Gary Hamel. They wrote that a core competency is "an area of specialized expertise that is the result of harmonizing complex streams of technology and work activity" (Hamel, *The Core Competence*).

In the article the authors suggested business functions not identified as one of an organization's "core competencies" should be outsourced to experts outside the organization, if and when economically feasible. It is safe to assume that awareness of ethnic and racial groups' cultures is not a core competency of most US organizations and businesses; ergo for the foreseeable future, outsourcing may be the way to ensure success in an increasingly diverse marketplace.

One definition of cultural competence in ethnic marketing is the ability to recognize, understand, and interact effectively with members of targeted cultural, ethnic and language groups. To fully understand cultural competence, it is important to know that it consists of four fundamental elements:

A. Awareness of one's own cultural perspective.

B. One's attitude towards other cultures.

C. One's knowledge of other cultural customs and mores.

Ñ. Command of cross-cultural skills or resources.

Culture is the range of activities, attitudes, and values of a group of people with shared traditions, language, and life experiences that are transmitted and reinforced by members of that group. It is the lens through which individual members of different ethnic, gender, nationality, political, racial, and other distinct societies view their respective worlds. These cultural lenses enable members of the group to focus on what they see, process what they see, and communicate that experience.

Many aspects of different cultures are readily apparent, even to the untrained eye: art, customs, food, language, and music. The most difficult to observe and decipher requires considerable time and interest in learning about intangibles like beliefs, values, expectations, attitudes, and assumptions. Such cultural predispositions influence both individual and group attitudes and determine what is "normal" for that particular group. It is intangibles like these that the dominant groups perceive as being abnormal and who frequently magnify differences between themselves and other groups, often leading to misunderstanding and/or conflict.

Culturally competent individuals tend to value *Emotional Intelligence* (EQ), one of the professional communication tools used to tap into the mindsets of targeted audiences. Another useful skill is *Cultural Intelligence* (CQ), the ability to function effectively in culturally diverse environments or social settings. Whereas EQ provides practitioners a set of skills that are increasingly necessary for dealing with a rapidly changing society and marketplace, CQ is the ability to appreciate various cultures (including one's own), using one's senses and adapting gestures and body language to mirror those of the targeted groups, thereby gaining desired results and strength from successful cultural interactions.

Together, EQ and CQ offer practitioners wishing to augment their core competencies the ability to recognize and choose the appropriate actions in order to obtain positive results in their interactions with people of different cultures. In communication circles, they encompass the skills necessary to say the "right thing" to the "right person" at the "right time" — regardless of their own cultural orientation. Our country's rapidly changing demographics underscores the need for cultural competency skills that will enable people to function more effectively in a culturally diverse society and marketplace.

EVALUATING YOUR OPTIONS

There are many thoughts on how to enhance cultural competency. The logical place to start is in expanding one's knowledge of those cultures that affect your personal, as well as your organization's, mission, goals, and objectives. The increased attention given Latino consumers and stakeholders has resulted in a series of questions from professionals who find themselves challenged by efforts on how to best reach out to them:

A. "What type of expertise do I really need?

B. "Can I get by with my general market skills and resources?"

C. "Should I hire a Latino agency or competent internal staff?"

Latino agencies and consultants are the obvious place to start. They generally possess an edge in experience and cultural relevance, making them more effective in reaching out to the Hispanic Consumer Market (HCM) and other non-white markets. The major advantage of most Latino agencies' is their innate cultural intelligence, especially if they share the same experiences as your targeted audience; they understand the influence of Hispanic, Latino, and *mestizo* culture on consumer behaviors and can identify the essential elements required to design and execute culturally relevant campaigns.

Increasingly, Latino agencies and consultants are demonstrating expertise in general market advertising, and public relations campaigns that allow them to efficiently adapt general market campaign themes into Spanish, *Spanglish*, and other culturally oriented messages to effectively reach the eyes, ears, and minds of targeted audiences and those who influence them.

Traditional business practices have created a dilemma for private and public executives under pressure to communicate with diverse segments of the population, while maintaining long-term relationships with their current general market agencies and consultants. Many client-side practitioners, who may have honed their professional skills while employed by general market agencies, now find themselves in positions of selecting those agencies to provide them marketing and communications services.

In order to retain business relationships with existing clients interested in the ethnic markets, many general market agencies have gone the merger and acquisition route to add cultural competency to their internal staffs' skills. Larger US and multinational agencies are purchasing and integrating "boutique shops" into their stable of affiliated companies. By allowing ethnic agency principals to retain at least 51 percent ownership of acquired agencies they retain "minority" status and qualify for a variety of private and public sector vendor/supplier business opportunities identified under corporate social responsibility goals.

Do corporate and nonprofit clients need to continue relying on general market expertise and long-term relationships with their traditional agencies, or do they want the ethnic and cultural competence Latino agencies and consultants bring to the table? These and other related questions are being more frequently posed by those who decide which agencies can best help them attract the $1 trillion HCM and improve their relationships with Latino employees, students, taxpayers, and voters. Examples of these fundamental questions are:

A. Which of these two agency options provide the most cost-effective and logical solutions to accomplish HCM outreach and related goals and objectives?

B. How will vendor/supplier opportunities designed to improve economic development in the Latino community affect public perceptions of my company?

C. Are corporate citizenship and social responsibility initiatives enough of a reason to warrant doing business with Hispanic-owned companies in the eyes of consumers, community leaders, shareholders and media?

Another historical strength of traditional marketing, advertising and public relations agencies has been their networks of (and access to) "influencers" who can affect their clients' businesses and/or interests. As the marketplace and political environments continue to reflect more diversity perhaps the more appropriate question might be: "Should the selection of communications resources be an "either/or" proposition?"

For the foreseeable future, general market agencies will continue to dominate the marketing and communications fields due to established business relationships (and personal networks) with their clients and staff members. However, as the US Hispanic population continues to grow, general market agencies must fend-off the encroachment and progress being demonstrated by culturally competent, Latino-owned firms that are also establishing positive relationships with clients interested in the nation's fastest-growing consumers, employees, entrepreneurs, students, taxpayers, and voters.

Historically, the most cost-effective general market campaigns have been those that have an aggregation of professional resources and specialists working in concert with agencies of record. General market campaigns and projects have utilized a host of "specialty" shops and consultants on their marketing and communication teams; it may be time to incorporate this same comprehensive practice to Hispanic marketing and Latino community outreach efforts to ensure cultural competence.

ACES IN THEIR PLACES

As the levels of sophistication in segmenting the HCM and Latino community audiences grow, so must the need to assign ethnic outreach to staff members with the highest levels of potential success. To effectively communicate and market to diverse consumers and targeted audiences, private and public organizations must avoid the pitfalls encountered by their predecessors in selecting individuals to oversee efforts and initiatives aimed at the Latino community.

Traditionally, Spanish-language skills or a Spanish surname have been the most popular criteria for selecting individuals to manage or monitor Latino outreach projects. While this approach has generally addressed the superficial issues, it has not uniformly provided the expertise to ensure effective, culturally relevant campaigns.

Consider that general market advertising and communication projects have seldom been assigned to staff members solely on the basis of being able to speak English or having a recognizable white European surname. Yet, an alarming number of organizations entrust their Hispanic marketing and communication initiatives to staff members on the basis of a Spanish surname (with the hope that it somehow equates to literacy in Spanish and cultural relevance to the targeted audience), rather than basing decisions on the professional expertise required for the position: education, bilingual proficiency, knowledge of the Latino marketplace and/or targeted audiences—plus demonstrated experience and success.

CASTE VS. CULTURE

Just as a Spanish surname or fluency in Spanish does not guaranty success for Latino initiatives, neither does being Hispanic, Latino, or a Spanish speaker. There are Latin Americans who do not appreciate or understand the experiences common to most US-born Latinos, nor do they identify with the economic, educational, political, and social issues associated with members of this community. Additionally, a substantial number of native- and foreign-born professionals do not wish to be relegated to Hispanic/Latino "career tracks" or assignments; many want the opportunity to succeed in ethnic- and race-neutral assignments. They want to be judged solely by the same job-related and performance standards as their non-Hispanic peers.

This attitude is often due to class status in their countries of origin, which helps to explain why many Latin American professionals distance themselves from stereotypic characteristics and traits attributed to Latinos and *mestizos* by non-Hispanic whites. Some even question the need for the US civil rights movement that resulted in diversity recruitment and "affirmative action" employment practices that may have indirectly resulted in their own career opportunities.

The short history of ethnic marketing and community outreach is replete with examples of individuals responsible for projects who had little in common with the targeted audience; or worse, demonstrated attitudes and behaviors indicating levels of indignation in working with segments of a community they perceived to be antithetical to their personal, social, or economic status. Such individuals may often be the ones expressing how they succeeded on their own and don't agree or understand complaints from "minorities" about the lack of equal opportunity or discrimination. Attitudes such as these do not require a quantum jump to understand them, especially if one recognizes the complex caste system created by the ruling classes hundreds of years ago throughout the Americas.

In an effort to facilitate assimilation into a majority white Eurocentric society, a substantial number of US-born Latinos abandoned their Spanish-speaking ability and cultural trappings in efforts to adapt to white Eurocentric values and behaviors and to ensure success in their chosen social and career paths. Some have elected to eschew all things Latino related to advocacy, heritage, and community involvement. In most cases, naming a disinterested Latino employee to direct ethnic initiatives can prove to be disastrous to your organization's image and bottom line.

Conversely, not everybody who oversees ethnic programs is required to be of that particular ethnicity. An individual with a high IQ (Intelligence Quotient), an above average EQ (Emotional Intelligence), and an interest in CQ (Cultural Intelligence) can become a valuable resource by virtue of the manner in which she/he conduct themselves with targeted audiences. Inasmuch as senior executives don't gamble on exceptions to meet their goals and objectives, it is critical that the professionals in charge of managing or monitoring efforts to reach Latino consumers, employees, students, taxpayers, and voters be as culturally relevant and competent as possible. But who will you trust to make that decision within your organization?

TALK THE TALK, WALK THE WALK

The type of individual in which an organization places its trust for communicating to its targeted audiences is critical to the success of that organization's mission. In too many instances the responsibility for these programs is too far removed from C-suite (an office for those with "Chief" in their titles) executives, leaving strategic marketing, outreach, and public relations matters in the hands of entry- to mid-level who may not fully comprehend management's strategies to promote products/services to ethnic and other targeted segments of the population.

But how do you go about selecting the right person for the job? First and foremost, understand there are a number of enthusiastic professionals already in the "pipeline" who can maintain the balance between an organization's mission and its relationship to the Latino community. Being "community oriented" does not imply disloyalty to an employees' organization or its goals. Due to their life experiences and commitments to reinvest in their families, friends, and community, these members of the team can provide employers with valuable insights into the "public square" and marketplace. This community advocate often results in helping to build consumer loyalties and ensures positive relationships between an organization and community-based organizations and leaders in increasingly diverse and competitive markets. Furthermore, they view community outreach skills as compatible with their professional careers.

Unfortunately, these employees have a "quit rate" higher than that of their non-Hispanic peers. To adequately address this attrition, employers should create inclusion and retention initiatives to improve advancement opportunities for Latinos and other non-white employees by providing support and mentoring—in much the same way they are made available to other members of their team. Research and "exit interviews" have found that most managers engage in work and personal relationships with their staffs and provide them greater work related rewards than those in ethnic and/or minority oriented jobs. Unless employers correct the reasons for their "quit rate" problems, efforts to attract culturally competent employees, executives, and board members may never get them to the levels of diversity they need to insure they remain competitive in a rapidly changing marketplace.

THE BUCK STOPS WHERE?

A survey conducted by global public relations firm Weber Shandwick in 2006 found many global executives assign nearly 60 percent of the blame to CEOs when companies encounter a loss of reputation after most types of conflicts or public relations issues. The survey also indicated many of the factors causing "reputation loss" was frequently self-inflicted and could have been averted.

Surveyors suggested companies must improve their public image and "reputation radar" systems to quickly identify and track impending or potential threats detrimental to their public image and stock value. The fact that one third of the global *Fortune 500* experienced damaged reputations in their "Most Admired" status the year previous to this survey reinforced the findings.

Surprisingly, corporations and nonprofits continue to overlook how poor relationships with community and special interest groups can be damaging to their sustainability; especially, if they are not prepared to address their issues quickly and decisively. These types of decision-making skills are not generally well honed among entry-level or middle management professionals. The survey also underscored how corporate, non-profit, and public sectors executives might be underestimating the need to identify "early warning" signs of challenges to their organizations' reputations and plan appropriate and timely steps to avoid them.

In increasingly competitive or politically contentious situations, it is not prudent for senior executives to assign critical Corporate Social Responsibility initiatives to low-level subordinates, especially those without the appropriate cultural competencies. There are basic steps an organization can implement in order to avoid potential public relations and image issues with the Latino community, its advocates, and its leadership:

A. Increase the levels of involvement in consumer and community outreach activities by senior management. If senior management doesn't consider this an important segment of the organization's stakeholder or consumer base, why should their direct reports and frontline employees?

B. Assign responsibility for Latino community initiatives to individuals who understand and demonstrate expertise in efforts related to both the targeted audience and the organization's internal operations—individuals who understand the goals and objectives of both internal and external agendas will be more effective. Your organization's representatives must be decision-makers, not messengers. This will create a more positive impression and lead to greater receptivity on the part of targeted audiences, particularly among community leaders and influencers.

C. Provide sufficient fiscal, staffing and technical resources to ensure the effectiveness and success of Latino outreach initiatives and projects. Allocating necessary external resources is considered "investment spending" and critical for developing trust and receptivity on the part of targeted audiences and potential customers. Leveraging and coordinating with other internal CSR initiatives may not even require incremental funding.

The failure of most Latino outreach efforts is directly related to inadequate expertise and/or resources allocated to the initiative. A review of resources made available to your organization's general market initiatives (including staff) compared to the amount being allocated to Latino efforts is a good place to begin when determining funding levels related to ethnic marketing and communication initiatives. This is especially true if Latinos represent a substantial share of your organization's customer base.

PUTTING YOUR BEST
FOOT FORWARD

Individuals charged with consumer and community outreach initiatives must be aware of the organization's overall mission and possess the knowledge of how best to integrate the organization's strategic initiatives—including those of key departments, such as human resources, marketing, philanthropy, and supplier/diversity—directed at Latinos. Meeting their goals and objectives is ensured when your organization speaks with one voice in its outreach efforts.

Strategically an organization's public image responsibility lies squarely on the shoulders of senior management and tactically on the backs of internal staff. Together they share the responsibility of synchronizing departmental messages into a seamless flow of outgoing information. The most effective integrated campaigns are those where an organization's senior staff is receptive to incorporating their respective departmental outreach initiatives into a comprehensive and coordinated external communication campaign. Integration and standardization of messages can be both cost-effective and build trust and confidence among stakeholders in a surprisingly short period of time. The best impression you can make with any targeted audience is that the right hand always knows what the left hand is doing, regardless of the language and cultural "spin" used to deliver the message.

An equally critical skill set is a practitioner's knowledge of, and access to, those who influence opinions of targeted audiences and leaders. Access to community leaders, awareness of community issues, and knowledge of how your organization's products or services are perceived can be helpful in creating campaigns to support marketing, employment recruitment, and other CSR initiatives.

A basic building block of effective communications is conveying to your target audiences that they and their respective communities are appreciated and valued by your organization. Research has found that such communications with the Latino segment often means going beyond the use of Spanish; it requires a substantial level of awareness and relevance to individual and community concerns.

The most effective communication programs are those that resonate with the target audience and reflect the world as seen through "their" eyes. Such insights can only be gained through personal relationships, along with continuously updated community intelligence. Ambassadorial relationships require considerable amounts of time dedicated to community involvement and volunteerism and should be incorporated into every employee's job description from executive to entry levels. This approach allows for the early detection of threats to your organization's reputation and/or image by involvement of senior management in key community activities and events related to business interests—an involved senior staff is a great complement to your culturally competent, frontline employees!

Frontline staff must possess high Cultural Quotients—firsthand knowledge of your organization's targeted Latino communities, which is generally gained by interacting with community leaders and becoming familiar with concerns and issues important to their constituents and neighborhoods. Latinos in particular don't only want to be spoken to, they also want to be heard, understood and appreciated; this requires more than the ability to speak to them in Spanish.

It is critical that your messages be packaged with appropriate amounts of cultural relevance. This requires listening to and interacting with them, an approach used by successful organizations for years and commonly referred to as civic involvement and volunteerism. If you doubt the effectiveness of such practices, check with the top executives of your organization to determine how many community service activities she/he attends or supports on a regular basis.

It is important for Latinos to feel corporations, public agencies, and nonprofits are interested in providing them the same attention and benefits they provide to other market segments. The presence of senior management and employees at Latino events is how community leaders and advocates evaluate an organization's commitment to community relations. Like members of the general market, Latinos are also receptive to messages that address their hopes and dreams. The challenge for practitioners and their organizations is in how accurately they can identify those hopes and dreams and present them in the proper cultural context.

The most successful companies and organizations go beyond Spanish-surnames or employees' Spanish skills when selecting individuals to manage their Latino outreach efforts. They increasingly rely on professionals who demonstrate high levels of empathy toward the targeted audiences and possess the cultural competence to manage communication campaigns and outreach initiatives as part of an organization's coordinated outreach efforts. Having culturally competent "aces in their places" ensures your competitiveness and sustainability in an increasingly diverse marketplace.

A willingness on the part of a company, organization or public agency to invest time and energy is key to driving trial, earning brand loyalty, and increasing stakeholder support. Private and public organizations must demonstrate their ability to "talk the talk" by recognizing the aspirations, culture, and needs of its targeted audiences. Whether you outsource, hire professional staff members, or train your existing staff to manage CSR and Latino outreach, select individuals that best complement the organization's core competencies. Adapt or perish remains nature's inexorable imperative.

Clearing the Path to Your Door

No dejes crecer la hierba en el camino de la amistad.
Translation: Don't allow weeds to grow on the path of
friendship.
Transcreation: Ensure the path to your door is not the one
least traveled.

Ralph Waldo Emerson is credited with coining the phrase:
"Build a better mousetrap, and the world will beat a path to
your door." It was adapted from his original works:

> "If a man has good corn or wood, or boards, or pigs, to sell,
> or can make better chairs or knives, crucibles or church
> organs, than anybody else, you will find a broad hard-
> beaten road to his house, though it be in the woods."

The phrase is a reference to the power of innovation and quality
of products/services that remains applicable to this day. However,
product innovation may no longer be as critical as the marketing of the assortment of modern products and services available
to increasingly diverse consumer preferences. Adapting to the
demographic changes of our nation's population and consumers
has become a major concern for businesses that continue to look
for a competitive advantage.

The nation's civil rights movement of the mid to late 1900s
resulted in many social and economic advancements for our
nation's racial and ethnic minority groups; one was the concept
of "economic reciprocity," which means to the extent a busi-

ness or organization receives its revenues from specific areas of the marketplace, the benefitting entities should reciprocate by reinvesting in those consumers' communities through any of their appropriate corporate social responsibility (CSR) initiatives: Employment, Economic Development, Governance, and Philanthropy. This "one hand washes the other" marketplace practice is representative of the world's most effective community reinvestment models that have been in place for centuries. CSR has become an admired private and public sector practice, one that provides shareholder value to those organizations that practice it best.

CSR is not new, nor foreign, to the private and public sectors in the US. The practice of supporting communities in which organizations operate and where their employees work, live, and play has become the bedrock upon which the most successful businesses have built their economic reciprocity initiatives. Today, CSR is practiced by most of the world's leading companies (and a growing number of public and nonprofit agencies) as a way of ensuring value for stockholders and stakeholders.

For years, major US corporations and public agencies have provided members of their respective communities (and nonprofit community-based organizations) a variety of business and economic perquisites. A quick scan of successful businesses—from product suppliers to constructors of buildings, roads, and bridges, to professional accounting, legal, marketing, and public relations services—that have historically contracted with the private and public sectors demonstrate how well this "reciprocal" arrangement has worked. The success of such businesses and their owners are proof that economic reciprocity has helped develop the health of our national economy.

This type of *quid pro quo* has been the model for US corporate-public partnerships and appears to have worked extremely well since the onset of our nation's Industrial Revolution. US businesses became a major source of employment for residents of communities in which they were established (or expanded into); they provided economic revenues to other local businesses and made charitable contributions to community service groups and nonprofit organizations that led to the overall well being of surrounding communities. These "corporate citizens" also appointed local community and business leaders to their respective boards of directors, resulting in added civic and political influence for their companies and board members in those communities.

CLEARING THE PATHWAY

Emergence of the Hispanic Consumer Market (HCM), which is growing faster than any other consumer segment in the US, is the major impetus behind the interest in establishing economic reciprocity relationships between Latinos and private and public organizations that benefit from Latinos' financial support. The Hispanic population increased by nearly 400 percent from 1970 to 2010 and has been growing at a rate of some 4,000 people per day, adding over 1.4 million individuals a year to the nation's total.

This consumer potential is being recognized in corporate boardrooms and C-suite offices across the country, especially among those wishing to increase revenues from the HCM. This heightened awareness of economic influence has also raised expectations among Hispanics, Latinos, and *mestizos* who have come to expect social, economic, and political benefits commensurate with their levels of consumer spending.

Even though growth in population and increased consumerism should have resulted in reassessments of the HCM's value to corporations, the marketplace, and society, Latinos are still underrepresented in these reciprocal relationships. From 2000 to 2010, foundation support for Latinos has held steady at an unbelievable "one percent" of total philanthropic funds allocated, despite the fact that Hispanics now are approaching 20 percent of the US population.

Latinos may be influencing society as consumers, taxpayers, and employees, but in the areas of charitable giving, most philanthropic donors haven't seemed to notice. Latinos and their advocates feel it is appropriate that this time-honored practice be expanded to include their communities. At the very least, Latino consumers and their community-based organizations have the same needs and expectations as all other consumers, as it relates to CSR initiatives. In exchange for its growing consumer spending—estimated in 2012 to be nearing $1.2 trillion annually—and customer loyalty, Corporate America, and other institutions that benefit from Latino consumer support, must begin to allocate employment, vendor/supplier contracts, board appointments, and charitable donations on an equitable and equitable basis as they have historically provided to mainstream society.

NEW LEVELS OF SOPHISTICATION

The CSR concept has gained traction among Latino advocacy organizations and community leaders who see the growing value of the HCM to the nation's marketplace and economy. They now are asking private and public sector organizations, "How does our community benefit from its consumer purchases and use of your products or services?"

One such advocate is the Hispanic Association on Corporate Responsibility (HACR) in Washington, DC. It is a coalition of national non-profit organizations representing the more than 50 million Hispanics in the US and Puerto Rico. The organizations represented on its board of directors collaborate with corporate partners and supporters, national nonprofit associations and public and governmental entities that monitor CSR and related economic reciprocity initiatives. HACR's Corporate Partners include many of the most respected and successful companies whose policy makers understand the benefits of CSR as a business practice.

Founded in 1986, HACR's mission is to advance the inclusion of Latinos in Corporate America at a level commensurate with their economic contributions as consumers. It focuses on the same four areas of corporate responsibility and market reciprocity as the nation's corporations: Employment, Procurement, Philanthropy, and Governance.

In pursuit of its mission, HACR offers Corporate America direct access to the Latino community and its professional talent, entrepreneurs, and national leadership by creating forums to ensure effective corporate responsibility and market reciprocity for the nation's Hispanic population, in essence: inclusion in all aspects of corporate operations commensurate with its consumer spending on a corporation's products or services. Through advocacy, education, capacity building, public policy support, resource development, and its political influence in the nation's capitol, HACR speaks on behalf of its coalition's 1,500 affiliated organizations across the nation. That includes more than 450 institutions of higher learning (whose enrollment accounts for approximately 75 percent of all Latino college students), as well as a substantial number of media publications with over 10 million readers—two major resources important to HACR's corporate partners.

It is generally accepted in business circles that economic reciprocity has helped develop and grow our national economy, while improving the quality of life for a great number of consumers whose spending ensures our country's fiscal vitality. Latinos are now looking for a place at the table that their consumer spending has earned them.

CRASHING THE BOARDS

Of the four basic pillars associated with CSR practices, the most difficult for Latinos to access is governance: the appointment to boards of directors. Resistance to inviting "outsiders" into policy-making decisions has been standard operating procedure (SOP) for many reasons, the most often cited is the time-honored need for experience in business, corporate governance, and policymaking. Needless to say, fraternal and business relationships have played a major role in keeping appointments a "good old boys" perk among our nation's corporate governing boards.

Historically vacancies on most boards had been filled by individuals with exposure, previous experience, and access to other corporate boards or directors. A good number of candidates were current or former senior executive officers, current or former board members, or related to (and associates of) current board members.

USA Today provided an insight into the process of board appointments in a 2002 article. It found: "... behind the controls of the nation's top businesses lurks an inner sanctum of friends, colleagues and partners who sit on our nation's corporate boards together." It reported that a cabal of business leaders and their colleagues, those charged with protecting the interests of their stockholders, were overseeing much of the business operations of our nation's major corporations. The article cited numerous examples of the ties that connected many of our nation's most powerful corporations and their directors (Krantz, *Web*).

Eleven of the fifteen largest companies, including Pfizer and Citigroup, had at least two directors who sat together on separate boards, and four had at least two board members in common with another of the top-tier firms.

USA Today reported how nearly 2,000 corporate boards (with more than 22,000 board members) were linked and showed some of the ties between the fifteen largest US companies:

- Pfizer, the giant drug maker, shared at least two board members each with MetLife, J.P. Morgan Chase, Williams, Prudential Financial and Dell Computer.

- Procter & Gamble was similarly connected with General Motors, Alcoa and Rockwell Collins, the latter specializes in electronics for airplanes.

- Telecommunications giant Verizon was linked this way with seven other companies, including fellow corporate giants Procter & Gamble and ExxonMobil.

In all, 200 of the 1,000 largest companies in the US shared at least one board member with another of the top one thousand. More than one thousand board members sat on four or more corporate boards, and 235 on more than six.

In a separate October 2011 article, *USA Today* reported, "Fortune 500 directors could receive median pay of nearly $234,000." The 235 directors who sat on six boards stood to make $1.4 million a year for what amounted to a handful of board and committee meetings—according to a National Association of Corporate Directors study, those meetings required just 4.3 hours a week on board work (Strauss, *Company Directors*).

Prior to the Sarbanes-Oxley Act of 2002—legislation designed to ensure transparency and accountability on the part of corporate and policy-making boards of directors—"outsiders" were few and far between. One of the objectives of the act was to better reflect a greater representation of the nation's consumers. Since Sarbanes-Oxley, efforts to diversity corporate boards has allowed for an increase in involvement by segments of the US population that had been historically excluded.

Among traditional board members and shareholders, a premium had always been placed on what a potential board member could contribute to a company's business objectives. In recent years a new paradigm related to governance has emerged among corporate leaders, thanks in part to Sarbanes-Oxley: the need for responsiveness among policymakers to the changing diversity of the marketplace and its affects on their companies.

Regarding non-white inclusion on corporate boards, in 1998 Walmart rocked both the US corporate and consumer worlds by announcing the appointment of two Latinos to its board of directors: Roland A. Hernández of Los Angeles, CA and José H. Villarreal of San Antonio, TX. The appointment of Hernández (then the President & Chief Executive Officer of *Telemundo*, the nation's second-largest Spanish-language television network) and Villarreal, a partner in the legal firm of Akin Gump Strauss Hauer & Feld, LLP and former board chairman of the National Council of La Raza, still reverberates as a major step by Walmart in its efforts to demonstrate its corporate responsibility commitment to Hispanic consumers, Latino communities and its own stockholders.

These appointments reflected Walmart's proactive efforts to recruit culturally competent directors and its recognition of the changing marketplace. With this single action, it demonstrated that its decision to seek different results required a change in the way it did business. It also underscored the growing importance of the Hispanic Consumer Market to its bottom line. The retail giant had communicated to the nation that like most business practices, the selection of an organization's policymakers must be continuously refined to reflect the marketplace in which an organization conducts its business.

An increasing amount of weight has subsequently been placed on prospective executives and potential board members regarding their levels of expertise about the evolving marketplace. Such objectives require a new type of director, one with skills above and beyond those normally associated with traditional legacy and business pedigrees.

Professional expertise notwithstanding, civic and community involvement—along with political access and influence—are now criteria used to decide which candidates will be invited to join the ranks of governance. Corporate policymakers using these criteria to measure the potential benefits of such directors are starting to reap the rewards of acting "outside the box." This is especially true among those that find themselves increasingly committed to CSR initiatives and their positive effects on "bottom lines."

THE C-SUITE SMELL OF SUCCESS

A growing number of senior C-suite officers and stockholders recognize the need for diverse perspectives in developing policies to meet the challenges of emerging markets. A quick scan of the nation's top corporations reveals a growing number of non-white male and female directors (and senior executives) being admitted into the world of policymaking. Understandably, the selection of prospective corporate executives must include the traditional requirements of business and financial management expertise; but it must also consider those who can help organizations become culturally relevant and competitive in relating to increasingly diverse stakeholders and markets.

Publisher and entrepreneur Malcolm S. Forbes described this approach to diversifying governance as "the art of thinking independently, together." Granted, management and executive officers of any organization should be experts in the management of their organizations' operations, but recruitment and use of professionals who possess added personal and professional knowledge of the changing marketplace is an area where "thinking independently, together" has not kept pace with our country's demographic changes.

USA TODAY ran a story in 2006 entitled "Cingular Calls on 3 Amigos," about a trio of high-powered telecommunication executives at Cingular Wireless in Atlanta, GA. Chief Operating Officer Ralph de la Vega, Chief Information Officer Thaddeus Arroyo and General Counsel Joaquin Carbonell were the "toast of the town" in Corporate America and in Latino communities across the nation (Iwata, *Cingular Calls on '3 Amigos'*).

In addition to maneuvering Cingular through its purchase of AT&T Wireless—a $41 billion merger that spawned the nation's top wireless carrier, with 57 million customers and $30 billion in yearly revenue—the three were instrumental in Cingular's efforts to attract the multibillion-dollar Hispanic Consumer Market in the US, and Latin America.

According to Cingular, family-oriented Latinos were using cell phones and related services at a higher rate than other US consumer groups. Cingular recognized that it needed a management team that understood the high technology wireless business, as well as the cultural nuances of this critical segment of a still untapped marketplace.

USA TODAY rated the three *amigos* as members of the *Fortune 500's* highest-ranking senior executives, which based on the history of corporate board appointments would logically lead to consideration of the three for corporate board appointments.

CAN'T TELL THE PLAYERS WITHOUT A SCORECARD

Why are Latinos so concerned with boardroom diversity? Essentially, it is the cohort of policymakers that determine the goals and objectives of CSR initiatives. At the beginning of the twenty-first century, of the 22,000 board members serving on 2,000 US corporate boards, less than 100 (or .01 percent) were Latino citizens, a situation that had caught the attention of community leaders, media, government regulators, and stakeholder organizations.

In 2004, *Hispanic Business* magazine reported there were only sixty-nine Hispanics listed on the boards of the *Fortune 500* companies and held a total of ninety-six board seats at eighty-eight different publicly-traded corporations. Nineteen of the board seats were at companies that were proactive in Spanish-language advertising; marketing experts pointed to this use of Spanish-language in marketing communications as a key corollary between these companies' targeted markets and the increasing diversity of their boards and C-suite executive ranks.

Hispanic Business found twelve of the board seats were associated with the utilities sector and nine others were from financial institutions (banks or US-sponsored lenders); both industries were government regulated and necessarily sensitive to the benefits of diversity within their respective spheres of influence. The ninety-six board positions filled by Latinos in 2004 represented slightly more than 1.5 percent of the estimated 5,900 seats listed by *Fortune 500* corporations. In 2005, the number remained unchanged.

In 2006, HACR surveyed members of the *Fortune 1000* corporations, ranked according to 2005 revenues, to gauge the most recent levels of "Hispanic inclusion" on corporate boards. A preliminary survey was conducted, followed by verification of the collected data, and concluded with interviews of participating corporations' board members. HACR found the interest in diversifying boards was greatest among the highest ranked *Fortune* companies.

HACR found that among the *Fortune 100*, forty-three Hispanics occupied fifty-one board seats, with seven individuals serving on more than one board. Representation declined dramatically when the survey's universe was expanded to include *Fortune's* 200 through 500 largest companies; only 142 of those 400 corporations reported having Latinos on their boards, for a total of 122 filling 168 board positions, with forty-six serving on more than one board.

There are many US corporations that have not included Latinos in their policymaking or senior executive positions, despite the fact that they account for nearly one in five of all consumers in the US, and by 2008 had already surpassed the $1 trillion per year benchmark in consumer spending. Granted, not all corporations or businesses make products or services that are purchased by Latinos; many have not yet decided if having Latinos on their boards or in high level, policy-making positions will benefit them.

Those companies that find themselves in the process of playing catch-up within their own consumer categories must find ways to become culturally relevant if they wish to attract the fastest growing consumers, future employees, and shareholders. Today, more and more Latinos judge companies, organizations and agencies by their CSR track record—often as much as the quality and cost of their products or services.

In our nation's current economic throes, it is critical that companies and institutions reflect the importance of customers in those marketplaces where they do business. Expanding the employee workforce and governing boards to mirror the actual customer base will help increase market share and revenues.

The path used by consumers and businesses is a two-way street that must be kept clear of obstacles in order to allow for easy and frequent access. Integrating your organization's personnel with people that reflect your customer base ensures the path to your door is not the one least traveled.

About Jim Estrada

Más sabe el diablo por viejo que por diablo.
Translation: The devil knows more because he's old, not
because he's the devil.
Transcreation: Experience teaches the ABCs and *Ñ* of all
things.

Jim Estrada is a nationally renowned practitioner of ethnic marketing, with nearly forty years of advertising, marketing, and public relations experience. In 1992, the Southern
California native founded Estrada Communications Group in
San Antonio, TX, a family-owned and operated agency special-
izing in Marketing Communications and Public Relations. ECG
created a unique niche for itself by providing clients with strategic marketing and culturally relevant insights needed to effectively reach diverse cultural markets. Now based in Austin, TX,
ECG provides its "blue chip" list of clients with counsel related
to the Hispanic Consumer Market (HCM) and its leadership
from throughout the US.

ECG has provided its services to many of the nation's most
respected corporations and private sector clients; among them:
Advantica (Denny's), Anheuser-Busch Companies, AT&T
Mobility (nee Cingular), HISPANIC Magazine, Lopez Foods,
Marathon Oil, McDonald's, MCI, Pizza Hut, Univision
Television Network, Walmart Stores, and Wells Fargo.

A partial list of ECG's nonprofit clients include: California
State University System, Hispanic American Police Command
Officers Association (HAPCOA), Hispanic Association on
Corporate Responsibility (HACR), Latino Institute on Corporate
Inclusion (LICI), National Association of Hispanic Publications
(NAHP), National Council of La Raza (NCLR), National

Society of Hispanic MBAs (NSHMBA), Texas Association of Chicanos in Higher Education (TACHE), Texas State Lottery (GSD&M), Texas State University-San Marcos (*Las Colonias* PBS documentary), Tomas Rivera Center (UT), U.S. Hispanic Chamber of Commerce (USHCC), and University of Texas, Austin (NPR programs *Latino USA, Universo* and *VOCES Oral History Project*).

Prior to ECG, the author oversaw national Hispanic market-ing for Anheuser-Busch beer brands (St. Louis, MO); launched Anheuser-Busch Companies' Corporate Relations programs in the Southwest (Houston, TX); and supervised Regional Marketing and Public Relations initiatives for McDonald's Corporation (San Diego, CA; Phoenix and Tucson, AZ, and Las Vegas, NV). In his public sector career he directed public infor-mation, citizen participation and community relations for the San Diego County Council of Governments and implemented the marketing strategies to gain community support for construction of the San Diego Trolley, one of the nation's most successful light rail systems in ridership and fare box revenues.

He served as California State Secretary of the Mexican American Political Association (MAPA), editor of MAPA's news-letter *El Mapista*, founding student member of the *Movimiento Estudiantil Chicano en Aztlán* (MEChA), founding board mem-ber of the San Diego County Burn Institute, Mayor's appointee to the City of San Diego Library Commission, and Chairman of the San Diego County Chicano Federation.

He currently serves as a board member of the American Association of Hispanics for Higher Education (AAHEE), Advisory Council member of the University of Texas Libraries, and co-chairs the Community Advisory Council of the UT-Austin School of Journalism's VOCES Oral History Project.

The former television news reporter and award-winning documentary film producer (La Raza Series, McGraw-Hill Broadcasting Company, 1972) is a nationally recognized speaker on issues related the US Latino community. The US Air Force veteran (1961-64) attended Mesa College (1967-69); San Diego State University (1970-71); Boston College (1988); and The Harvard School of Business (2006).

Works Cited

1855 in Law: *1855 Treaties, 34th United States Congress, Law Firms Established in 1855, United Kingdom Acts of Parliament 1855*, General Books, LLC, 2010.

Aix-la-Chapelle: *Full Text of the Ostend Manifesto*, October 15, 1854.

Alvarez, Robert R. Jr.: *The Lemon Grove Incident: The Nation's First Successful Desegregation Court Case*, San Diego Historical Society: The Journal of San Diego History, Spring 1986, Volume 32, Number 2.

Bauder, David–Associated Press: *Burns Documentary Angers Latino Veterans*, USA TODAY, Life section, April 8, 2007.

Bowden, J.J.: *Bowden Book I Chapter Six: Continuing Challenges Arising from the Southwestern Land Claims*, New Mexico Office of the Historian, 2004-2012.

Brennan, Brian: *Ode to the Irish: The Story of St. Patrick's Battalion*, Ventura County Reporter, March 10, 2010.

Carrigan, William D.: *The Making of a Lynching Culture: Violence and Vigilantism in Central Texas 1836-1916*, University of Illinois Press, 2004.

Cattan, Peter: *Moving Up the Economic Ladder: Latino Workers and the Nation's Future Prosperity*, State of Hispanic America 1999, National Council of La Raza, 2000.

Chavez, Cesár E.: *Education of the Heart-Culture Quotes*, UFW, http://www.ufw.org/.

Chicano Coordinating Council on Higher Education: *El Plan de Santa Barbara: A Chicano Plan for Higher Education*, La Causa Publications, 1970.

Chitel, David & Morse, David: *Young Latinos Reinforce their Immersion in American Popular Culture*, HispanicAd.com, http://www.hispanicad.com/cgi-bin/news/newsarticle.cgi?article_id=21861, May 14, 2007.

Coates, Paul V.: *Silver Starlight of G. Louis Gabaldon*, Los Angeles Times, April 8, 1957.

Collins, Phil: *The Alamo and Beyond: A Collector's Journey*, State House Press, March 6, 2012.

Cypess, Sandra M.: *La Malinche in Mexican Literature: From History to Myth*, p. 33, University of Texas Press, 1991.

Darwin, Charles: *On the Origin of the Species by Means of Natural Selection: Or, The Preservation of Favoured Races in the Struggle for Life*, Random House Digital, Inc., June 1, 1999.

Daum, Megan: *The White vs. Off-White election*, Chicago Tribune, May 20, 2008.

Department of the Army: *"Section 578.4, Medal of Honor"* Code of Federal Regulations, Title 32, Volume 2. Government Printing Office, July 1, 2002.

Domhoff, G. William: *Who Rules America? Power, Politics, and Social Change*, McGraw-Hill, 2006.

Dryden, John: *The Works of Vergil, Translated into English Verse*, Publius Vergilius Maro, 1806.

Dunham, Richard: *History is Made: Univision is Top Network in U.S. Among Viewers 18-49*, Express-News, San Antonio, TX, September 9, 2010.

Egan, Barry: *Eva Longoria: Unbelievable*, Independent News & Media, Dublin, Ireland, May 4, 2008.

Fahmy, Sam: *Despite Recession, Hispanic and Asian Buying Power Expected to Surge in U.S., According to Annual UGA Selig Center Multicultural Economy Study*, Selig Center for Economic Growth, University of Georgia Terry College of Business, November 4, 2010.

Fernandez, Manny and Savage, Charlie: *Court Blocks Texas Voter ID Law, Citing Racial Impact*, New York Times, August 30, 2012.

Garcia, John A.: *Panethnic Identity: Building Understanding By Taking on Complexities*, Latino Decision.com, June 4, 2012.

Gerstle, Gary: *American Crucible: Race and Nation in the Twentieth Century, Princeton*, 2001.

Gorman, Bill: *Lopez Tonight Scores Big First Week Ratings*, http://tvbythenumbers.zap2it.com/2009/11/16/lopez-tonight-scores-big-first-week-ratings/33705/, November 16, 2009.

Hamel, Gary and Prahalad, C. K.: *The Core Competence of the Corporation*, Harvard Business Review OnPoint Enhanced Edition, Download: PDF, Digital, March 3, 2009.

Hanner Lopez, Ian F.: *Racism on Trial - The Chicano Fight for Justice.* Belknap Press, Harvard University, 2003.

Harder, Kelsie B./Kingsbury, Stewart A./Mieder, Wolfgang: *A Dictionary of American Proverbs*, Oxford University Press, December 5, 1991.

Hayes-Bautista, David E.: *El Cinco de Mayo, An American Tradition*, UC Press, May 5, 2012.

Hewitt, Gregory: *Hispanics and the Oscar*, Special to the Star Tribune, Minneapolis-St. Paul, MN, February 27, 2011.

Hola or Hello? Debate Over Spanish Integration in America, Good Morning, America, ABC News, October 8, 2007.

Horsman, Reginald: *Race and Manifest Destiny: The Origins of American Racial Anglo-Saxonism*, Harvard University Press, 1981.

Humphreys, Jeffrey M.: *The multicultural economy 2009*, GBEC, University of Georgia, Volume 69, Number 3, p. 10, Third Quarter 2009.

Hunt, Kasie: *Gingrich: Bilingual Classes Teach 'Ghetto' Language*, Washington Post, Associated Press, April 1, 2007.

Immigration Policy Center: *Unauthorized Immigrants Pay Taxes, Too*, http://immigrationpolicy.org/just-facts/unauthorized-immigrants-pay-taxes-too, April 18, 2011.

Jackson, Bryce: *Help One Another by Recycling Dollars*, http://www.articlesbase.com/entrepreneurship-articles/help-one-another-by-recycling-dollars-4679513.html, April 26, 2011.

Jamieson, Patrick L. & Romer, Daniel: *The Changing Portrayal of Adolescents in the Media Since 1950*. Oxford University Press, pp. 31–32.

Jennings Bryan, William: *Heart to Heart Appeals*, p.36, Fleming H. Revell Company, 1917.

Johnson, Reed: *Remembering the Chicano Moratorium*, Los Angeles Times, August 27, 2010.

Krantz, Matt: *Web of board members ties together Corporate America*, USA TODAY, Money, November 11, 2012.

Lacey, Marc and Preston, Julia: *Latinos Reached Milestones in Midterm Races*, The New York Times, November 5, 2010.

Larralde, Carlos: *Josefina Fierro and the Sleepy Lagoon Crusade,1942-1945*, Southern California Quarterly, Vol. 92, No. 2, pp. 17-160, University of California Press, 2010.

Lewis, Hilary: *Rush Limbaugh Gets $400 Million To Rant Through 2016*. Business Insider, July 2, 2008.

Leypoldt, F.: *The Publisher's Weekly, Volume 49*, R.R. Bowker Co., Publishers' Board of Trade, Book Trade Association of Philadelphia, American Book Trade Union, 1896.

Lilley, Sandra: *Poll: 1 out of 3 Americans Inaccurately Think Most Hispanics are Undocumented*, NBC Latino News, September 12, 2012.

MacArthur, John D.: *E Pluribus Unum*, Latin Mottoes, The Great Seal.com, 2012.

Mandela, Nelson: *Mandela in His Own Words*, CNN.com/world, June 26, 2008.

McCullough, Kate: *Regions of Identity: The Construction of America in Women's Fiction, 1885-1914*, Stanford University Press, 1999.

McWilliams Carey: *North from Mexico: The Spanish-Speaking People of the United States*, Greenwood Press, Westport, CT, 1948.

Media Matters Action Network (MMAN): *Fear & Loathing in Prime Time: Immigration Myths and Cable News*, http://mediamattersaction.org/, 2007.

Meyer, K.: *Pundits, Poets, and Wits*. Oxford University Press, 1990.

Miller, Merle. *Plain Speaking: An Oral Biography of Harry S. Truman*, Berkeley Press, September 1, 1974.

Mock, Brentin: *Hate Crimes Against Latinos Rising Nationwide: Hate Crimes Against Latinos Flourish*, Southern Poverty Law Center, Intelligence Report, Issue Number 128, 2007.

Morley, Jefferson: *U.S.-Cuba Migration Policy, Frequently Asked Questions*, Washington Post, July 27, 2007.

Motel, Seth and Patten, Eileen: *The 10 Largest Hispanic Origin Groups: Characteristics, Rankings, Top Counties*, Pew Hispanic Center, July 12, 2012.

Nauert, Rick: PhD Senior News Editor: *Long-term Effects of Stereotyping*, Reviewed by John M. Grohol, Psy.D. , PsychCentral.com, August 11, 2010.

News Release: *Intuit Study Foresees Profiles of Small Business as Radically Different in 2017: 10-year Forecast by Intuit and Institute for the Future Redefines the Face of Entrepreneurs*, Mountain View, CA, January 24, 2007.

Novas, Himilce: *Everything You Need to Know about Latino History*, p. 98, Penguin, November 27, 2007.

O'Sullivan, John L.: *Annexation*, United States Magazine (July 1845) and Democratic Review, August 1845.

Ouaknin, Marc-Alain: *Mysteries of the Alphabet*, New York Abbeville Press, 1999.

Passel, Jeffrey/Livingston, Gretchen/Cohn, D'Vera: *Explaining Why Minority Births Now Outnumber White Births*, Pew Research Center, May 17, 2012.

Paz, Octavio: *The Labyrinth of Solitude*, Grove Press, NY (1961).

Pitts Jr., Leonard: *Separating Fact from Prejudice*, St. Louis Post-Dispatch, August 1, 2010.

Project for Excellence in Journalism, Pew Research Center: *Hispanics in the News: Event Drive the Narrative*, http://www.journalism.org/analysis_report/hispanics_news, December 7, 2009.

Ramirez Berg, Charles: *Latino Images in Film: Stereotypes, Subversion, and Resistance*, University of Texas Press, August 15, 2002.

Rodriguez, Gregory: *Mongrels, Bastards, Orphans, and Vagabonds: Mexican Immigration and the Future of Race in America*, Random House Digital, Inc, October 14, 2008.

Rutten, Tim: *Opinion: L.A.'s Political Predictor—the Latino Vote*, Los Angeles Times, November 12, 2008.

Salinas Stern, Rubén: *West Side Story Stereotypes Puerto Ricans*, The Tufts Daily, April 1, 2001.

Santiago, Roberto: *Boricuas: Influential Puerto Rican Writings; An Anthology*, p. 54, Random House Digital, Inc., 1995.

Scanlan, Christopher: *Reporting and Writing: Basics for the 21st Century.* Harcourt Brace College, p.79, 2000.

Schmal, John P.: *Are You Related to the Aztecs?: Uto-Aztecan Languages Spoken Throughout Mexico and the Western United States*, Houston Institute for Culture, http://www.houston-culture.org/mexico/aztec.html.

Schmal, John P.: *Hispanic Contributions to America's Defense*, Department of Defense, Washington, D.C. U.S. Printing Office, 1990.

Seidner, Stanley S.: *In Quest of a Cultural Identity: An Inquiry for the Polish Community*, Institute for Urban & Minority Education, Teachers College, Columbia University, New York, NY, 1976.

Smith, Tom: *Great American Trials: Sleepy Lagoon, 1942-43*, Encyclopedia.com, 2002.

St. Peter, Anthony: *The Greatest Quotations of All-Time*, Xlibris Corporation, p.367, October 28, 2010.

Strauss, Gary: *Company Directors see Pay Skyrocket*, USA TODAY, Money, October 26, 2011.

Terkel, Studs: *The Good War: An Oral History of World War II*, Ballantine, October 12, 1985.

The 4th Estate: *Newsroom Diversity: A look at Diversity in the Newsroom*, http://www.4thestate.net/bleached-lack-of-diversity-in-newsroom-front-page-election-coverage/, October 25, 2012.

The Brennan Center Voting Rights and Elections Project: *Analysis: Voter ID Laws Passed Since 2011*, The Brennan Center for Justice, New York University School of Law, October 3, 2012.

The Doctrine of Discovery and U.S. Expansion, Anti-Defamation League, http://www.adl.org/education/curriculum_connections/Doctrine_of_Discovery.asp.

The Heritage Foundation: *Why Catholic Schools Spell Success for America's Inner-City Children*, #1128, June 30, 1977.

Tomas Rivera Policy Institute, University of Southern California: *National Study Finds 80% Growth in Latino Middle-class over Past 20 Years*, http://www.hispanianews.com/archive/2001/March02/06.htm, March 2, 2006.

US Department of Labor: *The Latino Labor Force at a Glance*, April 5, 2012.

Vasconcelos Calderón, José: *La Raza Cósmica, Segunda edición*, México: Porrúa, 2003.

Walsh, Erin: *50 Years after Brown v. Board: San Diego County's Lost Connection*, North County Times, May 9, 2004.

Wang, Xia: *Undocumented Immigrants as Perceived Criminal Threats: A Test of the Minority Threat Perspective.* Criminology, 50: 743–776. doi: 10.1111/j.1745-9125.2012.00278.x, May 10, 2012.

WCC Executive Committee: *Statement on the Doctrine of Discovery and its Enduring Impact on Indigenous Peoples*, World Council of Churches, February 17, 2012.

Webb, Walter Prescott: *The Texas Rangers*, Houghton Mifflin, 1935/University of Texas Press, 1982.

Wolf, Eric R.: *Europe and the People Without History: With a New Preface*, p. 133, University of California Press, 1982.

Yen, Hope (Associated Press): *Hispanics One-fifth of K-12 Students*, USA Today, March 5, 2009.

Zach: *Silence Never Won Rights*, ACLU of Maine, www.aclu-maine.org/node/373, November 5, 2007.

CPSIA information can be obtained at www.ICGtesting.com
Printed in the USA
LVOW10s2119130916

504425LV00003B/431/P